Economics
Peace
and
Laughter

A CONTEMPORARY GUIDE TO

Economics
Peace
and
Laughter

John Kenneth Galbraith

Essays edited by
Andrea D. Williams

HOUGHTON MIFFLIN COMPANY BOSTON

Second Printing   c

Material from this book first appeared, often in somewhat different form,
in various publications:
"Economics and the Quality of Life," *Science*, July 10, 1964. "The Language of Economics," *Fortune*, December 1962. "How Keynes Came to
America," *New York Times Book Review*, May 16, 1965. "Economics as a
System of Belief," *American Economic Review, Papers and Proceedings*, May
1970. "Inflation, Recession or Controls," *New York Times Magazine*, June 7,
1970. "The Nixon Administration and the Great Socialist Revival," *New
York*, September 21, 1970. "On the Grave and Frightening Perils of Finan-
cial History," Introduction to the 2nd Edition, *The Great Crash 1929*,
Houghton Mifflin, 1961. "Financial Genius Is Before the Fall," *Harper's*,
November 1969. "Some Reflections on Public Architecture and Public
Works," *New York Times*, October 9, 1960. "Foreign Policy: The Plain
Lessons of a Bad Decade," *Foreign Policy*, December 1970. "The American
Ambassador," *Foreign Service Journal*, June 1969. "The Proper Purpose of
Economic Development," chapter of *Economic Development*, Harvard Uni-
versity Press, 1964. "Poverty and the Way People Behave," *The Under-
developed Country*, Canadian Broadcasting Corporation publication of the
Massey Lectures, 1965. "The Causes of Poverty: A Classification," *The
Underdeveloped Country*, Canadian Broadcasting Corporation, Massey Lec-
tures, 1965. "A Differential Prescription," *The Underdeveloped Country*,
Canadian Broadcasting Corporation, Massey Lectures, 1965. "The Day
Nikita Khrushchev Visited the Establishment," *Harper's*, February 1971.
"Dean Acheson," *Book World*, October 12, 1969. "Dwight D. Eisenhower,
General," *Book World*, June 28, 1970. "Richard Nixon," *Life*, March 27,
1970. "A Retrospect on Albert Speer," *New York Times Book Review*, January
10, 1971. "Ed O'Connor," *The New Yorker*, June 24, 1961. "William F.
Buckley, Jr.," *New York Herald Tribune*, October 16, 1966. "John Stein-
beck," *The Atlantic*, November 1969. "The Nicest Village in the Country,"
Esquire, December 1967. "Why Do You Go to Gstaad?" *Holiday*, January
1970. "Berkeley in the Thirties," *The Atlantic*, June 1969.

for Sarah and Alan

Contents

Contemporaries and Amusements

Points of a Compass

Introduction

ALL OF THESE ESSAYS were written in the sixties or during the past year. Through much of this time I was working out the ideas which I published as *The New Industrial State*. The economic essays are a history of this effort. The third essay, on the Keynesian revolution — for whatever reason by far the most extensively reprinted piece I have ever written — gives the point of departure not only for my system (if I can use that word) but for all modern economics.

However, it was in the first essay, "Economics and the Quality of Life," that I first outlined the ideas that developed into the later book. The essay holds that the test of economic achievement is not how much we produce but what we do to make life tolerable or pleasant. A simple-minded concentration on output makes life disagreeable, perhaps dangerous. This is a case that the recent concern over ecology and the environment has made wonderfully familiar. I thought, accordingly, that it would be appropriate and rewarding to my vanity to call this book *Economics and the Quality of Life*. I found that the phrase had succeeded too well. The title which had seemed so wonderfully apt when I first used it sounded egregiously trite to everyone to whom I suggested it for this book. I'm not at all sure, incidentally, that I should claim priority for the phrase. I am a sensitive though inadvertent plagiarist.

The last of the economic essays in time of writing is "Economics as a System of Belief." I suppose it to be the most important in this book. It gives in short form the ideas that have matured out of the criticism of *The New Industrial State* and it deals extensively with their practical application. It is not an altogether easy piece to read. But there are compensations. Those who give it enough attention will know a great deal of what is in *The New Industrial State* and much of what I have thought of since.

II

At the beginning of the fifties, Cambridge was a Mecca and Jerusalem for students from Asia, Africa and Latin America. I concluded that our pedagogy at Harvard, related as it was, more or less, to the sophisticated economy of the United States, had remarkably limited relevance to the poor agricultural countries whence they came. So I launched a seminar on the subject of economic development. It must have been one of the first in the country. I continued it, with some accretion of pessimism, after I returned from being Ambassador to India. The essays here on economic development, which should be read as a unit, summarize (really summarize) the subject matter of this course. I first gave them as a series of lectures — the Massey Lectures — over the Canadian Broadcasting Corporation network. It was then my intention to publish them as a small book (they were so published in Canada) but in the end I kept them for this volume. They are part of its claim to be about peace. So also is the review of our foreign policy disasters in the sixties. So, more marginally, are my reflections on being an ambassador. These essays neither exhaust the subject nor ensure peace as the result.

Much of what I wrote during the sixties had to do with peace in Vietnam. Like so many others I supposed that if one could prove that our presence there was unnecessary, unwise and even idiotic, it might influence the government to alter its course. I did not realize, as Hans Morgenthau has recently said in the same connection, that it only led those who were wrong to wish we would shut up — or be discredited by sudden victory. I haven't reproduced any of that writing — for two reasons. At the time, to maximize the persuasion, I published every piece not once but several times — one article appeared simultaneously in *Christianity and Crisis,* the *ADA World* and *Playboy* and then as a pamphlet and was then rewritten for the *New York Times,* published as a paperback book, syndicated in newspapers and then extensively reprinted abroad. The only people who could have missed it are those who wished to do so or who could not read. And so gloomy is this history, I could not bear to reread these pieces myself. I by no means regret them — nor should the hundreds of others who wrote in opposition to our belated seizure by the fervor first aroused by Pope Urban II. We did not influence President Johnson, Secretary Rusk or the generals and our effect on President Nixon was at best ambiguous. But they did not answer — or not very effectively. And having the field so largely to ourselves we unquestionably helped to persuade the people of the United States of the unwisdom of the Vietnam crusade. It is harder and certainly less politically rewarding to have to fight a war without any appreciable public support.

III

The last essays, as I note, have mostly to do with laughter. This is a delicate business. It is my amusement, not that of the reader, that is the test. And, as it took me some years to discover, the two are not the same. Where I have the help of such genuinely funny men as John Steinbeck or Ed O'Connor, I am fairly safe. John Steinbeck's fable of the model diplomat who meets the man with a wife from Green Bay, Wisconsin (page 329), is the finest thing in this book and one would have to be pretty obtuse to think otherwise. But principally I must count on the central tendency of our public life which is to thrust a succession of richly comic figures into unbelievable prominence. No other country has ever produced such reliably hilarious figures as Bernard Baruch, Douglas MacArthur, John J. McCloy, J. Edgar Hoover, Roman Hruska or Joseph Alsop. All are superbly solemn except where they are magnificently fraudulent. A note of minor cruelty heightens one's enjoyment. All, one knows, feel (or felt) that it was their destiny to guide and instruct and be an example to their fellow Americans and not, as in fact, to lighten their days. Perhaps the joy they cause me here will not be shared by everyone. But I can hope, and do.

Economics

1

Economics and the Quality of Life*

IN THIS ARTICLE, I suggest the social problems, and therewith the political tasks, which become most important with
a relatively advanced state of economic development. To
see these tasks in proper perspective, one must have in mind
the relation of economic circumstance to social thought and
therewith to political action. In the poor society, this relationship is understandably powerful and rigid. For various
reasons, the rich society also continues to assume that economic condition must be the dominant influence on social
thought and action. This assumption becomes, in turn, a
barrier both to rational thought and needed action. It is exploited by vested intellectual and pecuniary interests. Let
me summarize the matter briefly.[1]

Economic circumstance has a dominant influence on social
attitudes in the poor society because for those who are poor,
nothing is so important as their poverty and nothing is so
necessary as its mitigation. In consequence, among the poor,

---

* This article was originally the AAAS Distinguished Lecture at the annual
meeting of the American Association for the Advancement of Science in
Cleveland, Ohio, December 27, 1963, and was later changed considerably for
publication.
[1] I have discussed the matter at some length in *The Affluent Society*, 2nd
ed. (Boston: Houghton Mifflin, 1969), Chapter II.

only religion, with its promise of a later munificence for those who endure privation with patience, has been competitive with economic circumstance in shaping social attitudes. And since for nearly all time nearly all people have lived under the threat of economic privation, men of all temperaments and views have stressed the controlling and permanent influence of economic need. "The mode of production in material life determines the general character of the social, political and spiritual processes of life."[2] "Here and there the ardour of the military or the artistic spirit has been for a while predominant; but religious and economic influences . . . have nearly always been more important than all others put together."[3]

In the poor society, not only do economic considerations dominate social attitudes but they rigidly specify the problems that will be accorded priority. Under conditions of scarcity and human privation, there is obvious need to get as much as possible out of the productive resources that are available — to use the labor, capital, natural resources and intelligence of the community with maximum efficiency. Such effort enlarges the supply of goods and thus mitigates the most pressing problem of the society which is the scarcity of needed things. There is similar concern over who gets the revenues from production and who thus can buy what is produced, for one man's happy advantage will be another man's exploitation. Thus the two classical concerns of normative economics — how to increase productive efficiency and how to reconcile this with distributive equity — are the natural consequences of general poverty.

[2] Karl Marx, "A Contribution to the *Critique of Political Economy*," Author's Preface to the 1859 German edition of *Capital*.

[3] Alfred Marshall, *Principles of Economics*, 5th ed. (London: Macmillan, 1907), p. 1.

In the past in poor countries, all whom feudal prerogative, private fortune, exceptional personal accomplishment, imaginative larceny or military or political reward exempted from the common privation quickly became subject to noneconomic preoccupations — military adventure, political ambition, artistic patronage, sexual or other physical achievement, social intercourse or horsemanship. To be accomplished in these matters was to prove economic emancipation.

When people generally experience improved economic well-being, there is a similar and general loosening of the grip of economics on their social attitudes. No longer does increased production mean lessened pain. And no longer does the fact that one person gets more than he needs mean that someone else gets less than enough. Yet economic compulsion continues to have a highly influential bearing on social attitudes and resulting political behavior in the generally affluent community. Although they release their absolute grip, economic goals retain, nonetheless, much of their original prestige.

This is partly for reasons of tradition. Economic goals having been so long considered paramount, they are thought immutable. Economists have also long equated physical with psychic need; for many years, none might pass a Ph.D. qualifying examination who said that the wish of a poor family for adequate shelter was superior in urgency to that of a rich family for a mansion rivaling that of the still richer family next door. To do so was to interpose unscientific judgments and invite immediate discredit. Psychic need being on a parity with physical need and infinitely extensible, the urgency of increased production and thus of the economic problem did not diminish with increased well-being.

Economics also retained its grip on social attitudes because of compassionate appeal to the problem of unemployment and racial disadvantage. As living standards have risen, consumption has pressed less insistently on income. Corporations have had increased freedom to save for their own purposes — notably their expansion which rewards the corporate bureaucracy. Failure to offset the resulting savings has become a cause of unemployment. Against the well-being of the majority has therefore to be set the misfortune of those whom increasing affluence has left without work and reliable income. And this disadvantage, it has come more recently to be observed, is suffered in special measure by blacks and other minority groups. So even though improvement in living standards might be less urgent, improvement in economic performance to provide jobs for the unemployed and the minorities remains of high importance and appeals to this purpose have a high moral content. Increasingly, the purpose of the economy has become not the goods it produces but the jobs it provides.

Economic goals are also strongly, if not always visibly, supported by vested interest. The prestige of important groups in the community depends on the priority accorded to their function. If nothing is so important as production, no one is as important as the producer — the businessman. If other goals take precedence, so do other people. The importance of economic goals for the prestige of the economist needs scarcely to be emphasized.

Economic goals also serve vested interest in a very practical way. For if such goals take precedence, public questions will be decided according to economic tests. These are much less complicated than other tests. A road can be cut through a park, the countryside turned over to industry, waste turned into the air or a lake, a welfare measure rejected, a change in work habits commanded, all on a simple showing of beneficial economic effect. This is a great simplification. To validate noneconomic goals is to risk a very different decision with different benefits and beneficiaries.

Finally, economic goals remain important for the vacuum they fill. A society must have a purpose. A highly tangible purpose is to produce goods for private consumption. The annual increase in this production can be measured. The result can be taken as an index of national vigor and success. This measure we now employ.

We are, to be sure, allowed occasional doubts about this index of national achievement. And there are anomalies that are a trifle embarrassing. As more basic requirements are filled, expansion naturally occurs in less urgent items. There is diminished emphasis on steel or bread grains (these or the capacity for producing them may even be redundant) and there is more emphasis on electric golf carts and electric toothbrushes. Questions may arise — as I have noted on other occasions — whether national vigor is to be measured by the ability to have dental hygiene without muscular effort or athletic endeavor while sitting down. However, this is a minor embarrassment. Though economic growth consists increasingly in items of luxury consumption, we have successfully converted the enjoyment of luxury into an index of national virtue. Or almost so.

Some concern is also allowed as to whether all of the important tasks of the society are being equally well performed. The contrast between public penury and private affluence is remarked. The starvation of the public services, notably those of the cities, and the ample consumption of those who live in the adjacent suburbs are increasingly apparent.

But, in general, we remain subject to economic preoccupations. Economic goals are paramount. The guidance of economists on how to achieve them is accepted as a matter of course. There are, I believe, serious dangers in this delegation. This we see if we look more closely at the sociology and the mystique of economics. We then see how this most developed and influential of the social sciences can be influential also in misguidance when the society is subject to change and when the social problem has ceased to be primarily economic.

II

Unlike the natural sciences, which have long been viewed as the behavioral norm by economists, economics is subject to two types of change. The first is in the interpretation of given phenomena. The second is in needed accommodation to change in economic behavior or institutions. The development of the social accounts (national income, gross national product and their components) in the thirties, the evolution of the input-output matrix in the forties and the application of computer techniques to economic data in the fifties and sixties are all examples of the first type of change. The accommodation of economic theory to the rise of the trade union, to the development of the large corporation or to the changing behavior resulting from the transition of the average person from comparative privation to, by past standards, comparative well-being are examples of the second type of change.

Economics is progressive as regards the first type of change — conceptual advances or innovations in interpretive apparatus are promptly examined, enthusiastically discussed and, where useful, willingly adopted. From index numbers through the social accounts to modern quantitative methods, these developments have contributed greatly to the guidance of the American economy and also to the conduct of business. Both modern public and business administration are deeply dependent on them.

By contrast, economics is rigorously conservative in accommodating to underlying change. Until quite recently, wage theory did not recognize the unions. Their importance was not denied. But, by an agreeable convention, one was allowed in pedagogy and scientific discourse to assume away their effect. "Let us suppose," the lecture began, "there are no unions or other impediments in the labor market." The modern corporation has not yet been assimilated into economic theory, although the corporate system is all but coterminus with mining, communications, public utilities and manufacturing — in short, the largest part of economic life. The theory of the firm makes little distinction between a Wisconsin dairy farm and General Motors Corporation except to the extent that the latter may be thought more likely to have some of the technical aspects of monopoly.[4] All economists agree that there has been a revolutionary increase in popular well-being in the past thirty or forty years. Most textbooks have yet to concede that this has altered economic calculation or affected economic motivation. This means that the shape of the economic problem is not assumed to be changed by being solved.

The reasons for this reluctance to admit to the effects of underlying change are three: There is, as always, the tendency to protect vested interest; there is the imitative scien-

[4] " . . . the functioning of the modern corporate system has not to date been adequately explained or, if certain explanations are accepted as adequate, it seems difficult to justify." Edward S. Mason, ed., *The Corporation in Modern Society* (Cambridge: Harvard University Press, 1959), p. 4.

tism of the social sciences which is, perhaps, carried farther in economics than in any other discipline; and there is the natural wish of the scholar to avoid controversy.

On vested interest there need be little comment. We all have a deep stake in what we understand. Moreover, much underlying change — this is especially true of the movement to higher levels of well-being — diminishes the urgency and scope of economic judgment. Well-being reduces the importance of economic choice and therewith of economic advice based on economic calculation. Unions and large corporations make the dynamics of organization as important as the authority of the market in telling what will happen. This, in turn, diminishes the authority of economic judgment. So, like cavalry generals, locomotive firemen and fundamentalist preachers, economists deny the existence of what it is professionally disadvantageous to concede.

The natural sciences are not subject to underlying institutional or behavioral change. In consequence, economics seems more scientific if it is deemed to have a similar immutability. This explains, in turn, the considerable scientific self-righteousness with which sophisticated scholars avow the irrelevance of, say, the advent of modern advertising for the theory of demand. It is a libel on the scientific integrity of economics to suppose that its scientific verities are affected by such superficial change. Moreover, the first steps to bring institutional changes within the framework of economic analysis are invariably tentative, oral rather than mathematical and lacking the elegance of a methodological innovation. Hence they are readily dismissed by the men of scientific reputation or pretension as being rather sloppy.[5]

[5] One thinks here of Adolf Berle's efforts to bring the corporation within the framework of economic analysis. Though it had many shortcomings, it had

Thus does a scientific or pseudoscientific posture direct economics away from accommodation to underlying social and institutional change. And it does so with the blessing of presumptively scientific attitude, method and conscience.

But an instinct to caution also plays a role. Methodological change rarely has implications for public policy; if it does, they are likely to be minor. Adaptation to social and institutional change, by contrast, may have large and radical policy implications.

Economists who have been associated with such change and the related policy — the late Lord Keynes in Britain, Alvin Hansen and Seymour Harris in the United States — have led a rather controversial existence. This is not to the taste of all. I do not suggest that economists are peculiarly craven. Other disciplines have far less experience with controversy because they are not under attack at all. But many economists do find harmony agreeable. In the years following World War II, having just come through the Keynesian revolution which was a major accommodation to major underlying change and having discovered that the critics who once dissented had become acquiescent and were indeed finding a common ground with economists on the conservative consequences of according priority to economic goals, there was a special reluctance among economists to look for new trouble. In the intellectual backwaters, the name of Keynes still struck a radical note. Surely it was possible to bask a bit longer in the reputation for living dangerously that his name thus invoked.[6]

---

much greater relevance to the behavior of the firm than theoretical models which ignored questions of size and corporate structure. But among the economic cognoscenti his work has enjoyed much lower standing.

[6] I should like to stress again that in discussing the reluctance of economists to accommodate to underlying change my motive is not criticism but to

III

This reluctance to accommodate to underlying change is not new. Its consequence is that, in time of social and institutional change, the advice on practical matters which reflects the accepted economic view will often and perhaps usually be in error. The advice will relate to previous and not to present institutions: The needed action, unfortunately, must relate to the reality. If it does not, it will be at best inadequate or useless and at worst, damaging.

The danger here can be illustrated by reference to the last great change in underlying behavior and institution and the related watershed in economic decision. In this century, as I have observed, unemployment — the failure to use resources — replaced the problem of efficiency in resource use. In the autumn of 1929, when unemployment began to grow rapidly, President Hoover's first instinct was to cut taxes and to urge corporations to maintain purchasing power by not reducing wages. This was completely in conflict with accepted economic views. The economists continued to respond to the belief that efficient use of productive resources, not full employment, was the central need. This required

---

isolate a fact of some contemporary consequence. And while I am identified with the notion that increased well-being has had a profound effect on economic behavior, I am not entering a personal complaint of neglect. On the contrary, it was the view of significant economists that these contentions received too much attention. Thus Professor George Stigler, a past president of the American Economic Association, once expressed "shock" that so many more Americans had read *The Affluent Society* than *Wealth of Nations*. (*The Intellectual and the Market Place;* University of Chicago, Graduate School of Business, *Selected Papers* No. 3, 1963.) I was reluctant to reply to Professor Stigler for to do so could have seemed to be urging the claims of my book against those of a classic. (And I could have conceivably been missing the deeper cause of Professor Stigler's sorrow which might have been not that so many read Galbraith and so few read Smith but that almost no one reads Stigler at all.)

that there be no interference with the labor market. Or with prices. And since the system was believed to supply itself adequately with its own purchasing power — as in an earlier and simpler day it did — nothing need be done to increase demand by public action. It was sufficient to balance the budget and adhere to the gold standard. This advice was of no value for preventing unemployment; nearly all economists would now agree that if followed, it would only make matters worse. In time, Mr. Hoover himself surrendered to the accepted economic view. The subsequent reversal of the approved policies by Roosevelt in 1933 was viewed with skepticism and even hostility by most economists of acknowledged reputation.[7,8] This outcome was to be expected. There had been extensive underlying change leading to change in the problem to be solved. Accommodation was, as usual, slow. Prescription was, accordingly, for the wrong problem. As a matter of prudence, this tendency of economists must be expected in any time of change.

[7] The Roosevelt economists were largely without professional prestige. None of them — Rexford G. Tugwell, Gardiner C. Means, Mordecai Ezekiel, Lauchlin Currie — ever fully survived the premature identification with policies that nearly all economists now consider right. All were righteously excluded from professional honors. In 1936 the Harvard Department of Economics dismissed as eccentric a suggestion from its junior members that John Maynard Keynes be numbered among the leading economists of the day who were being endowed with an honorary degree at the Tercentenary celebrations of that year. The honors went to men who, in general, urged wrong but reputable policies.

[8] Cf. for example, Douglass V. Brown, Edward Chamberlin, Seymour E. Harris, Wassily Leontief, Edward S. Mason, Joseph A. Schumpeter, Overton H. Taylor, *The Economics of the Recovery Program* (New York: Whittlesey House, McGraw-Hill, 1934).

The preoccupation of economists now continues to be with
the volume of output of goods and services both for itself
and as the remedy for unemployment. Once again underlying change has made the preoccupation partially obsolete;
as a result, the recommendations of economists are again
either irrelevant or damaging. I have used the phrase "partially obsolete." The tendency of institutional change is to
introduce new preoccupations without entirely dispensing
with the old ones. In the nineteen-thirties, though unemployment became the central problem, inefficiency did not
become unimportant. A high level of employment remains
important now. But the need is to prescribe first for the
most important problems. Though production and employment were the central problems of the Great Depression,
they have not by any available standard of measurement
been so serious since. It is logical, accordingly, to ask if
underlying circumstances may not have made other goals
more urgent. The question is especially in order if there are
obvious shortcomings in the lives of those who are employed
— if education is deficient, regional development is unequal,
slums persist, health care is inadequate, cultural opportunities
unequal, entertainment meretricious or racial inequality is
glaring. And the need for prior concern for education, slum
abatement, improved health, regional development or racial
equality would be even more clear if these could be shown to
be the cause of unemployment and retarded economic
growth. In fact, all of the conditions for a shift from the
preoccupation with unemployment and growth do exist. The
primary prescription must henceforth be for the improve-

ment of what may broadly be called the quality of life. This should now be the foremost goal.

Reference to the quality of life will be thought replete with value judgments; the condemnation of value judgments, in turn, is one of the devices by which scientific pretension enforces adherence to traditional preoccupations.[9] But even economists must agree with a social goal which accords the individual the opportunity of providing for all of his needs, not merely for a part of them. And most must agree that the individual should be the end in himself and not the instrument of the business firm or public bureaucracy which was created to serve him. By both standards, imperfections are easily visible. They are the result of the priority now accorded economic goals and the considerable power of the machinery we have created to pursue these goals.

v

There is first the continuing imbalance in the way needs are met. We identify economic performance with the production of goods and services. Such production is, in the main, the task of the private sector of the economy. As a result, privately produced goods and services, even of the most frivolous sort, enjoy a moral sanction not accorded to any public service except defense. Desire for private goods

[9] It is held that the provision of an expanding volume of consumer goods, among which the consumer exercises a sovereign choice, involves no value judgments. This might be approximately true if everything the consumer needs were available from the market and if no attempt were made to manage his choice. Conservatives instinctively but wisely insist that almost all important needs can be provided by the market, and that management of the consumer is of negligible importance. This enables them to rest their case on an impersonal manifestation of individual choice. It is also evident that the preconditions for their case are far from being met.

is subject to active cultivation — a point to which I will
return. And the equation of psychic with physical need
excludes any notion of satiety. It is a mark of an enfeebled
imagination to suggest that two automobiles to a family is
sufficient. Public services, by contrast, are the subject of no
similar promotion; that there are severe limits to what
should be expended for such services is, of course, assumed.

The consequence of this difference in attitude is a sharp
discrimination in favor of one and against another class of
needs. Meanwhile a series of changes in the society increases
the pressure for public services. A growing population, and
particularly a growing urban population, increases the friction of person upon person and the outlay that is necessary
for social harmony. And it is reasonable to suppose that a
growing proportion of the requirements of an increasingly
civilized community — schools, colleges, libraries, museums,
hospitals, recreational facilities — are by their nature in the
public domain.

And increasing private production itself adds to the urgency of public services. The automobile obviously demands
streets and highways, traffic control and control of air pollution. From the pressure of mining, fishing, lumbering and
other resource industries on the public agencies responsible
for regulation and conservation to the needs imposed by the
container industry on trash removal, the effect is similar.

It should also be observed that if appropriate attention
is not accorded to public needs, the private sector itself will
suffer in technical performance. Much of its knowledge and
technology is supplied from the public sector. Modern industry has come, in particular, to require its own type of man.
One consequence is that a major part of the unemployment

is now of people whose place of birth, family characteristics, childhood environment or race denied them access in their youth to normal opportunities for education and training.[10] The same is true of individuals and families which fall below the poverty line.[11] Thus it comes about that the remedy for unemployment and individual privation depends to a very considerable degree on the balance between public and private services — or, more generally, on measures to improve the quality of life.

I have dealt with a number of these concerns before; one must not overdo that particular manifestation of scholarship which consists in repeating one's self and other people. But there is a new danger in this area which is now urgent.

If unemployment is deemed to be the dominant problem, and if as in the past, expansion of the economy is deemed a complete remedy, it will not matter much how this is achieved. Tax reduction and an acceleration of the expansion in demand for the output of the private sector will be entirely appropriate. Even some reduction in public services if offset by a larger increase in private outlays will be

[10] In March, 1962, 40 percent of the unemployed had eight years of schooling or less. This educational group accounted for only 30 percent of the total labor force. At a time when national unemployment was 6 percent among males aged eighteen and over, it was 10.4 percent of those with four years of schooling or less and 8.5 percent of those with five to seven years of schooling. Unemployment dropped to 4 percent among those with thirteen to fifteen years of schooling and to 1.4 percent of those with college training. (Testimony of Charles Killingsworth, *Automation, Jobs and Manpower*, Subcommittee on Employment and Manpower, United States Senate [The Clark Committee] September 20, 1963.)

[11] In 1956, 13 percent of families had incomes of less than $2000. Of those with eight or fewer years of education, 33.2 percent had incomes of less than $2000. Among all unattached individuals 54.1 percent had incomes of under $2000. Of those with eight or fewer years of education, 80.3 percent had incomes under $2000. (National Policy Committee on Pockets of Poverty, Washington, D.C., mimeographed, December 6, 1963.)

sound policy. However, if the problem is the quality of the society, it will matter a great deal how the expansion of demand is managed. Improvement in needed public services, given the tendency to imbalance, improves the quality of the society. Expansion of private services without expansion of public services brings, prima facie, no similar improvement. It could lead to distortions that would mean a reduction in the quality of life. And plainly an expansion of the private sector which is won at the expense of the public sector is intolerable. It provides what we least need at the expense of what we most need. And since the ultimate remedy for much unemployment depends on public sector investment in the unemployed (or their children), the policy may fail in even its avowed purpose.

There may be times when tax reduction will be a legitimate measure for securing improved economic performance. Defense expenditures are a large share of all public outlays and also are protected by special attitudes and a powerful constituency. Should it be possible to reduce these, it would be possible and perhaps necessary to reduce taxes — even while improving other services. But tax reduction for the express purpose of expanding production and employment must be regarded with the greatest suspicion.[12] The crude Keynesian case is that any source of spending is acceptable for it acts equally to expand the economy. But by bringing unbalanced production, tax reduction will ordinarily add to output at the expense of the quality of life. This effect will be increased because the expansion may well be without the added public services that the expansion itself requires. Also, the policy invites a coalition between those who seek

[12] Taxes were reduced on such grounds in 1964 at approximately the time this article was being prepared for original publication.

tax reduction for purposes of Keynesian policy and those who simply want lower taxes and less government. This could be a formidable and damaging coalition.[13]

VI

The quality of life will also suffer if the individual is not an end in himself but an instrument of some purpose that is not his own. This too is a danger in our situation. We have developed an economic system of great power. We have reason to be grateful for its achievements. But it has its purposes and it seeks naturally to accommodate people and the society to these purposes. If economic goals are preoccupying, we will accept the accommodation of society to the needs of the great corporations and the supporting apparatus of the state. We will regret our surrender but we will reconcile ourselves to the inevitable. If we have economic goals in proper perspective, we will question the desirability of such subordination.

One part of this subordination is that of the individual to the organization, specifically the corporation, by which he is employed. This has been considerably discussed[14] and none can doubt the tendency. The corporation requires its own type of man; he must be willing to subordinate his own

---

[13] "There is mounting realization of the injury to incentives and economic growth arising out of the magnitude of taxation. From this has come increasing determination to do something about it. This is all to the good. There is also a rising realization that there is something wrong about reducing taxes unless something also is done about curbing expenditures to avoid the need for big deficits in budgets. This also is good. But the general insistence on reducing expenditures falls short of that on reducing taxes. This failure to place equal emphasis on expenditure reduction can mean a danger of continuing big deficits." "Important Trends in Our Economy," United States Steel Corporation, *Annual Report*, 1963, p. 38.

[14] Notably in William H. Whyte, Jr., *The Organization Man* (New York: Simon and Schuster, 1956).

goals to those of the organization. And it is necessary if
the organization is to succeed. It is what makes possible
group performance of tasks. And by combining experience,
knowledge, technical skills and art, such group performance
greatly improves on what an individual can accomplish, popular myth to the contrary. It is, of course, regularly combined
with vehement protestations of the most muscular individ-
uality on the part of the participants.

We must keep this part of the problem in perspective. The
competitive market also has its type. It is not clear that
the wary, uncompassionate, self-regarding, wit-matching rug
dealer, in whom both deviousness and cupidity may have
been as often rewarded as penalized, would have been kept
in the Temple while the organization man was expelled. Also
the corporation executive commits himself voluntarily to
what Mr. Whyte has called the social ethic of the corporation.[15] He can readily escape if he is willing to forgo the
compensation which purchases his conformity.

The most serious problem is not the discipline imposed by
organization on its members but the discipline imposed on
society to make the latter accord better with its needs. The
behavior and beliefs of society are, in fact, subject to extensive management to accord with economic need and convenience. Not even scientific truth, much as our culture
presumes to canonize it, is exempt. The tobacco industry
has not yet ceased to reveal its discontent with scientists
who, on the basis of rather impressive evidence, aver that
cigarettes are a cause not only of lung cancer but a disconcerting assortment of other fatal or disabling maladies. The
economic well-being of the industry requires the active and
energetic recruitment of new customers. This need is para-

[15] Ibid.

mount. So there is no alternative to impeaching the scientists and their evidence.[16]

Similarly, and in conceivably a more dangerous area, we have come to assume that our defense strategy, and even in some degree our foreign policy, will be accommodated to the needs of the industries serving the defense establishment. Before leaving office, President Eisenhower warned of the rise of the military-industrial complex, a concern which had previously been pressed somewhat less influentially by the late C. Wright Mills.[17] The Eisenhower-Mills contention was, in essence, that defense budgets and procurements were being influenced not by national need but by what served the economic interests of suppliers.

However, these are only the extreme cases; they highlight an effort that is pervasive and inherent. No producer, in our present state of economic development, would be so naive as to launch a new product without appropriately attempting to reconstruct the pattern of consumer wants to include the innovation. He cannot be sure of succeeding. But he would never be forgiven if he failed to try. Nor does any commercially viable producer leave the consumer to unpersuaded choice among existing products. The management of consumption in accordance with economic in-

---

[16] On March 31, 1963, Zach Toms, President of Liggett & Myers Tobacco Company, said of the Surgeon General's Report: "We think . . . (it) went beyond the limits of the problem as now understood by other qualified scientists." At the same time the President of the American Tobacco Company, Mr. Robert B. Walker, dismissed the scientific evidence as ". . . first of all the frustrations of those who are unable to explain certain ailments that have accompanied our lengthening span of life on earth and who see in tobacco a convenient scapegoat." On April 14, 1963, Joseph F. Cullman III of Philip Morris, Inc., said that his advisers "do not feel the prime conclusion is justified on the basis of available scientific knowledge and evidence."

[17] C. Wright Mills, *The Power Elite* (New York: Oxford University Press, 1956).

terest has become one of the most complex arts of our time.
The participants urge their virtuosity in uninhibited terms
save, perhaps, when it becomes a subject for social criticism.
At this stage, consumer persuasion ceases to be such and
becomes a bland but indispensable exercise in providing
the public with greatly needed information.

In a well-to-do community, we cannot be much concerned
over what people are persuaded to buy. The marginal utility
of money is low; were it otherwise, people would not be
open to persuasion. The more serious conflict is with truth
and aesthetics. There is little that can be said about most
economic goods. A toothbrush does little but clean teeth.
Aspirin does little but dull pain. Alcohol is important mostly
for making people more or less drunk. An automobile can
take one reliably to a destination and back, and its further
features are of small consequence as compared with the
traffic encountered. There being so little to be said, much
must be invented. Social distinction must be associated with
a house or a swimming pool, sexual fulfillment with a particular shape of automobile, social acceptance with a hair
oil or mouthwash, improved health with a hand lotion or,
at best, a purgative. We live surrounded by a systematic
appeal to a dream world which all mature, scientific reality
would reject. We, quite literally, advertise our commitment
to immaturity, mendacity and profound gullibility. It is the
hallmark of the culture. And it is justified as being economically indispensable.

The conflict with aesthetics is even more serious. As the
economic problem is resolved, people can be expected to
become increasingly concerned about the beauty of their
environment. From getting goods, people can be expected to
go on to getting the surroundings in which the goods can be

enjoyed. But harmony between economic and aesthetic accomplishment cannot be assumed. On the contrary, conflict must be assumed at least in the short run.

With rare and probably accidental exceptions, an aesthetically attractive environment requires that economic development take place within an overall framework. Thus agreeable urban communities are invariably those in which law or fashion allow of variant treatments within a larger and symmetrical design. Such communities must be related to properly protected open space, for parks and countryside lose their meaning if they are invaded at random by habitation, traffic, industry or advertising. Segregation of industry and commerce from living space is essential if the latter is to be agreeable — neither a steel mill nor a service station is an aesthetically rewarding neighbor. Likewise, good theater and good music require the protection of a mood; they cannot be successfully juxtaposed to rhymed jingles on behalf of a laxative.

All of this is in conflict with short-run economic priority.[18] Economic efficiency rightly accords the greatest possible freedom for uninhibited use and uncontrolled dissonance. It is handicapped by the framework that aesthetic goals require. And economic organization strongly affirms its need for freedom. Proposals for control are pictured as subversive; concern for beauty is pictured as effete. Purely as a matter of tactics, this makes sense.

We see, however, that this need not necessarily be accepted. The priority of economic goals will, of course, continue to be defended. The vigor of the defense will increase as people come to see the price that they pay for it. But

[18] Given the self-destructive character of much unplanned investment, the longer-run conflict is not so clear.

we can have the social control that establishes the necessary framework for economic development and which erases or segregates industrial squalor and which preserves and even enhances beauty. A price in industrial efficiency must be assumed. But economic development enables us to pay the price; it is one of the advantages of development. It cannot be supposed that we have development in order to make our surroundings more hideous and our culture more meretricious.

Nor should scholars and scientists be detained for a moment by the protest that this is a highbrow view and that people must be allowed to have what they want. This is the standard defense of economic priority. It is the argument not of those who want to defend the public choice. It is the argument of those who want no interference in their management of the public choice.

It will be sensed that these are controversial matters — much more controversial than the questions surrounding economic growth and full employment. Important questions of social policy inevitably arouse passion. A consensus is readily reached on things that are unimportant or on their way to solution. That these matters are controversial and that expansion of output and employment is not is very good proof that economics is now concerned with the wrong problem.

Escape from the commitment to economic priority has, it will be clear, a broadly emancipating role. It enables us to consider a range of new tasks from the improvement of our cities to the cleaning up of roadside commerce, to the enlargement of cultural opportunity, to the redemption of mass communications from the hucksters, to the suppression of the influence of weapons makers on foreign policy. The political and social power that is available for these tasks is not negligible. Scientists, humane scholars, teachers, artists and the community that is identified with these preoccupations have been asserting themselves with increasing influence and self-confidence. Given a clear view of the issue and need and given release from the assumption of economic priority, that influence will surely deepen and expand. Nothing is more to be wished, welcomed and urged.

2

The Language of Economics

AMONG THE SOCIAL SCIENCES, and indeed among all reputable fields of learning, economics occupies a special place for the reproach that is inspired by its language. The literate layman regularly proclaims his discontent with the way in which economists express themselves. Other scholars emerge from the eccentricities of their own terminology to condemn the economist for a special commitment to obscurity. If an economist writes a book or even an article in clear English, he need say nothing. He will be praised for avoiding jargon — and also for risking the rebuke of his professional colleagues in doing so. And economists themselves, in their frequent exercises in introspection, regularly wonder whether they are making themselves intelligible to students, politicians and the general public. Committees are occasionally impaneled to consider their communication with the world at large. Invariably they urge improvement.

My purpose in this essay is to go into these charges and assess their substance. My ambition is to put a period, or at least a semicolon, to this discussion. For I hope to show that the transgressions of the economists in transmitting their knowledge, though some must be conceded, are not remarkable. Some of the fault lies in the attitudes, including the insufficient diligence, of those who lead the attack. Some is in the sociology of the subject and is not wholly peculiar to economics.

The language of economics is commonly indicted on three different counts. It is of some importance that these charges, which often are mixed together, be kept separate. They are:

1. That the ideas and terminology of economics are complex and artificial and exceedingly confusing to the layman.

2. That economists are bad writers. And it is said that proficiency in obscure and difficult language may even enhance a man's professional standing.

3. That arcane concepts and obscure language are the symptoms of a deeper disorder. So far from seeking communication with the world at large, the tendency of economics is to divorce itself therefrom and construct an unreal universe of its own.

I shall take up these several charges in turn. Each calls for a progressively more detailed examination.

II

That economics has a considerable conceptual apparatus with an appropriate terminology cannot be a serious ground for complaint. Economic phenomena, ideas and instruments of analysis exist. They require names. No one can reasonably ask a serious scholar in the field to avoid reference to index numbers, the capital gains tax, the consumption function, acceleration effects, circular money flows, inflation, linear programming, the progressive income tax, the pure rate of interest or the European Common Market. Nor should he be expected to explain what these are. Education in economics is, in considerable measure, an introduction to this terminology and to the ideas that it denotes. Anyone who has difficulties with the ideas should complete his education or, following an exceedingly well-beaten path, leave the subject alone. It is sometimes said that the economist has a special obligation to make himself understood because his subject is of such great and popular importance. By this rule the nuclear physicist would have to speak in monosyllables.

A physician, at least in the United States, does not tell you that a patient is dying. He says that the prognosis as of this time is without significant areas of encouragement. The dead man becomes not that to his lawyer but the decedent. Diplomats never ask. They make representations. Economists have similar vanities of expression and an accomplished practitioner can often get the words parameter, stochastic and aggregation into a single sentence.[1] But it would be hard to prove that the working terminology of the subject is more pretentious or otherwise oppressive than that of jurisprudence, gynecology or advanced poultry husbandry. One indication that it is not is the speed with which the really important words and ideas — gross national product, compensatory fiscal policy, GATT, international liquidity, product differentiation, balance of payments deficit — pass into general use.

I turn now to the quality of writing in economics.

III

Anyone who wishes to contend that economists are bad writers is faced with the fact that no learned discipline unconnected with literature or the arts has had such distinguished ones. Everyone has his own test of good writing. I would urge a multiple test for economists in which particular

[1] Arcane terminology and esoteric concepts do play a certain role in the prestige system of the subject to which I shall return.

excellence in one respect is allowed to offset lesser achievement in others.

Thus power and resourcefulness of language are important, as is purity of style. Style means that the writing is identified with personality — that it does not have the rigid homogeneity sometimes associated with scientific prose. Nor should it. Language has many dimensions. It does not convey meaning better or more accurately by being flat and colorless.

Good writing, and this is especially important in a subject such as economics, must also involve the reader in the matter at hand. It is not enough to explain. The images that are in the mind of the writer must be made to reappear in the mind of the reader, and it is the absence of this ability that causes much economic writing to be condemned, quite properly, as abstract.

Finally, I doubt that good economic writing can be devoid of humor. This is not because it is the task of the economist to entertain or amuse. Nothing could be more abhorrent to the Calvinist gloom which characterizes all scientific attitudes. But humor is an index of a man's ability to detach himself from his subject and such detachment is of considerable scientific utility. In considering economic behavior, humor is especially important for, needless to say, much of that behavior is infinitely ridiculous.

The writing of an impressive number of English-language economists qualifies by these standards. At the head of the list, I would put the work of Adam Smith. In purity and simplicity of style, and certainty in his command of language, he is inferior to John Stuart Mill. But he is more resourceful than Mill and much more amused by his subject. Smith sensed that a trip into the pin factory to see the division of labor in operation would establish the importance of the phenomenon for good. Pins, "a very trifling manufacture," were also an excellent selection; had the product been more portentous it would have competed with the process by which it was made. In competition with pins, the division of labor could not be less than triumphant. Similarly a less amused man would have stressed the penchant of businessmen for getting together to fix prices. (A halfway decent modern scholar would have isolated an instinct for antisocial behavior.) The businessmen would then have defended themselves, not without indignation. As the men of influence and admitted respectability, their views would have prevailed; Smith would have been dismissed as anti-business. Or, more likely, he would have been ignored. Instead, in one brilliant sentence, he noted that, "People of the same trade seldom meet together, even for merriment and diversion, but the conversation ends in a conspiracy against the public, or in some contrivance to raise prices." [2] Though the tendency is wholly innocent and convivial, the impulse to wickedness is overpowering. Neither anger nor reproach is in order; only sorrow at the inability to resist an improper penny. So expressed, the indictment has never been lifted. To this day, in the United States at least, anyone observing an exchange of words between two competitors assumes it is costing the public some money. Those so engaged feel obliged to make some embarrassed comment to the same effect when they are finished. Such craftsmanship was far beyond the reach of Mill.[3]

[2] Adam Smith, *Wealth of Nations* (New York, Modern Library, 1937), p. 128.

[3] I have always been enchanted by another observation of Smith's: "The late resolution of the Quakers in Pennsylvania to set at liberty their negro

Mill, of course, was a greatly talented writer, a standard by which others have long been judged. And to the list I would add the name of Thorstein Veblen. In one sense it is hard even to think of him in the same terms as Mill; his prose, unlike Mill's, is involuted and pretentious. One reads Veblen with the constant impression of a struggle for effect. But few men have ever so resourcefully driven home a point. What had always seemed commonplace and respectable became, after Veblen, fraudulent, ridiculous and (a favorite word of his) barbaric. This is high art. The American rich never recovered from the sardonic disdain with which Veblen analyzed their behavior. The manners of an entire society were altered as a result. After he made the phrase "conspicuous consumption" a part of the language, the real estate market in Newport was never again the same. What had been the biggest and best was henceforth the most vulgar. "Conspicuous leisure" made it difficult even for the daughters of the rich to relax. Their entertainment had thereafter to be legitimatized by charitable, artistic or even intellectual purpose or, at a minimum, sexual relief. Here is Veblen's account of the effect of increasing wealth on behavior:

> . . . Since the consumption of these more excellent goods is an evidence of wealth, it becomes honorific; and conversely, the failure to consume in due quantity and quality becomes a mark of inferiority and demerit.
>
> This growth of punctilious discrimination as to qualitative excellence in eating, drinking, etc. presently affects not only the manner of life, but also the training and intellectual ac-

---

slaves, may satisfy us that their number cannot be very great." Adam Smith, *Wealth of Nations,* Book 3 (New York: Modern Library, 1937), chapter 2.

tivity of the gentleman of leisure. He is no longer simply the successful, aggressive male, — the man of strength, resource, and intrepidity. In order to avoid stultification he must also cultivate his tastes, for it now becomes incumbent on him to discriminate with some nicety between the noble and the ignoble in consumable goods. He becomes a connoisseur in creditable viands of various degrees of merit, in manly beverages and trinkets, in seemly apparel and architecture, in weapons, games, dancers, and the narcotics. This cultivation of the aesthetic faculty requires time and application, and the demands made upon the gentleman in this direction therefore tend to change his life of leisure into a more or less arduous application to the business of learning how to live a life of ostensible leisure in a becoming way.[4]

The list of good if less than inspired writers — the elder Mill, Thomas Malthus, Henry George, Alfred Marshall and (subject to some reservations to be mentioned presently) John Maynard Keynes — is also an impressive one. So it would be difficult, on the general evidence, to find fault with the literary qualifications of the English-writing economists.

IV

Perhaps, however, this does not quite settle things. It will be said that when economists have gone to the technical heart of the matter, as did Ricardo in *Principles*, or as they have come up against the full complexity of modern economic problems, as did Keynes in *The General Theory*, they have become less than lucid and accessible. Some will surely think it significant that the best writer by my accounting was so nearly the first. Were Smith or Mill writing about the economy today, they would, it will be said, be either as in-

[4] Thorstein Veblen, *The Theory of the Leisure Class* (New York: Macmillan, 1912), pp. 74–75.

comprehensible or as condescending in their prose as their contemporaries.

This confuses the problem of complex exposition or scientific perception with bad writing. Ricardo's problems were no more difficult than those which were lucidly discussed by Malthus or Mill and he did not go into them very much more deeply. Ricardo's reputation as a bad writer is greatly deserved. He was, in addition, an unscientific one. His prose was awkward, uncertain and unpredictable as to meaning conveyed, and it was his habit to state strong propositions and then qualify them to possible extinction. His natural price of labor was such as to "enable laborers, one with another, to subsist and perpetuate their race." But within a page or two the application of this heroic (and historic) law was suspended in "improving" societies, of which contemporary England was obviously one as were all others to which he had relevance. The notion of subsistence was simultaneously enlarged to include conveniences, these being any luxuries to which the worker had become or might become accustomed. And the population theory on which the proposition depended was modified to exclude Englishmen although it was deemed to have full force and effect for the Irish. This is neither good writing nor good scientific method. It is bad writing based on incomplete thought.

The writing in Keynes's *General Theory* justifies similar if somewhat less severe comment. Keynes has been widely acclaimed as a master of English prose. A good part of this applause has come from economists who are not the best of judges. Much of it approved his criticism of the Versailles Treaty, or Winston Churchill, or his pleasant memoirs on academic contemporaries. But the real test of a writer is whether he remains with a difficult subject until he has thought through not only the problem but also its exposition. This Keynes did not do. *The General Theory* is an acrostic of English prose. The fact that it was an important book should not cause anyone to say that it was well written. In a real sense it was not even finished. Though new, the ideas were not intrinsically more complex than those presented with competence by A. C. Pigou and a certain churchly eloquence by Alfred Marshall. Other writers — Mrs. Joan Robinson, Professors Hansen, Harris and Samuelson — turned Keynes's ideas into accessible English, thus showing that it could be done. A better writer — patience has a certain notoriety as a component of genius — would have done the job himself.[5] The ideas of *The General Theory* could have been stated in clear English.

The influence of this book, combined with its unintelligibility, does bring up another question. It is whether clear and unambiguous statement is the best medium for persuasion in economics. Here, I think, one may have doubts.

v

Had the Bible been in clear, straightforward language, had the ambiguities and contradictions been edited out and had the language been constantly modernized to accord with contemporary taste, it would almost certainly have been, or

[5] Those who think this underestimates the difficulty of the ideas with which Keynes was dealing will do well to notice the carelessness of his nontechnical expression in this volume. The following is from a summary of his position in an early chapter: "The celebrated optimism of traditional economic theory, which has led to economists being looked upon as Candides who, having left this world for the cultivation of their gardens, teach that all is for the best in the best of all possible worlds provided we will let well enough alone, is also to be traced, I think, to their having neglected to take account of the drag on prosperity which can be exercised by an insufficiency of effective demand." *The General Theory of Employment Interest and Money* (New York, Harcourt, Brace, 1936), p. 33.

have become, a work of lesser influence. In the familiar or King James version it has three compelling qualities. The archaic constructions and terminology put some special strain on the reader. Accordingly, by the time he has worked his way through, say, Leviticus, he has a vested interest in what he has read. It is not something to be dismissed like a column by Alsop or even Lippmann. Too much has gone into understanding it.

The contradictions of the Old Testament also mean that with a little effort anyone can find a faith that accords with his preferences and a moral code that is agreeable to his tastes, even if fairly depraved. In consequence, dissidents are not extruded from the faith; they are retained and accommodated in a different chapter.

Finally, the ambiguities of the Scriptures allow of infinite debate over what is meant. This is most important for attracting belief, for in the course of urging his preferred variant on a particular proposition, the disputant becomes committed to the larger Writ.

Difficulty, contradiction and ambiguity have rendered precisely similar service in economics. Anyone who has worked his way through Ricardo, Marx or Keynes needs to feel that he has got something for such an effort. So he is strongly predisposed to belief. Ricardo is sufficiently replete with qualification and Marx with contradiction so that the reader can also provide himself with the interpretation he prefers.[6] All three lend themselves marvelously to

---

[6] No great figure since Biblical times has lent himself to such varied interpretation as Marx. This arises partly from the manner of expression, partly from the contradiction inherent in some of the ideas and partly from the fact that so much of his work was uncompleted at his death and conflicts that might otherwise have been cleared up by revision or deletion were carried into print. It is for this reason that the interpretation and reinterpretation of Marx has been not a scholarly pursuit but a profession.

argument as to what they mean. Thousands read these authors less for wisdom than because of need to participate in a suitably impressive way in arguments over what they said.

The case of Keynes is especially interesting because prior to the publication of the immensely difficult *General Theory*, he had advocated its principal conclusion — fiscal policy as an antidote for depression — in clear English in both the United States and Great Britain. He had not been greatly influential. Then in *The General Theory* he involved economists in a highly professional debate on technical concepts and their interpretation. His practical recommendations were not central to this discussion. But the participants carried his practical program to Washington and Whitehall. Would a simple, clearly argued book such as later produced by (among others) Professor Alvin Hansen have been as influential? My reluctant inclination is to doubt it.

Yet ambiguity is a tactic which not everyone should try. Economists will seize upon the ill-expressed ideas of a very great man and argue over what he had in mind. Others had better not run the risk.

VI

So far I have been dealing with (by broad definition) classical rather than contemporary writing in economics. The time has come to consider the complex language and the difficult mathematics of the current contributions not only to *Econometrica* and *The Review of Economic Studies* but also of many of the articles in *The Economic Journal* and *The American Economic Review*. And here the question ceases to be purely one of language. These articles are obviously beyond the reach of the intelligent layman. Is it possible that they are also out of touch with reality and that it is the ambition of some scholars to construct a world of their own choosing and exclusive understanding? Doubt is not confined to non-economists. Professor Samuelson, in his presidential address to the American Economic Association several years ago, noted that the three previous presidential addresses had been devoted to a denunciation of mathematical economics and that the most trenchant had encouraged the audience to standing applause. Once when I was in Russia on a visit to Soviet economists, I spent a long afternoon attending a discussion on the use of mathematical models in plan formation. At the conclusion an elderly scholar, who had also found it very heavy going, asked me rather wistfully if I didn't think there was still a "certain place" for the old-fashioned Marxian formulation of the labor theory of value.

What is involved here is less the language of economics than its sociology. Once this is understood, the layman can view what he does not understand with equanimity.

Professional economists, like members of city gangs, religious congregations, aboriginal tribes, British regiments, craft unions, fashionable clubs, learned disciplines, holders of diplomatic passports and, one is told, followers of the intellectually more demanding criminal pursuits, have the natural desire of all such groups to delineate and safeguard the boundary between those who belong and those who do not. This has variously been called the tribal, gang, club, guild, union or aristocratic instinct.

The differentiation of those who belong from those who do not is invariably complemented by a well-graded prestige system within the tribal group. And — a vital point — the two are closely interdependent. If the members of the tribal group are sufficiently conscious of the boundary that separates them from the rest of the world, the tribe becomes *the* world to its members. Its limits and the mental horizons of its members are coterminus. This means, in turn, that the prestige system of the tribe is the only one that has meaning to a member and it is all important. The most honorific position in the tribal group then becomes the most honorific position in the universe. If the school is all that counts, then the head boy is a person of the greatest possible grandeur. In the Barchester Close the eminence of the Bishop was absolute because no one took cognizance of the world beyond. Similarly those who are privileged to the secrets of the CIA or who work in the White House. In each case, everything within depends on the exclusion of what is without.

The prestige system of economics is wholly in accord with these principles. It assigns, and for good reason, the very lowest position to the man who deals with everyday policy. For this individual, in concerning himself with the wisdom of a new tax or the need for an increased deficit, is immediately caught up in a variety of political and moral judgments. This puts him in communication with the world at large. As such, he is a threat to the sharp delineation which separates the tribal group from the rest of society and thus to the prestige system of the profession. Moreover, his achievements are rated not by his professional peers but by outsiders. This causes difficulty in fitting him into the professional hierarchy and argues strongly for leaving him at the bottom.[7,8]

---

[7] In the United States, at least, a similar disposition is made of members who, being good teachers, are accorded the approval of their students.

[8] Thus during his life Keynes was held in rather low regard. In his *History of Economic Analysis,* which he intended to be an authoritative view of professional precedence, Professor Schumpeter affirms this judgment and bases his disapproval on Keynes's unscholarly preoccupation with useful and practical matters. He condemns Ricardo on similar grounds.

At the time of his election to the United States Senate, Professor Paul Douglas had a very high position in the prestige system of the profession and, indeed, had just completed his term as President of the American

A very low position is also assigned to economists who, even though forswearing any interest in practical affairs, occupy themselves with related disciplines — urban sociology, education, the social causes of poverty or juvenile delinquency. The reason is the same. These men are also inimical to the tribal delineation for their achievements depend on the judgment of noneconomists and thus cannot be integrated into the established scale. They are assumed by their colleagues to be escaping the rigors of their own subject.

At the higher levels, economics divorces itself fully from practical questions and from the influence of other fields of scholarship with the exception of mathematics and statistics. One can think of the full prestige structure of the subject as a hollow pyramid or cone, the sides of which, though they are transparent and with numerous openings at the base, become increasingly opaque and impermeable as one proceeds to the apex. Positions near the apex are thus fully protected from external communication and influence. Work here is pure in the literal sense. Questions of practical application are excluded as also the influence of other disciplines. And this being so, tasks can be accommodated to the analytical techniques which the scholar wishes to use. These techniques may not be mathematical but the absence of extraneous practical considerations is conducive to mathematical techniques. Needless to say, communication is closely confined to those within the pyramid and advancement to

---

Economic Association. While economists continued to take pride in his accomplishments, and especially welcomed his demonstration of the versatility of their craft, no grave professional importance could any longer be attached to his writing or his stand on technical issues. From being a leading economist, he became the leading economist in politics. This resolution of the matter, no doubt, is a sensible one. To fit a United States Senator into the prestige system of the profession would be very difficult. Better to compromise on purely nominal rank.

higher levels within the pyramid is exclusively by the agency of the other occupants. The standards of accomplishment which lead to recognition are thus self-perpetuating. It is no criticism of this work that it is unrelated to the real world. Such divorce is its most strongly intended feature.[9]

VII

It is not part of my present task to pass judgment on this prestige structure or to compare it with that of other learned disciplines. In a world where for pedagogic and other purposes a very large number of economists is required, an arrangement which discourages many of them from rendering public advice would seem to be well conceived. Otherwise there would be more such advice than could possibly be heard let alone used. Much of the discussion in the upper reaches of the pyramid is idle — economic models unrelated to reality are constructed, criticized, amended, on occasion commended and then, alas, completely forgotten. But, as often happens, there is no ready way of separating valueless work here from the possibly valuable and any effort to do so would be intrinsically damaging. And it is the good fortune of the affluent country that the opportunity cost of economic discussion is low and hence it can afford all kinds. Moreover, the models so constructed, though of no practical value, serve a useful academic function. The oldest problem in economic education is how to exclude the incompetent.

[9] This explains why professional economists of the highest standing often come forward with proposals — for the abolition of corporations or trade unions, the outlawing of oligopoly, the enforcement of free competition, therapeutic unemployment, cathartic deflation, elimination of central banks, ending of income taxes — of the most impractical sort with no damage whatever to their reputations. No store is set by ability to assess such measures in their political and social context. On the contrary, such preoccupation is discrediting.

A certain glib mastery of verbiage — the ability to speak portentously and sententiously about the relation of money supply to the price level — is easy for the unlearned and may even be aided by a mildly enfeebled intellect. The requirement that there be ability to master difficult models, including ones for which mathematical competence is required, is a highly useful screening device.[10]

What is clear from this brief excursion into the sociology of economics, and this is the matter of present importance, is how the intelligent layman or the scholar from another discipline should regard contemporary economic writing. Its relevance to the real world is not great. Much of it, and more especially that exchanged in the upper levels of the pyramid, is not meant to be. So it may be ignored.[11] It being designed to exclude practical questions, there is no practical loss. It being designed to exclude the outside scholar, the outsider may safely take the hint. The work at the less prestigious lower edges, since it must take account of information from other disciplines and also take account of political reality, does not lend itself to highly technical and mathematical treatment. This is the part that is important to the outsider. While he may not find it easy, he is not excluded.

[10] There can be no question, however, that prolonged commitment to mathematical exercises in economics can be damaging. It leads to the atrophy of judgment and intuition which are indispensable for real solutions and, on occasion, leads also to the habit of mind which simply excludes the mathematically inconvenient factors from consideration.

[11] The layman may take comfort from the fact that the most esoteric of this material is not read by other economists or even by the editors who publish it. In the economics profession the editorship of a learned journal not specialized to econometrics or mathematical statistics is a position of only moderate prestige. It is accepted, moreover, that the editor must have a certain measure of practical judgment. This means that he is usually unable to read the most prestigious contributions which, nonetheless, he must publish. So it is the practice of the editor to associate with himself a mathematical curate who passes on this part of the work and whose word he takes. A certain embarrassed silence covers the arrangement.

None of this excuses anyone from mastering the basic ideas and terminology of economics. The intelligent layman must expect also to encounter good economists who are difficult writers even though some of the best have been very good writers. He should know, moreover, that at least for a few great men ambiguity of expression has been a positive asset. But with these exceptions he may safely conclude that what is wholly mysterious in economics is not likely to be important.

3

How Keynes Came to America

I believe myself to be writing a book on economic theory
which will largely revolutionize — not, I suppose, at once
but in the course of the next ten years — the way the world
thinks about economic problems.

Letter from John Maynard Keynes to
George Bernard Shaw,
New Year's Day, 1935.

THE MOST INFLUENTIAL BOOK on economic and social
policy so far in this century, *The General Theory of Employment Interest and Money* by John Maynard Keynes, was
published in 1936 in both Britain and the United States. A
paperback edition became available in America for the first
time not long ago and quite a few people who took advantage of this bargain must have been puzzled at the reason for
the book's influence. Though comfortably aware of their own
intelligence, they could not read it. They must have wondered, accordingly, how it persuaded so many other people
— not all of whom, certainly, were more penetrating or diligent. This was only one of the remarkable things about this
book and the revolution it precipitated.

By common, if not yet quite universal, agreement, the
Keynesian revolution was one of the great modern accom-

plishments in social design. It brought Marxism in the advanced countries to a total halt. It led to a level of economic performance that inspired bitter-end conservatives to panegyrics of unexampled banality. Yet those responsible have had no honors and some opprobrium. For a long while, to be known as an active Keynesian was to invite the wrath of those who equate social advance with subversion. Those concerned developed a habit of reticence. As a further consequence, the history of the revolution is, perhaps, the worst told story of our era.

It is time that we knew better this part of our history and those who made it, and this is a little of the story. Much of it turns on the almost unique unreadability of *The General Theory* and hence the need for people to translate and propagate its ideas to government officials, students and the public at large. As Messiahs go, Keynes was deeply dependent on his prophets.

The General Theory appeared in the sixth year of the Great Depression and the fifty-third of Keynes's life. At the time Keynes, like his great contemporary Churchill, was regarded as too candid and inconvenient to be trusted. Public officials are not always admiring of men who say what the right policy should be. Their frequent need, especially in foreign affairs, is for men who will find persuasive reasons for the wrong policy. Keynes had foreseen grave difficulty from the reparations clauses of the Versailles Treaty and had voiced them in *The Economic Consequences of the Peace,* a brilliantly polemical volume, which may well have overstated his case and which certainly was unjust to Woodrow Wilson but which nonetheless provided what proved to be a clearer view of the postwar economic disasters than the men of more stately view wished anyone to expect.

Later in the twenties, in another book, he was equally un-
tactful toward those who invited massive unemployment in
Britain in order to return sterling to the gold standard of its
prewar parity with the dollar. The man immediately responsible for this effort, a highly orthodox voice in economic
matters at the time, was the then Chancellor of the Exchequer, Winston Churchill, and that book was called *The
Economic Consequences of Mr. Churchill.*

From 1920 to 1940, Keynes was sought out by students
and intellectuals in Cambridge and London; was well known
in London theater and artistic circles; directed an insurance
company; made, and on occasion lost, quite a bit of money;
and was an influential journalist. But he wasn't really trusted
on public questions. The great trade union which identifies
trustworthiness with conformity kept him outside. Then
came the Depression. There was much unemployment, much
suffering. Even respectable men went broke. It was necessary, however unpleasant, to listen to the candid men who
had something to say by way of remedy. This listening is
the terrible punishment the gods reserve for fair weather
statesmen.

It is a measure of how far the Keynesian revolution has
proceeded that the central thesis of *The General Theory* now
sounds rather commonplace. Until it appeared, economists,
in the classical (or nonsocialist) tradition, had assumed that
the economy, if left to itself, would find its equilibrium at
full employment. Increases or decreases in wages and in interest rates would occur as necessary to bring about this
pleasant result. If men were unemployed, their wages would
fall in relation to prices. With lower wages and wider mar-
gins, it would be profitable to employ those from whose toil
an adequate return could not previously have been made. It

followed that steps to keep wages at artificially high levels, such as might result from (as it was said) the ill-considered efforts by unions, would cause unemployment. Such efforts were deemed to be the principal cause of unemployment.

Movements in interest rates played a complementary role by ensuring that all income would ultimately be spent. Thus, were people to decide for some reason to increase their savings, the interest rates on the now more abundant supply of loanable funds would fall. This, in turn, would lead to increased investment. The added outlays for investment goods would offset the diminished outlays by the more frugal consumers. In this fashion, changes in consumer spending or in investment decisions were kept from causing any change in total spending that would lead to unemployment.

Keynes argued that neither wage movements nor changes in the rate of interest had, necessarily, any such benign effect. He focused attention on the total of purchasing power in the economy — what freshmen are now taught to call aggregate demand. Wage reductions might not increase employment; in conjunction with other changes, they might merely reduce this aggregate demand. And he held that interest was not the price that was paid to people to save but the price they got for exchanging holdings of cash, or its equivalent, their normal preference in assets, for less liquid forms of investment. And it was difficult to reduce interest beyond a certain level. Accordingly, if people sought to save more, this wouldn't necessarily mean lower interest rates and a resulting increase in investment. Instead, the total demand for goods might fall, along with employment and also investment, until savings were brought back into line with investment by the pressure of hardship which had reduced saving in favor of consumption. The economy would find its equilibrium not at full employment but with an unspecified amount of unemployment.

Out of this diagnosis came the remedy. It was to bring aggregate demand back up to the level where all willing workers were employed; and this could be accomplished by supplementing private expenditure with public expenditure. This should be the policy wherever intentions to save exceeded intentions to invest. Since public spending would not perform this offsetting role if there were compensating taxation (which is a form of saving), the public spending should be financed by borrowing — by incurring a deficit. So far as Keynes can be condensed into two paragraphs, this is it. *The General Theory* is more difficult. There are nearly 400 pages, some of them of fascinating obscurity.

Before the publication of *The General Theory*, Keynes had urged his ideas directly on President Roosevelt, most notably in a famous letter to the *New York Times* on December 31, 1933: "I lay overwhelming emphasis on the increase of national purchasing power resulting from government expenditure which is financed by loans." And he visited FDR in the summer of 1934 to press his case, although the session was no great success; each, during the meeting, developed some doubts about the general good sense of the other.

In the meantime, two key Washington officials, Marriner Eccles, the exceptionally able Utah banker who was to become head of the Federal Reserve Board, and Lauchlin Currie, a recent Harvard instructor who was its assistant director of research and later an economic aide to Roosevelt (and later still a prominent victim of McCarthyite persecution), had on their own account reached conclusions similar to those of Keynes as to the proper course of fiscal policy. When *The General Theory* arrived, they took it as confirmation of the course they had previously been urging. Currie, a brilliant economist and teacher, was also a skilled and influential interpreter of the ideas in the Washington community. Not often have important new ideas on economics entered a government by way of its central bank. Nor should anyone be disturbed. There is not the slightest indication that it will ever happen again.[1]

Paralleling the work of Keynes in the thirties and rivaling it in importance, though not in fame, was that of Simon Kuznets and a group of young economists and statisticians at the University of Pennsylvania, the National Bureau of Economic Research and the United States Department of Commerce. They developed from earlier beginnings the now familiar concepts of National Income and Gross National Product and their components, and made estimates of their amount. Included among the components of National Income and Gross National Product were the saving, investment, aggregate of disposable income and the other magnitudes of which Keynes was talking. As a result, those who were translating Keynes's ideas into action could now know not only what needed to be done but how much. And many who would never have been persuaded by the Keynesian abstractions were compelled to belief by the concrete figures from Kuznets and his inventive colleagues.

However, the trumpet — if the metaphor is permissible for this particular book — that was sounded in Cambridge, England, was heard most clearly in Cambridge, Massachusetts. Harvard was the principal avenue by which Keynes's ideas passed to the United States. Conservatives worry about

---

[1] Currie failed of promotion at Harvard partly because his ideas, brilliantly anticipating Keynes, were considered to reflect deficient scholarship until Keynes made them respectable. Economics *is* very complicated.

universities being centers of disquieting innovation. Their
worries may be exaggerated but it has occurred.

In the late thirties, Harvard had a large community of
young economists, most of them held there by the shortage
of jobs that Keynes sought to cure. They had the normal confidence of their years in their ability to remake the world
and, unlike less fortunate generations, the opportunity. They
also had occupational indication of the need. Massive unemployment persisted year after year. It was degrading to
have to continue telling the young that this was merely a
temporary departure from the full employment norm, and
that one need only obtain the needed wage reductions.

Paul Samuelson, who subsequently taught economics to
an entire generation and who almost from the outset was the
acknowledged leader of the younger Keynesian community,
has compared the excitement of the young economists, on
the arrival of Keynes's book, to that of Keats on first looking
into Chapman's Homer. Some will wonder if economists are
capable of such refined emotion, but the effect was certainly
great. Here was a remedy for the despair that could be seen
just beyond the Yard. It did not overthrow the system but
saved it. To the nonrevolutionary, it seemed too good to be
true. To the occasional revolutionary, it was. The old economics was still taught by day. But in the evening and almost
every evening from 1936 on, almost everyone in the Harvard
community discussed Keynes.

This might, conceivably, have remained a rather academic
discussion. As with the Bible and Marx, obscurity stimulated
abstract debate. But in 1938, the practical instincts that
economists sometimes suppress with success were catalyzed
by the arrival in Cambridge from Minnesota of Alvin H.
Hansen. He was then about fifty, an effective teacher and a

popular colleague. But, most of all, he was a man for whom economic ideas had no standing apart from their use.

Most economists of established reputation had not taken to Keynes. Faced with the choice between changing one's mind and proving that there is no need to do so, almost everyone gets busy on the proof. So it was then. Hansen had an established reputation, and he did change his mind. Though he had been an effective critic of some central propositions in Keynes's *Treatise on Money*, an immediately preceding work, and was initially rather cool to *The General Theory*, he soon became strongly persuaded of Keynes's importance.

He proceeded to expound the ideas in books, articles and lectures and to apply them to the American scene. He persuaded his students and younger colleagues that they should not only understand the ideas but win understanding in others and then go on to get action. Without ever seeking to do so or being quite aware of the fact, he became the leader of a crusade. In the late thirties Hansen's seminar in the new Graduate School of Public Administration was regularly visited by the Washington policy-makers. Often the students overflowed into the hall. One felt that it was the most important thing currently happening in the country and this could have been the case.

The officials took Hansen's ideas, and perhaps even more his sense of conviction, back to Washington. In time there was also a strong migration of his younger colleagues and students to the capital. Among numerous others were Richard Gilbert, later a principal architect of Pakistan's economic development, who was a confidant of Harry Hopkins; Richard Musgrave, later at Princeton and other universities, and now once again back at Harvard, who applied Keynes's and

Hansen's ideas to the tax system; Alan Sweezy, now of the California Institute of Technology, who went to the Federal Reserve and the WPA; George Jaszi, who went to the Department of Commerce; G. Griffith Johnson, who served at the Treasury, the National Security Resources Board and the White House; and Walter Salant, now of the Brookings Institution, who served influentially in several Federal agencies. Keynes wrote admiringly of this group of young Washington disciples.

The discussions that had begun in Cambridge continued through the war years in Washington where most of the earlier participants were now serving. One of the leaders, a close friend of Hansen's but not otherwise connected with the Harvard group, was the late Gerhard Colm of the Bureau of the Budget. Colm, a German refugee, had made the transition from a position of influence in Germany to one of major responsibility in the United States government in a matter of some five years. He played a major role in reducing the Keynesian proposals to workable estimates of costs and quantities. Keynesian policies became central to what was called postwar planning and designs for preventing the re-emergence of massive unemployment.

Meanwhile, others were concerning themselves with a wider audience. Seymour Harris, another of Hansen's colleagues and an early convert to Keynes, became the most prolific exponent of the ideas in the course of becoming one of the most prolific scholars of modern times. He published half a dozen books on Keynes and outlined the ideas in hundreds of letters, speeches, memoranda, Congressional appearances and articles. Professor Samuelson, mentioned above, put the Keynesian ideas into what became (and remains) the most influential textbook on economics since the last great exposition of the classical system by Alfred Marshall. Lloyd Metzler at the University of Chicago applied the Keynesian system to international trade. Lloyd G. Reynolds gathered a talented group of younger economists at Yale and made that university a major center of discussion of the new ideas.

Nor was the Harvard influence confined to the United States. At almost the same time that *The General Theory* arrived in Cambridge, Massachusetts, so did a young Canadian graduate student named Robert Bryce. He was fresh from Cambridge, England, where he had been in Keynes's seminar and had, as a result, a special license to explain what Keynes meant in his more obscure passages. With other Canadian graduate students, Bryce went on to Ottawa and to a succession of senior posts ending as Deputy Minister of Finance. Canada was perhaps the first country to commit itself unequivocally to a Keynesian economic policy.

Meanwhile, with the help of the academic Keynesians, a few businessmen were becoming interested. Two New England industrialists, Henry S. Dennison of the Dennison Manufacturing Company in Framingham, Massachusetts, and Ralph Flanders of the Jones and Lamson Machine Company of Springfield, Vermont (and later United States Senator from Vermont), hired members of the Harvard group to tutor them in the ideas. Before the war they had endorsed them in a book, in which Lincoln Filene of Boston and Morris E. Leeds of Philadelphia had joined, called *Toward Full Employment*. It was only slightly more readable and even less read than Keynes.[2] In the later war years, the Committee for Economic Development, led in these matters by Flanders

² I drafted it.

and Beardsley Ruml, and again with the help of the academic Keynesians, began evangelizing the business community.

In Washington during the war years, the National Planning Association had been a center for academic discussion of the Keynesian ideas. At the end of the war Hans Christian Sonne, the imaginative and liberal New York banker, began underwriting both the NPA and the Keynesian ideas. With the CED in which Sonne was also influential, the NPA became another important instrument for explaining the policy to the larger public. (In the autumn of 1949, in an exercise combining imagination with rare diplomacy, Sonne gathered a dozen economists of strongly varying views at Princeton and persuaded them all to sign a specific endorsement of Keynesian fiscal policies. The agreement was later reported to the Congress in well-publicized hearings by Arthur Smithies of Harvard and Simeon Leland of Northwestern University.)

In 1946, ten years after the publication of *The General Theory*, the Employment Act of that year gave the Keynesian system the qualified but still quite explicit support of law. It recognized, as Keynes had urged, that unemployment and insufficient output would respond to positive policies. Not much was said about the specific policies but the responsibility of the Federal Government to act in some fashion was clearly affirmed. The Council of Economic Advisers became, in turn, a platform for expounding the Keynesian view of the economy and it was brought promptly into use. Leon Keyserling, as an original member and later chairman, was a tireless exponent of the ideas. And he saw at an early stage the importance of enlarging them to embrace not only the prevention of depression but the maintenance of an adequate rate of economic expansion. Thus in only a decade had the revolution spread.

Those who nurture thoughts of conspiracy and clandestine plots will be saddened to know that this was a revolution without organization. All who participated felt a deep sense of personal responsibility for the ideas; there was a varying but deep urge to persuade. There was a strong feeling in Washington that key economic posts should be held by people who understood the Keynesian system and who would work to establish it. Currie at the White House ran an informal casting office in this regard. But no one ever responded to plans, orders, instructions or any force apart from his own convictions. That perhaps was the most interesting feature of the Keynesian revolution.

Something more, however, was suspected. And there was some effort at counterrevolution. Nobody could say that he preferred massive unemployment to Keynes. And even men of conservative mood, when they understood what was involved, opted for the policy — some asking only that it be called by some other name. The Committee for Economic Development, coached by Ruml on semantics, never advocated deficits. Rather, it spoke well of a budget that was balanced only under conditions of high employment. Those who objected to Keynes were also invariably handicapped by the fact that they hadn't (and couldn't) read the book. It was like attacking the original Kama Sutra for pornography without being able to read Sanskrit. Still, where resisting social change is involved, there are men who can surmount any handicap.

Appropriately Harvard, not Washington, was the principal object of attention. In the fifties, a group of graduates of mature years banded together in an organization called the

Veritas Foundation and financed a volume called *Keynes at Harvard.* It found that "Harvard was the launching pad for the Keynesian rocket in America." But then it damaged this highly plausible proposition by identifying Keynesianism with socialism, Fabian socialism, Marxism, communism, fascism and also literary incest, meaning that one Keynesian always reviewed the works of another Keynesian.[3] Like so many others in similar situations, the authors sacrificed their chance for credibility by writing not for the public but for those who were paying the bill. The university was comparatively unperturbed, the larger public sadly indifferent. The book continued for a long while to have some circulation on the more thoughtful fringes of the John Birch Society.

As a somewhat less trivial matter, a more influential group of graduates pressed for an investigation of the Department of Economics employing as their instrument the Visiting Committee that annually reviews the work of the Department on behalf of the Governing Boards. The Keynesian revolution belongs to our history; so accordingly does this investigation.

It was conducted by Clarence Randall, then the unduly articulate head of the Inland Steel Company, with the support of Sinclair Weeks, a leading zipper manufacturer, onetime Senator and long a tetrarch of the right wing of the Republican Party in Massachusetts. In due course, the Committee found that Keynes was, indeed, exerting a baneful influence on the Harvard economic mind and that the Department of Economics was unbalanced in his favor. As always, there was the handicap that the investigators, with one or two possible exceptions, had not read the book and

---

[3] The authors also reported encouragingly that "Galbraith is being groomed as the new crown prince of Keynesism [sic]."

were thus uncertain as to what they attacked. The Department, including the members most skeptical of Keynes's analysis — no one accepted all of it and some not much, unanimously rejected the Committee's findings. So, as one of his last official acts before becoming High Commissioner to Germany in 1953, did President James Bryant Conant. In consequence of the controversy, there was much bad feeling between the Department and its critics.

In ensuing years there was further discussion of the role of Keynes at Harvard and of related issues. But it became increasingly amicable, for the original investigators had been caught up in one of those fascinating and paradoxical developments with which the history of the Keynesian (and doubtless all other) revolutions is replete. Shortly after the Committee reached its disturbing conclusion, the Eisenhower Administration came to power.

Mr. Randall then became a Presidential assistant and adviser. Mr. Weeks became Secretary of Commerce and almost immediately was preoccupied with the firing of the head of the Bureau of Standards over the question of the efficacy of Glauber's salts as a battery additive. Having staked his public reputation against the nation's scientists and engineers on the issue that a battery could be improved by giving it a laxative (as the late Bernard DeVoto put it), Mr. Weeks could hardly be expected to keep open another front against the Harvard economists. But much worse, both he and Mr. Randall were acquiring a heavy contingent liability for the policies of the Eisenhower Administration. And these, it soon developed, had almost as strong a Keynesian coloration as the Department at Harvard.

President Eisenhower's first Chairman of the Council of Economic Advisers was Arthur F. Burns of Columbia University and the National Bureau of Economic Research (and later adviser and Chairman of the Federal Reserve Board under Richard Nixon). Mr. Burns had credentials as a critic of Keynes. A man who has always associated respectability with mild obsolescence, his introduction to the 1946 annual report of the National Bureau was called "Economic Research and the Keynesian Thinking of Our Time." He made his own critical interpretation of the Keynesian underemployment equilibrium and concluded, perhaps a trifle heavily, that "the imposing schemes for governmental action that are being bottomed on Keynes's equilibrium theory must be viewed with skepticism." Alvin Hansen replied rather sharply.

But if Burns regarded Keynes with skepticism, he viewed recessions (including ones for which he might be held responsible) with antipathy. In his 1955 report as Chairman of the Council of Economic Advisers, he said, "Budget policies can help promote the objective of maximum production by wisely allocating resources *first between private and public uses;* second, among various government programs." (My italics.) Keynes, reading these words carefully — government action to decide as between private and public spending — would have strongly applauded. And, indeed, a spokesman for the National Association of Manufacturers told the Joint Economic Committee that they pointed "directly toward the planned and eventually the socialized economy."

After the departure of Burns, the Eisenhower Administration incurred a deficit of $9.4 billion in the national income accounts in the course of overcoming the recession of 1958. This was by far the largest deficit ever incurred by an American government in peacetime; it exceeded the total peacetime expenditure by FDR in any year up to 1940. No administration had ever given the economy such a massive dose of Keynesian medicine. With a Republican administration, guided by men like Mr. Randall and Mr. Weeks, following such policies, the academic Keynesians at Harvard and elsewhere were no longer vulnerable. Keynes ceased to be a wholly tactful topic of conversation with such critics.

Presidents Kennedy and Johnson continued what is now commonplace policy. Advised by Walter Heller, a remarkably skillful exponent of Keynes's ideas, they added the new device of the deliberate tax reduction to sustain aggregate demand. And they abandoned, at long last, the double talk by which advocates of Keynesian policies combined advocacy of measures to promote full employment and economic growth with promises of a promptly balanced budget. "We have recognized as self-defeating the effort to balance our budget too quickly in an economy operating well below its potential," President Johnson said in his 1965 report.

Now, as noted, Keynesian policies are the new orthodoxy. Economists are everywhere to be seen enjoying their new and pleasantly uncontroversial role. Like their predecessors who averted their eyes from unemployment, many are now able to ignore — often with some slight note of scholarly righteousness — the new problem, which is an atrocious allocation of resources between private wants and public needs, especially those of our cities. (In a sense, the Keynesian success has brought back an older problem of economics, that of resource allocation, in a new form.) And there is the dangerously high dependence on military spending. And there is the problem of the wage-price spiral. But these are other matters.

The purpose of this essay is to pay respect to those who pioneered the Keynesian revolution in America. We should take pride in the men who brought it about. It is hardly fitting that they should have been celebrated only by the reactionaries. The debt to the courage and intelligence of Alvin Hansen is especially great. Next only to Keynes, his is the credit for saving what even conservatives still call capitalism.

4

Economics as a System of Belief

A RECURRING and not unsubstantiated charge against economics over the last century has been its employment not as a science but as a supporting faith. In this latter role it is held to serve not the understanding of economic phenomena but the exclusion of lines of thought that are hostile or unsettling to the discipline or, a related matter, to an influential economic or political community. "Economists," Marx described as "the scientific representatives of the bourgeois class,"[1] and he held that after the bourgeoisie conquered power in England, "it was no longer a question [for political economy] whether this theorem or that was true, but whether it was useful to capital or harmful, expedient or inexpedient, politically dangerous or not. In place of disinterested enquirers there were hired prize-fighters; in place of genuine scientific research, the bad conscience and the evil intent of the apologetic."[2] Thorstein Veblen, after saying that the competitive model of classical economists "affords the test of absolute economic truth," went on to assert that "the standpoint so gained selectively guides the attention of

[1] Karl Marx, *The Poverty of Philosophy* (1847), Chapter 2.
[2] Karl Marx, *Capital*, 2nd ed. (1873), Author's Preface.

the classical writers in their observation and apprehension of facts . . ."[3] Tawney observed that during most of the last century the conflict between "individual rights and social functions was marked by the doctrine of the *inevitable harmony* (my italics) between private interests and public good."[4]

This view of economics is not confined to the great dissenters. There would now be considerable agreement that market theory until the early thirties[5] excluded from consideration market structures which could not readily be reconciled with either the competitive model of many small sellers or the limiting case of single firm monopoly. This affirmed a view of economic society in which firms (by implication small) were numerous in the market and without market power and in which the tendency was to an equilibrium of normal profits and optimal resource allocation. In the United States, this was over a period — say, from 1880 to 1930 — when industrial firms were becoming very large and, by all outward signs, wielding great market and political power. In denying scientific recognition or even legitimacy to this trend, economic theory was not being politically and socially neutral. It was persuading its communicants to avert their eyes from reality. Except where monopoly or intent to monopolize could be shown, the theory denied the need for

[3] "The Place of Science in Modern Civilization: The Preconceptions of Economic Science." First published 1899, 1900, in *What Veblen Taught* (New York: Viking Press, 1947), p. 111.
[4] R. H. Tawney, *The Acquisitive Society* (New York: Harcourt, Brace, 1920), p. 27. He added that it was the further achievement of economics that "Competition was an effective substitute for honesty."
[5] At which time Edward Chamberlin and Joan Robinson, following the earlier work of Piero Sraffa, introduced the notion of a various blend of monopolistic and competitive influences in most industrial markets.

any social response to economic power. It was playing an active — an actively conservative — role in the political process.

The social and political role of economic belief was at least equally great in the case of Say's Law of Markets, the practical consequences of which were profound. If, as Say's Law held, there could be no deficiency or excess in aggregate demand (if, in fact, any other solution meant that a man was unlearned in the fundamentals of economics),[6] there could be no case for increasing or decreasing public outlays or revenues to affect the level of output or employment. The alternative possibilities allowed only for a self-correcting theory of the business cycle or one that permitted (or encouraged) the adjustment, i.e., reduction, of wage levels or the correction of other special equilibrium error. On grounds that were avowedly scientific, the discipline thus helped to exclude from consideration what are now commonplace measures of fiscal policy. And, pari passu, it defended a minimal role for the state. This was accomplished by a proposition which, in the context of the modern industrial economy, virtually all economic scholarship holds to be wrong and even derisory.

One further aspect of this history is important. Popular perception of the shortcoming ran well ahead of the theoretical economic accommodation. While economic theory had no appreciable reaction to the rise of the great industrial firm prior to the nineteen-thirties, the case of single firm monopoly apart, the ubiquity and omnipotence of "big business" had been a source of popular discussion and concern for

[6] Consigned, Keynes said, "to live furtively, below the surface, in the underworlds of Karl Marx, Silvio Gesell or Major Douglas." John Maynard Keynes, *The General Theory of Employment Interest and Money* (New York: Harcourt, Brace, 1936), p. 32.

forty years. It was the basic fare of the muckrakers and the political base of the Populists. Journalists and politicians and the public at large had sensed what the theory denied or ignored, namely that where the participants in an industry were large and few, they wielded great power not explained by the occasional case of single firm monopoly. Similarly, long before Keynes made it reputable for economists, the lesser breeds without the law — politicians, journalists, liberal businessmen — had argued that in a depression affirmative action should be taken by the state to increase aggregate demand.[7,8] A not wholly irrelevant consequence of the rigid and enduring commitment to Say's Law was that the economics profession, through the early years of the Great Depression — indeed, until rescued by Keynes — had a reputation for doctrinaire negativism. When asked for remedies for the depression, it was without useful response. And those who continued to find truth only in the established belief were doomed to live out their lives in a state of obsolescence that was all too cruelly manifest, and which, one trusts, will be a sobering lesson for the future.

In yet other instances economics has excluded socially inconvenient analyses, at least until some combination of pressure — the need for practical action, the social intuition of the nonprofessional, competent heresy within the profession — has upset the accepted view. But I am not concerned with making a catalogue. I wish to argue that present professional belief — the neoclassical model of economic process — as

[7] It was also, one senses, the desperation bred of the Great Depression and the willingness so induced to look anew at old truths, as much as the cogency of Keynes's argument, which led to the rejection of Say's Law.
[8] In the United States both Presidents Hoover and Roosevelt (and also the Hearst press) had embraced a policy of either tax reduction or public spending to raise the level of aggregate demand before Keynes made the idea generally acceptable to economists.

profoundly accepted as was once the competitive model or Say's Law, is now similarly excluding urgent as well as politically disturbing questions from professional economic vision. It is important that all be reminded that there is nothing novel about this. On the contrary, it is quite normal — a recurring aspect of the sociology of the discipline. So, also, is vehement insistence that economics is wholly scientific and neutral when it is being politically quite purposeful. Say's Law was most indignantly asserted as a test of scientific integrity and professional respectability in the years of the Great Depression just before its demise. It was then that it most needed energetic defense. But let me summarize. The accepted economic models, in the past, have not necessarily been the ones that illuminated reality. They have frequently served to divert attention from questions of great social urgency which, in the established view, had alarming implications for political action. In doing this, they and the subject of economics have served a political function. Economics has been not a science but a conservatively useful system of belief defending that belief as a science. And knowing, and indeed agreeing, that this has occurred before, our minds must be open (or less incautiously closed) to the possibility that it may happen again.

II

The assumption that economics must now abandon, subject to some later definition, is that of consumer sovereignty — and, in light of the role of the modern state in the economy, what may also be called citizen sovereignty. If this is not done the discipline will serve, indeed is now serving, not as an elucidation of social phenomena but as a design for suppressing inconvenient social conclusions and action. And given the pressure of present circumstance, that of popular intuition and (one trusts) the growth of dissent among economists themselves, it will not so serve for very long. My intention in this article is to put the case for, and consequences of, the changed assumption in the shortest form consistent with necessary qualification and technical precision of argument.[9]

There are three plausible views of the individual in economic society of which two are broadly consistent with the neoclassical model. In the first view, the individual in economic life is regarded as a neutral or passive participant

[9] The surrender of the sovereignty of the individual to the producer or producing organization is the theme, explicit or implicit, of two books, *The Affluent Society*, 2nd ed. (Boston, Houghton Mifflin, 1969), and *The New Industrial State* (Boston, Houghton Mifflin, 1967). In both of these books I faced the problem of discarding ideas, much beloved, that had long been part of my habit of thought and also the tendency to recoil when one's analysis suggests or seems to suggest practical action well outside the accepted modalities. I was also, as I have said before, faced with the peculiar problem of persuasion that is here involved. A scientific proposition is refuted by proof to the contrary. Belief, especially if it is playing a functionally protective role in the society, is by no means so vulnerable. The strategy of persuasion thus required, as I have also elsewhere made clear, repays some thought. All social disciplines, and perhaps especially economics, are naturally jealous of the larger framework of assumptions in which they operate. For if assumptions become obsolete, so does the knowledge subtended thereon. This vested interest is further reinforced by the functional role of the ideas in excluding inimical lines of thought and action. It follows that to attack such a framework of assumptions from within the discipline is a perilous matter. The jury, or most of it, is a party at interest. The fate of all who attacked Say before Keynes is a warning.

The alternative is to engage a larger public and thus, as it were, force the issue on the discipline. For, if the assumptions being attacked are vulnerable — if they are visibly at odds with reality — the public intuition will be responsive. So will be that of the social radical. And if enough such support can be enlisted, the old framework can be broken. The use of this technique naturally incurs a certain measure of professional discomfort. It bypasses the system by which ideas and innovations are submitted for professional scrutiny and winnowing before being passed along to students and the lay public. At the same time it renders nugatory the defenses by which the intellectual vested interest is protected. To the legitimate rebuke for the first is added the personal outrage inspired by the second. For all this irregularity one must make such apology as may be appropriate.

in a process for transmitting change. This change may begin with the individual — it may be a change in taste reflecting some change in his life design — and its effects are reflected in his purchases and thus transmitted through the market to the producer. Or the change may originate with the producer, e.g., some change in the production function arising from spontaneous technical innovation, and in consequence of the effect on cost, output and price, it is transmitted through the market to the individual. In each case there may be secondary or tertiary reverberations. In each, concern is with the process; no special assumption is made as to the source of the change or the purpose of the process. It should be noted that all changes are transmitted through the market; there is no significant extramarket persuasion by which the producer is brought to accept changes sought by the consumer or by which the consumer is conditioned to accept changes sought by the producer. Most modern mathematical models of microeconomic relationships are, broadly speaking, of this kind. Public goods are not very satisfactorily embraced by this model.[10]

The second view of the individual in economic society is still of a process. Though in principle this process is still a neutral transmitter of change, including change that originates with the producer, the ultimate guidance is assumed to come from the individual. It is to him that the ultimate accommodation is made. The accommodation to changes in the producer's cost function is neutral and technical; the accommodation to changes in the consumer's demand function is functional and moral and embodies the purpose of the system. A similar though less precise accommodation is made

[10] I am grateful for suggestions on this model from my colleague, Leonid Hurwicz.

to the preferences of the individual citizen and voter for public goods.

None of this need be absolute. The consumer is admitted to be subject to influences that are external to the market. Some of these originate with the producer or the process by which he is supplied. These include specific persuasion, i.e., advertising, by the producer and the competitive, emulative and cultural influences which bear on consumption and which, as Professor Duesenberry pointed out many years ago, associate it with success in life and thus make a high level of consumption an end in itself.[11] And for private and even more especially public goods, information is transmitted imperfectly by the market or political process. In consequence, one technical branch of economics (welfare economics so-called) concerns itself with how the final budget of goods produced can be made to accord more precisely with the individual's preference for kinds and quantities of goods. However, both the extramarket effects and the shortcomings that must be so corrected are peripheral; one concedes them while accepting the larger fact. That larger fact is the ultimate accommodation of the economic system to an individual choice that is original and innate. That accommodation is inhibited and diverted and modified but only as the brush along the banks and the rocks along the bottom inhibit and divert and modify the flow of a stream.

This accommodation, it should specifically be noted, is broadly consistent with the accepted theory of monopoly or oligopoly. The demand function of the individual is given, which is to say that it originates with him and not with the producer. The producer seeks to maximize revenues — a

[11] James S. Duesenberry, *Income, Saving and the Theory of Consumer Behavior* (Cambridge, Harvard University Press, 1949), p. 28.

vital point. He does this by responding to the aggregated demand of individuals. This response is no less reliable than in the competitive market. The resulting distribution of productive resources and income is different and so is the resulting consumption. But it is not different in being less responsive to the ultimate authority of the consumer.

The third possible view sees the process as one in which the ultimate accommodation in significant measure is to the producer. The individual's wants, though superficially they may seem to originate with him, are ultimately at the behest of the mechanism that supplies them. In the practical manifestation of this accommodation, the producing firm controls its own prices in the market. And it goes beyond this control to persuade the consumer to the appropriate responding behavior. And it also selects and designs products with a view to what can be so priced and made subject to such persuasion. And it does this in a society in which the strongly iterated and reiterated praise of goods makes them seem important for happiness and thus makes the individual attentive to claims in this regard. And the persuasion proceeds in the context of a generally affluent supply of goods which means that their contribution is to psychic rather than to physical need. The further consequence is that the individual is open to persuasion — to appeals to his psyche — as he would not be were physical effects alone involved.[12] On

[12] Some will be aware of the energy with which I have pressed this distinction. Cf. *The Affluent Society*, 2nd ed., p. 134 ff. It is one of those naïvely crucial matters (as Keynes once noted) on which much turns. Economics generally denies the distinction between physical need and psychic satisfactions — taking advantage in part of the undeniable fact that the line between the two lends itself to no precise conceptual demarcation. Thus, it excludes from consideration the notion of a class of wants which, originating in the psyche, are subject to management by psychological means, as wants originating in physical need are not. This greatly defends the values of a society which measures achievement by output. There being no

occasion the state will supply related services that support the requisite behavior of the individual — its provision of highways as an aspect of the management of consumer behavior by the automobile industry is an obvious example. By regulating aggregate demand the state also ensures that the microeconomic or market management of demand will not be nullified by macroeconomic changes in purchasing power in the economy as a whole.[13]

This view of economic process has great importance as regards public goods. For important classes of products and services — weapons systems, space probes and travel, a supersonic transport — decisions are taken not by the individual citizen and voter and transmitted to the state. They are taken by the producers of public services, i.e., by the armed services and the weapons firms. It is their goals that, primarily, are served. The Congress and the public are then persuaded or commanded to acceptance of these decisions.[14]

The need to manage consumer behavior, as I have argued in detail elsewhere,[15] arises from the circumstances of mod-

---

valid difference in the wants being served, there is no lessening of the urgency of output. The notion of production for frivolous purposes is almost completely elided. Thus, the importance of production remains above question. Once again one sees economics overriding a commonsense view to defend what is, unquestionably, a most convenient conclusion.

[13] The one is obviously dependent in a highly practical way on the other and it is a curiosity of economics that the two — the need to ensure that people will want GM cars and the need to ensure that they will be able to buy GM cars — has been so little associated. Employment, not industrial need, has carried by far the major burden of this policy.

[14] The most meaningful distinction between a market and a planned economy, so it seems to me, turns on whether and to what extent accommodation is to producer or consumer choice. The more responsive the producer must be to consumer choice, the more it is a market economy. The greater his power to establish prices and to persuade, command or otherwise arrange the consumer response at these prices, the more it is a planned economy. Intervention by the state does not alter the fact of planning; it changes only its nature, extent or efficacy.

[15] *The New Industrial State,* pp. 1–97.

ern industrial life — sophisticated technology, large commitments of capital, longtime horizons in product development and production and, in consequence, large, inflexible and vulnerable organization. These lead, in turn, to the need to control as many as possible of the parameters (costs, prices, demand, costs and risks of technological innovation) within which the firm operates. The development and the need for control are greatly different in different parts of the economy — the range is from the producer of modern weapons systems or automobiles at one extreme to the small shopkeeper or vegetable farmer at the other. (One can think of roughly half of the economy as being characterized by large organizations and producer sovereignty.) The extent of the accommodation of the individual to producer need varies with the power of the producing organization. This difference is not something to be minimized; on the contrary, it is itself of practical consequence for economic behavior, as I will argue in a moment. The efficacy of the management of the consumer or the public in any industry will also vary over time. On occasion, it will partly fail or be frustrated.

In this model the firm does not maximize profits to the exclusion of other and more important interests. It defends or maximizes, in some compromise, all of the things that are important to it — the security and the autonomy of its management, the growth of the firm and therewith the opportunity of the guiding technostructure for new responsibility and for promotion and pay increases, its reputation for technical achievement, its public prestige and, of course, its earnings. The particular compromise between these interests will, it may be supposed, differ as between different firms.

Finally, it remains possible, at least in the private sector of the economy, for the individual to contract out or partially out of the management to which he is subject. This, more than incidentally, allows him, if he is so disposed, to deny the existence of such management and to point to his own immunity as proof. A certain part of the case for unmanaged consumer choice rests subjectively on such grounds. All of these qualifications are essential, for only the inexperienced rejoice those who are resistant to an idea by allowing themselves the catharsis of overstatement.

III

So far as anything in economics is certain, it is that the *first two* of the foregoing views have a monopoly of established belief. Formal microstatic and mathematical models emphasize the first view; the less formal, more intuitive and more influential writing and textbook instruction assume the second. It is not impossible (though not altogether easy) to find work antedating the very recent discussion that concedes the management of consumer taste. Tibor Scitovsky[16] has shown how consumer markets are managed on behalf of the majority taste — an argument with more than parenthetical importance for the economics of the arts, for such management by its nature rejects the minority preference for high artistic excellence. Jerome Rothenburg has held of advertising that while it "is probably not acccountable for drastic changes, it is reckless to assume only trivial impact."[17] Noting that there are "endogenous taste changes — changes induced by producer investments designed to effect such changes," he concludes that "Few would insist

[16] *Papers on Welfare and Growth* (London: George Allen and Unwin, 1964), pp. 241–249.
[17] "Consumer's Sovereignty Revisited and the Hospitality of Freedom of Choice," *American Economic Review*, Papers and Proceedings, Vol. 52, No. 2 (May 1962), p. 280.

that the consumer is sovereign in any useful sense." [18] In more recent times other scholars, some of them accepting my arguments, have agreed. But these are still exceptions. In the established view economic life remains a process by which the individual imposes his will on the producer — as Fisher, Griliches and Kaysen have put it, "there is *always* an assumption of consumer sovereignty in the market economy." [19] (My italics.) And, although the process is confused, indirect and inefficient, the citizen is equally assumed ultimately to impose his will on the selection of public goods and services provided by the state. The world of the textbook is of special importance when one is concerned with economics as it serves functionally through its assumptions to influence belief and thus action. Here the commitment to consumer (and citizen) sovereignty remains virtually absolute.[20]

---

[18] Ibid., p. 279.

[19] Franklin M. Fisher, Zvi Griliches and Carl Kaysen, "The Costs of Automobile Model Changes Since 1949." *The Journal of Political Economy*, Vol. 70, No. 5 (October 1962), p. 434.

[20] "What things will be produced is determined by the votes of the consumers — not every two years at the polls but every day in their decision to purchase this item and not that." Paul Samuelson, *Economics*, 7th ed. (New York: McGraw-Hill, 1970), p. 42. However, in this edition Professor Samuelson subsequently softens this proposition and I sense, otherwise, that his commitment to consumer sovereignty is far from rigid. Others are more categorical. ". . . only [the consumer] can make the crucial decision on what goods he most prefers; thus, in the final analysis, consumers collectively decide what industry is to produce. The choices of consumers provide the basis on which business makes its decisions." C. E. Ferguson and Juanita M. Kreps, *Principles of Economics*, 2nd ed. (New York: Holt, Rinehart and Winston, 1965), p. 80.

"As buyers, individually but totally millions, react to prices, they also change prices. Consumers vote with their dollars. The buyer, himself guided by relative prices in making his choices, is directing the allocation of productive resources." C. Lowell Harris, *The American Economy*, 4th ed. (Homewood, Illinois: Richard D. Irwin, 1962), p. 380.

IV

It is not my purpose here to argue that the accepted views are incognate with reality, that the third view is right. This I have done at length elsewhere.[21] I doubt that the uncommitted reader will find the case for producer sovereignty as I have just outlined it wholly implausible. The case is strongest for public goods; there can be few men of accessible mind who have recently looked at the way weapons are provided without wondering if the notion of ultimate citizen sovereignty is above reproach. This is not a detail; it is half the Federal budget. Many must have wondered if the conventional doctrine of citizen sovereignty does not deliberately divert attention from the disenchanting reality — if it does not accord the public the myth of power while giving the military bureaucracy and the weapons industries the reality of power. But in the large scale consumer goods industries the case for producer sovereignty is not greatly less convincing. There is the massive outlay on persuading the consumer.[22] This persuasive effort increases with increas-

---

[21] *The Affluent Society*, especially pp. 134–167, and *The New Industrial State*, especially pp. 159–218.

[22] There is a marked tendency, especially among the unconsciously tendentious defenders of the market and thus of consumer and citizen sovereignty, to denigrate and even dismiss the role of advertising. One recent critic disposes of my interest in it by saying that it is concerned with "the most hackneyed theme in modern social literature — the power of advertising." (Scott Gordon, "The Close of the Galbraithian System," *Journal of Political Economy*, July–August 1968, p. 642.) So to minimize the role of so vast, obtrusive, expensive and integral an aspect of the modern market must surely provoke question. One notes also that advertising has continued to be a somewhat indigestible lump in conventional microeconomic theory. To see it, as does the most commonly accepted oligopoly theory, essentially as a functionless but safe alternative to price competition which ultimately cancels itself out, is not altogether satisfying and leads inevitably to the question, ill-received by advertisers and media when not tactfully elided

ingly complex technology and organization. It is a tenet of the more developed consumer goods industries that products must be selected, designed and produced with a view to what lends itself to persuasion. Accordingly, it requires a determined mind to conclude that the taste so expressed originates with the consumer. What the consumer deems to be a desirably shaped and chromatically compelling automobile is substantially different this year from what it was five years ago. But few would wish to argue that this represented a change in the consumer's intrinsic and improving vision of a vehicle — that, indeed, it was accomplished other than by rare skill, art and expense on the part of the automobile producers. It is not necessary to argue that the management of the consumer by the producer is complete, only that it makes consumer behavior conform in broad contours to producer need and intent. This is plausibly in accord with everyday observation of marketing practice and the commonplace claims of its practitioners. Nor will many resist the idea that these industries can bring the state to the support of their efforts in creating and managing consumer wants — that the automobile companies can get the highways that are essential for a consumer preference for automobile transportation; that the aircraft companies (under military disguise or more openly in the case of the SST) can win financing for the planes necessary for a public preference for air travel; or that

---

by economists, as to why such a portentous waste is not prohibited or mightily taxed. But there is also the fact, as Professor Rothenburg points out, that advertising is the most direct and visible attack on the concept of consumer sovereignty. This, one at least suspects, may be a reason for wanting to ignore it or, failing that, to follow Professor Gordon in suggesting that concern with it is unfashionable or otherwise intellectually unworthy. I count it an important part of the case for producer sovereignty that its exercise gives to so important an activity as advertising a wholly functional role in economic life.

the tobacco companies can still obtain a measure of immunity from the scientific evidence on the causes of cancer.

Finally, few will doubt the enormous stress which the process of persuasion places upon the importance of goods and the belief so created of the nexus between goods (including those that are technically innovative or can be so represented) and happiness. This, most will suppose, increases the susceptibility of consumers to persuasion. For if goods are firmly established as the cause of happiness, the public will be both attentive and responsive to claims on their behalf. And the relentless propaganda on behalf of goods must greatly increase the importance attached to production. This, in turn, it will surely be agreed, strengthens the position of producers in the exercise of their sovereignty especially as regards the community and the state. What can be so important as what they do? And economics again assists by making the level of output the formal, measurable accomplishment of the society.

But my purpose here is not to argue the case for producer sovereignty but to assume it — to assume it, though less comprehensively, as consumer sovereignty is now assumed. And that being done, I want to look at the problems of the society which, while excluded from view by the assumption of consumer sovereignty, now come spectacularly into view. What is so solved makes my case.

v

By far the most important matter that thus becomes clear concerns the relation of the individual to industrial society in the largest sense. In the accepted economics no general conflict can arise here. The individual or citizen is sovereign. There may be differences between different individuals as to whose commands are heeded. By ancient classical assent the rich speak more authoritatively in markets than the poor. And there may be friction or aberrations in the response of institutions to the ultimate authority of the individual. But none of this is systemic. The individual is ultimately and fundamentally in command; he cannot be at war with an economy he controls for he cannot be at war with himself.

When producer sovereignty is assumed the result is very different. This sovereignty is exercised, we have seen, by large and complex organizations. Their exercise of power is to serve their own goals — goals that include the security of the organization and its growth, convenience, prestige, commitment to technological virtuosity as well as its profits. There is every probability that these goals will differ from the aggregate expression of individual goals. Individuals are then accommodated to these goals, not the reverse. This normally will involve persuasion. But it may involve resort to the state or, in the manner of a utility marching its lines across the countryside, it may involve power that is inherent in institutional position.

The plausible consequence of economic development, so viewed, is not harmony between the individual and economic institutions but conflict. The conflict is modified by the persuasion — but not for the unpersuaded and those who sense what is happening. This conflict is sharply at odds with accepted economic (and political) interpretations of the reality. But it is not at odds with the reality. In the United States and the other industrial societies, it is a commonplace explanation of tension and discontent that the individual feels himself in the grip of large, impersonal forces whose purposes he senses to be hostile and in relation to which he feels helpless. The Pentagon pursues wars and builds weapons systems in accordance with its own dynamic. Similarly NASA. So the Department of Transportation in relation to the SST. So General Motors as a producer of automobiles that threaten to smother cities and as a sponsor of highways that have already gone far to devour them. So other industry as it subsumes countryside, water and air. This and the resulting discontent could not occur in a society in which the consumer or the citizen is sovereign. It is predictable in a society in which producing organizations are sovereign — in which they have power to pursue purposes of their own that are different from those of the consumer or citizen.

This conflict comes to a peculiarly sharp focus in the universities. This also is what the model would lead one to expect. In the universities large numbers of students are brought together by the unprecedented demands of the industrial system for qualified manpower. They are given a sense of personality as the older industrial proletariat was not; the older proletariat, indeed, was taught by the unions to submerge personality into a sense of class — to be class-conscious. And students are also exposed to social doctrine — to economic and political theory — which holds with some righteousness that the individual is possessed of ultimate power. And then they see a world in which organization exercises large, even seemingly plenary power and to which they, as citizens, soldiers, consumers or organization men are expected to be subordinate. It would be surprising — a triumph of indifference to both education and environment — if they did not react.

The notion of producer sovereignty, then, is not only empirically plausible — a seemingly logical response to the needs of the modern, highly technical, highly capitalized, very complex industrial organization — but it also sharply illuminates our major present concern. This is a good thing for any social theory to do. But economic and associated political theory in remaining with the notion of consumer and citizen sovereignty are not merely failing to interpret reality. By contributing to a contrast between what is taught and what exists, they are making these the servant not of an understanding of reality but of a conservatively useful myth that conceals the reality. And since, in fact, this cannot be concealed they are adding to frustration and conflict. They are also, it might be added, doing nothing for the reputation of economics for objectivity.

But this is not all. The notion of consumer and citizen sovereignty is otherwise diverting attention from fundamental problems of the economic and political system in a fashion that serves to strengthen the very producer sovereignty that the discipline denies. Let me cite eight specific examples, each of them of considerable contemporary concern.

1. If the mix of goods being produced at any given time seems unsatisfactory — if there are too many automobiles, too little mass transport, much television, few houses — consumer sovereignty holds that this reflects the dominant consumer will. The person who expresses doubt is seeking, in undemocratic elitist fashion, to substitute his preferences for those of the majority. But if producer sovereignty is assumed, the product mix will be the expression of comparative power in different industries. If there appear to be too many automobiles, insufficient intercity or commuter rail service or urban rapid transit, this will plausibly be because the automobile industry exercises its sovereignty — its power to persuade people that they want automobiles — more effec-

tively than do the producers of mass transport. We have more household appliances than houses because General Electric and Westinghouse are more powerfully sovereign than the housing industry. Except to the theoretically devout, none of this will seem unreasonable. But, by emphasizing consumer sovereignty, economics makes itself a shield for the exercise of producer sovereignty by the automobile industry. For by making questions about too many automobiles an elitist and undemocratic interference with consumer choice, it effectively excludes questions about the power of the automobile industry to impose its preference. It gives scientific and moral sanction to social indifference.

2. The concept of consumer sovereignty acts with marked force to inhibit questions concerning the cultural achievements of the system. It will surely be agreed that whatever the effects of advertising its ultimate effect is an extremely powerful and sustained propaganda on the importance of goods. No similar case is made on behalf of artistic, educational or other humane achievement. And the notion of consumer sovereignty suppresses any criticism.[23] While it may be conceded that the popular taste is biased toward goods, it holds that the popular taste must be respected. Again, to intervene is to substitute an elitist and snobbish preference for the honest democratic philistinism of the masses. The notion of producer sovereignty, by contrast, forces us to recognize that the sources of the popular taste, so-called, lie in the producing organizations that promulgate it for the

---

[23] With a peculiarly righteous indignation, in fact. I made this case in less sharp form and with much stronger emphasis on public goods in *The Affluent Society*. The rebuke differed only in emphasis. A few held that I was presuming to set an admittedly informed judgment against the democratic manifestation of the market. The rest held that I was presuming to interpose a precious, narcissistic, arrogant or otherwise grossly pretentious judgment for that of the market.

community. Economics renders a yet further conservative
service here. To the microeconomic doctrine of consumer
sovereignty it adds the macroeconomic test of output, not
art, as the measure of social achievement. The good society
is, very simply, one that increases gross national product at a
goodly rate.

3. The concept of consumer and citizen sovereignty allows
of no organic likelihood of a bias in the economy for private
as opposed to those public goods that do not serve producer
sovereignty. At most, there will be blockages and error in
the allocation of resources to the public sector. Producer
sovereignty, coupled with the fact that the instruments of
its exercise, advertising for example, are elaborately and ex-
pensively available to the private economy and not available
in any similar fashion to the public sector, makes this bias
systemic. At the end of 1969, the United States Senate reduced taxes in face of the seemingly unprecedented need of
the civilian public services. In the background was the doctrine that, unprecedented private consumption notwithstanding, taxes now bear on people with unprecedented
weight. Back of this was the formidable persuasion of producer sovereignty on behalf of private goods. There had
been no similar conditioning of the public on behalf of public goods — even though the cities were in a state of de-
terioration and disorder for want of funds. Again, it cannot
be bad to have a theory that accords with the contemporary
reality.

4. Consumer and citizen sovereignty sanctions the current
claims on resources of the military and associated industrial
power. These are in response to the perceived need and expressed demand of the public. Possibly they are excessive
but if so, this is an imperfection in the system — a sui generis

error. That military spending responds to citizen perception and action will tax the belief of even the most committed supporters of the received model; imperfection and error as an explanation for any part of the economy that is so large in both claim on resources and social portent as the military sector must lack something in scientific appeal. The notion of producer sovereignty increasing in effect with increasingly complex organization and military technology brings the power of the producers of military goods and services wholly into focus.

5. Consumer sovereignty makes pollution and other environmental disharmony a diseconomy external to the industry. In consequence, the cost of damage to air, water and surroundings is borne by the community, not by the producing firm which causes the trouble. Since the market is assumed to be an efficient expression of public taste and need, external diseconomies have long been viewed as of peripheral significance to be corrected by essentially cosmetic public regulation. With producer sovereignty environmental damage becomes a normal consequence of the conflict between the goals of the producing firm and those of the public. The goals of the firm place emphasis on growth and freedom for its organization, for autonomous decision unhampered by community or public constraints. Here again economic theory strongly supports producer sovereignty. Production and productive efficiency are the test of social performance. These give the power line or the industrial effluent or pollutant a natural priority. The burden of proof is strongly on anything, including the ecological preferences of the community, that interferes.

6. Consumer sovereignty allows of no question as to a socially desirable upper limit to the consumption either in

general or of particular products. The instruction of the
neoclassical model to the economist on this is strikingly clear.
The consumer wants more. Theirs not to reason why, theirs
but to satisfy. With producer sovereignty the view again
changes sharply. The level of consumption is seen to be a
derivative of producer goals, including the commitment of
the producing firm to continuous expansion of output. Consumer attitudes are substantially formed by producer persuasion. This emphasizes the satisfaction from continuing
increases in consumption. The question immediately arises
as to whether General Motors is the proper agency to decide
the proper level of consumption for its products. And since
the matter is not decided by the collective inner will of the
public, the question also arises as to the optimal upper level
of production and consumption in general. Such questions
should, perhaps, have been faced before now. For a host
of reasons, including the effect on environment, it is unlikely
that we can continue to increase physical output at recent
past rates for the next, say, twenty years. The proper level
of automobile use in cities is a matter of immediate urgency.
Once again, economics has rendered conservative service.
By holding these matters to be resolved by the inner and
unchallengeable will of the public, it has effectively banned
from public discussion all question as to how much a community should produce or consume.

7. Consumer sovereignty goes some way to sanction income inequality. Differences in income for personal services
reflect ultimately the willingness of the community to pay
for such services. This willingness, in turn, is derived from
individual market preferences. Inequality in nonproperty
incomes is thus legitimatized by the community. This too is

a considerable conservative service especially at a time when inequality in income distribution is increasing.[24] Producer sovereignty, by contrast, makes this income inequality, at least in part, the product of bureaucratic self-arrangement. It reflects not the needs and preferences of consumers but the needs and preferences of organization. Such a cause of inequality enjoys no similarly high sanction. It does correspond, however, with the everyday appreciation of the matter. That the General Motors hierarchy (or before its collapse that of Penn Central) has more to do with the distribution of income to its members than the buying public will not seem entirely improbable.

8. Finally, if consumer sovereignty is assumed, there will be a strong presumption that actions directly or indirectly affecting the consumer's market behavior will have a strong and reliable market response. It is to the consumer that the market responds. If by either fiscal or monetary policy his outlays are directly or ultimately curtailed, there will be confidence in the ensuing effect on prices and production. With producer sovereignty there will be no similar confidence. The producing firm is pursuing its own goals, which is to say that it is maximizing not necessarily its profits but its organizational interests. If this has caused it to subordinate profit maximization to growth, it can, if it must, increase revenues by increasing prices. And its organizational interests will include the security of the organization as opposed to the dangers inherent in labor conflict or interrupted production. So, given producer sovereignty, it is quite predictable that efforts to limit consumer expenditure in an

[24] Joseph A. Pechman, "The Rich, The Poor and The Taxes They Pay," *The Public Interest*, No. 17 (Fall 1968), pp. 21–43.

inflationary context, even if successful, will be accompanied by continuing price and wage increases in the highly industrialized, highly organized sector of the economy. The fact that this sector is not coordinate with the whole economy is of especial importance here. It means that the part of the economy characterized by producer sovereignty in effect exports its tensions to the more vulnerable sector where consumer sovereignty is still relevant.[25] A measure of index stabilization may even be accomplished at the expense of the latter.

This is a point of immediate interest — it is a compressed but wholly accurate description of what has been happening as this book goes to press. Here accepted economic theory serves to divert attention from the needed action which is some form of public control of wages and prices in that sector of the economy that is characterized by producer sovereignty. It has also blinded the economists responsible for the policy. In consequence, month after month, they have continued to avow their hope of ending inflation by measures appropriate to consumer sovereignty. And not surprisingly, month after month, they have been roundly defeated by a reality reflecting producer sovereignty.[26] In an age when public officials are often thought averse to personal immolation in pursuit of principle, they have been strikingly willing

[25] In *The New Industrial State,* influenced by the comparative success in the first half of the sixties in stabilizing prices in the organized sector of the economy through the guideposts and by the parallel resort of numerous other industrial countries to some form of wage-price restraint, I concluded that this was one of the parameters (like minimum prices or stable aggregate demand) where large organization would accept and even seek public stabilizing action. I still think public opposition to inflation as well as balance of payments and other reasons will eventually force such action. I am no longer so certain that it is one of the things that large organization needs.

[26] Until, quite possibly, they may achieve stabilization, as previously noted, at the cost of the nonindustrial and vulnerable sector of the economy.

to surrender their professional reputations on the altar of established doctrine. One regrets only that it is not in defense of a valid doctrine.

VI

None will doubt that this article leaves many important questions unanswered. There is, notably, the question as to the theory of the state that is here implied. The state as here envisaged comes close to being the executive committee of the large producing organization — of the technostructure. It stabilizes aggregate demand, underwrites or socializes expensive or risky technology, reflects the will of large organization in the mix of military and nonmilitary public goods, provides such needed public artifacts as highways for the management of specific consumer demand, supplies qualified manpower, otherwise stabilizes those parameters or does that planning which the large producing organization cannot do for itself. This being so, one must ask if the industrial state can separate itself from organization — if it can be the instrument of individual will. Let no one imagine that it will be easy.

One must ask also if there is a trade-off between increased technology, increased complexity of organization and increased production on the one hand and increased power of individual expression on the other. If so, is there a substantial measure of social perception in the behavior of the young who (at least while young) see in the rejection of physical artifacts an avenue to greater self-expression?

One must ask further if there is a possibility of meeting the power of organization with the power of anti-organization. If the automobile industry is sovereign in the market and thus in its decisions on automobile population and its effect on environment, can it be made less sovereign by countering organization — by political organization to exclude the internal combustion engine from urban areas? If the weapons industry is sovereign in the Congress, can it be made less sovereign by countering organization which removes its servants from the Congress?

Finally, and of high interest for this article, what is the effect on economics as a discipline, after years of comfortable coexistence with industrial and associated public bureaucracy, of making the power of the producer a central preoccupation? What happens when economics views the mix of products, the level of production, the autonomous exercise of power by the weapons industries, the effect on the environment not to mention the resolution of the wage-price bargain, as an exercise of bureaucratic power in the interest of bureaucratic goals and not as a reliable if sometimes obstructed response to the ultimate consumer will? Can economic theory embrace such issues? Can it stand up to the resulting contention? Clearly these matters have consequences for economics that are not slight. Indeed, they present an interesting choice for our discipline. We can remain with consumer sovereignty and be comfortable, non-controversial, increasingly sophisticated in our models and increasingly, and perhaps even dramatically, unrelated to life. Or economics can accept the implications of producer power — of the sovereignty of the great organizations. Then it will be contentious, politically perilous and for a long while, perhaps, intellectually inelegant in its models. But it will in compensation be relevant to the most immediate and formidable concerns of the industrial society.

I have little doubt as to the choice. Among my generation it will be, in principle, for comfort and its associated refinements. We have had one revolution; Keynes was enough. There are elements of truth in the emphasis on producer sovereignty, it will be said, but nothing that should require one to change his mind or his pedagogy. I say this will be the choice in principle for it will not be so in fact. Mention of Keynes reminds me that he stressed the ultimate power of ideas. In degree, he was right. But he could wisely have stressed the far greater authority of circumstance. Circumstance has given us the great private and associated public organizations. They have great power of the sort I have described. Divorced of this circumstance — as an abstract model interesting for itself — the ideas I am urging here would be nothing. Reinforced by such circumstance they are ineluctable.

And one trusts that for the young in our discipline professional comfort is not yet too much of a consideration. And comfort must contend with vanity. For, while one can exist decently in obsolescent maturity, the world rightly makes fun of the *young* fogy.

5

Inflation, Recession or Controls

*The Unpleasant Choice That Heaven Has
Arranged for Americans*

THE EARLY MONTHS of 1970 were just possibly decisive in
the modern history of economics. Ideas in which economists
reposed the greatest confidence were proved wrong and
therewith, not surprisingly, the associated policy. And this
happened under circumstances which allowed of no really
plausible explanation, rationalization or alibi — things in
which we economists are more than minimally accomplished.
There was, to be sure, more than a suspicion of error before;
the evidence was highly adverse to the reputable ideas. But
the heretics were a minority and the adverse evidence could
be attributed to a lag. In economics, any inconvenient dis-
association of effect from cause is always attributed to a lag.
But not even lags can last forever.

The doctrine was, of course, that the U.S. economy could
be regulated by *general* measures in such manner that employment would be adequate and prices would be approximately stable. A "trade-off," a new and popular word among
economists, would exist between price stability and employment. The closer the approach to level prices, the more
people who would be out of work; the lower the unemployment, the greater the rate of price increases. This relationship had been given quantitative expression by the so-called

Phillips curve. This showed the annual rate of price increase which, on the basis of historical data, could be expected to accompany any particular percentage of unemployment in the labor force. The choice between unemployment and inflation so shown *seemed* to be essentially benign — reasonable price stability could be combined with a tolerable level of unemployment. Also, a tactfully unspoken point, the unemployment would be among the unskilled, uneducated, mostly young and black, who are also unorganized. These are assumed to accept unemployment philosophically, there being nothing they can do about it. There were no other decisively adverse side effects from the stabilization measures.

The difference of opinion was not over the efficacy of the general measures but over technique. Since Keynes, most economists had placed major reliance on fiscal measures — on control of total spending in the economy by means of the Federal budget. Inflation being the problem, this consisted in making Federal taxes and spending a sufficient restraining force on total demand in the economy. But in recent times there had been the so-called monetary revival. This made control of spending from borrowed funds the key instrument in the control of prices. The difference between the exponents of fiscal and monetary management could not be exaggerated. Both believed in the efficacy of general measures. Both urged some combination of fiscal and monetary measures. The difference was in the mix.

The Nixon economists came to office in January, 1969, in a state of superlative confidence in the efficacy of general measures as they would employ them. The President promised never to interfere with wages and prices. Fiscal and especially monetary policy, precisely applied, would serve. In one of the more ecstatic examples of economic phrase-making, he said that inflation would be ended by "fine-tuning" the American economy; one could as well speak of fine-tuning a major Mississippi flood. The current inflation was blamed on the previous bad management of the economy — on tuning that was too coarse. With all wage and price restraint so ruled out, Pierre Rinfret, the consulting economist, dispatched a letter to his clients telling them that the lid on wages and prices was now off. It may be assumed that quite a few others reached the same conclusion. It is possible that in these first weeks the Administration did more to promote inflation than it accomplished in the next year and a half in controlling it.

Then came a steady flow of promises that inflation would soon end. Advising the President of the United States on economic policy, since few Presidents find the subject at all interesting, is tedious work. The tedium is relieved, after a fashion, by the liturgical functions of the office. Every week in the year, some convocation of businessmen, bankers, investment counselors, market researchers or economic necromancers is assembling somewhere in the United States. Often, combining business with tax deductibility, they meet at the better spas. All of these — the South Florida Savings Bank Association, the John Hancock Million Dollar Club, the Associated Sport and Saddle Shoe Manufacturers of America — have a prescriptive right to economic education by a member of the Council of Economic Advisers. The speeches so given are not always informative. But they are firmly repetitious and during the first year and a half of the Nixon Administration, all promised that inflation would end, that prices would become stable.

Always the stability would come approximately two quarters in the future. As the promises continued, so at an increasing rate did the inflation. (In time, the date when the promise would give way to performance was given a little more lag.) Dr. Paul W. McCracken, the head of the Council of Economic Advisers, became perhaps the most overpromised man in the history of the economics profession. There is a well-recognized tendency in public life when you want something to happen, to predict that it will happen. And then when it doesn't happen you escalate the predictions. Not since Herbert Hoover predicted the turning of the immortal corner was prediction therapy so remorselessly pursued as in the first eighteen months of the new Administration. The policy being pursued was called the "game plan" for defeating inflation. There had been no game quite like it since the Rose Bowl of 1929 when Roy Riegels ran 75 yards toward the wrong goal.

Outside the Administration, the view was slightly less sanguine. But the economists who had served the Kennedy-Johnson Administrations did not strongly question the reliance on general measures. In the early sixties — the Kennedy years — prices were fairly stable. Unemployment, though initially high, was falling — from an annual average of 6.7 percent of the labor force in 1961 to 4.5 in 1965. The so-called guideposts were then in effect which meant that wage increases were held on the average to what industry generally could afford from productivity gains. And industry accordingly was persuaded to forgo price increases. Enforcement was hortatory; it was a price increase by U.S. Steel in violation of this general understanding that provoked President Kennedy's inspired denunciation of the Corporation in April 1962. The economics underlying the guideposts obviously accords a prime determining role in price-making to unions and corporations. That is why wages and prices must be restrained. But this power (as other essays in this volume have told) is not much stressed in standard macroeconomic doctrine — roughly the economics of the textbooks. This holds that prices are set in markets, and respond well to changes in demand. If demand is restricted by general fiscal and monetary measures, price increases come to an end. Even in the Kennedy-Johnson years, the guideposts were the poor relation of economic policy. We economists greatly prefer to believe what we teach. When the guideposts later came under pressure from the Vietnam war, they were not strengthened but abandoned. And when the Kennedy-Johnson economists returned to the campus, their interest in wage and price restraint declined. The guideposts were defended as a useful adjunct to the policy but more cosmetic than real. It was fiscal and monetary policy that really counted. Almost no one talked about making the guidelines mandatory, i.e., making them work. That was too radical.

There was never any strong proof that high employment and stable prices could be combined in the absence of such control. Much of the evidence antedated modern corporate price-making and collective bargaining. Rather, there were hope and faith. But in economics, hope and faith coexist with great scientific pretension and also a deep desire for respectability. Fiscal and monetary measures in whatever mix are impeccably respectable, and the question of the particular mix is the kind of thing that can be resolved in a quiet office around a large table between gentlemen. Control of wages and prices has no similar standing. Its advocates have been thought to lack subtlety of mind and manners — to go too abruptly to the point. It requires tedious and even bitter negotiations with union leaders and corporations. Congress will of course get involved. As always, the sociology of economics is not without interest and not unimportant.

The flaw in the respectable doctrine is the appalling obduracy of circumstance. Wages do shove up prices. Prices do pull up wages. The bargaining that produces the wage and price increases continues even under conditions of severe fiscal and monetary restraint. It can be stopped but only by a considerable recession. It is almost as though those engaged in collective bargaining and corporate price-making were out to discredit the very best economic scholarship. One wonders why men should be so cruel.

So despite the most rigorous application of the general measures, prices continued to rise and for many months at a record rate. Dr. McCracken and his colleagues were forced to take comfort from the fact that the rate at which the inflation was getting worse was declining — or, as did Herbert Stein of the Council of Economic Advisers, from the even more exiguous fact that "the behavior of prices in the past year has been consistent with [the] expectation of a decline in the rate of inflation." Meanwhile unemployment rose steadily and exceedingly uncomfortable side effects of the policy appeared. Smaller businessmen who had to borrow money were punished with a highly selective brutality. Tight money does not much hurt the big well-managed corporation. It has a large internal cash flow that may make borrowing unnecessary and a favored position at the bank if it does need money. In contrast, tight money puts the housing industry into an acute depression and is hard on other businesses that depend on borrowed funds. The price increases in the private sector of the economy are also exported to the public sector as increases in living costs. And there among teachers, police, firemen and sanitation workers, they cause predictable turmoil. They also have an adverse effect on the balance of payments.

Finally, there was the effect on the financial markets. These had been made fragile by the putting together of jerry-built and debt-ridden conglomerates, previously called holding companies; by the ridiculous bidding up of the so-called glamour stocks; by the exfoliation of performance funds, hedge funds and "go-go" funds; and by the arrival of a new generation of money managers whose qualification, like that of their predecessors in past speculative orgies, consisted entirely in the eagerness of fools to be separated from their money. Under the pressure of the tight money policy, this speculative bubble collapsed. This had to happen sometime. But it was something that the proponents of the policy did not foresee. And it was something that could have further and very uncomfortable consequences for business investment, consumer spending and for the solvency of the more vulnerable corporations. As this is written (in the early summer of 1970) these consequences seem by no means improbable.

The effect of general measures is, thus, to combine inflation with recession. And once this combination is established, no modification of the policy allows of an escape. Looking at the recession the obvious course is to allow an increase in loanable funds at lower interest rates. This would ease unemployment, encourage home construction and mitigate the sorrow in Wall Street. But because of the price-wage spiral, inflation would continue. Easier money would make it worse. To tighten up on interest rates and the budget would be to make the recession worse. To continue as before is to combine and possibly worsen the combination of inflation and recession that the existing policy had contrived. There are many misfortunes that can befall an economist. The worst, by far, is to have a theory in which he devoutly believes, and which is wrong, put into practice.

The response of the Administration economists to their entrapment in the early months of 1970 was a rewarding study — or it would have been were the matter not so serious. Economics, like foreign policy, allows for an escape from error through what may be called the Indochina effect. This generous device enables a man who has been wrong to denounce his previous position without admitting error and, by becoming right, thus greatly to enhance his reputation. Dr. Arthur F. Burns, the Chairman of the Federal Reserve Board, took this route. He urged the wage-price guideposts he had previously and with great force condemned. (His transmigration was incomplete for he proposed something less strong than the Kennedy-Johnson measures which themselves had proved too weak.) Dr. McCracken was more complex. He conceded that the wage-price spiral was the cause of inflation but argued against doing anything about it. In a speech in Dallas in April, 1970, he noted that in the fourth quarter of 1969, labor costs per unit of output (which were about 75 percent of total costs) were rising at an annual rate of 7 percent. He then went on to say that "both evidence and theory are pretty clear that a rising cost level tends to mean a rising price level." Then he condemned controls. Later, in June, the President adopted a similar formula. He too accepted that the wage-price spiral is a cause of inflation and even established a committee to draw attention to inflationary wage settlements. But then he sternly rebuked those who proposed action to restrain wages and prices. One thinks, somehow, of a fireman who finds fire to be a cause of property loss and water a remedy but who, on grounds of principle, greatly opposes water as a way of putting the fire out.

In fact, the only answer is the one that has for so long been dismissed as so disreputable. That is to act directly on the wage-price spiral — to have wage and price control where the spiral contributes actively to inflation.

This must be real control. Dr. Burns and the economists of the Kennedy-Johnson period duck reality when they talk about a return to the voluntary guideposts. The guideposts won't do. They were not strong enough in the early sixties. Since then inflation has become part of everyone's expectation. Only if there is absolute assurance that it will come to an end can unions be persuaded to accept wage increases that reflect only prospective gains in productivity. Also, voluntary measures are highly discriminatory. They favor the individual or organization which refuses to comply and penalize those that are cooperative. This also guarantees their eventual breakdown. And there is nothing to be said for Presidential billingsgate as an enforcement device. It is much better public practice to lay down fair, firm rules after careful consultation with all concerned and then, when someone violates the rules, have resort to law.

With wage and price controls, interest rates can be reduced before price stability is brought about by recession. High interest rates will not have to carry the burden of controlling the wage-price spiral, a burden which they cannot carry anyway. With lower interest rates, home construction will increase, the pressure on small business will be reduced, employment will rise, and all without a new surge of inflation. Were such a policy combined at this writing with a prompt withdrawal from Indochina — which would ease the pressure of demand and, a more important matter, restore our reputation for elementary good sense — the immediate economic problem would be largely solved.

Such price and wage action, it is said, interferes with free markets. This is self-evident nonsense. The policy interferes with markets in which the interference of unions and corporations is already plenary. It fixes in the public interest prices that are already fixed.

Only prices that are so set by unions and strong corporations need to be (or should be) controlled. Prices of farm products, of most services and of products of small manufacturers are still subject to market influences. Where prices are still set by the market, general measures to restrict demand still work — or they do as much as can be done. As one must fix prices that are already fixed by private firms, one does not need to interfere with the market where the market still governs.

I am not without experience in the practical side of price control or in the difficulties involved. During World War II, price control was under my direction from its inception until mid-1943. No one else, I suppose, has ever fixed so many prices. In the past I have made various proposals for handling the problem but, as this is written, the best plan is a modification of one offered by Robert Roosa, former Undersecretary of the Treasury under Kennedy and now a leading Wall Street banker. He would begin by freezing all prices and wages for six months. This would break the structure of inflationary expectations and assure the unions that they could bargain on the assumption of stable living costs. During this six-month period there would be active consultation with corporations and unions to work out a more durable system of restraint. Steps would also have to be taken to iron out gross inequities — as for example between unions that had just won a new contract and those that were at the end of an old one. During the course of the freeze, all small enterprises — those employing, say, fewer than a hundred people, or even a thousand people — should be exempted. So also the wages of all workers not covered by collective bargaining contracts. I would also exempt all retail firms whatever their size for they have little independent market power. The objective is not perfectly level prices but the elimination of the grossly inflationary thrust of the present wage-price spiral.

Controls are not a temporary expedient. There must, alas, be a permanent system of restraint. That is because we will continue to have strong unions and strong corporations and a desire to minimize unemployment. The combination, in the absence of controls or serious recession, is inflationary. It will not become otherwise in the future.

No one who has had experience with wartime price control will be casual about the problems in managing it. Nor is it a formula for popularity; everyone eventually unites in disliking the price-fixer. But economic policy cannot be made as now with a primary eye to the comfort, convenience and general relaxation of those who guide it. The public interest must also be consulted. And if the controls are confined to the unions and to the corporations with market power, as here proposed, the administrative structure need not be vast. Dealings will be with only a few hundred unions and a few thousand firms and for the latter it is sufficient to specify the limits within which average as distinct from individual prices may be moved. All price and wage control involves an arbitrary exercise of public power. But this is not an objection, for it replaces an arbitrary exercise of private power and one that has further and exceedingly arbitrary effects for those who suffer from the resulting inflation.

Eventually economists, including those who advise the President if they are jealous of their reputations, will have to accept the idea of controls — and devote themselves to making them work. Up until now they have been substituting hope for reality, and hope unrequited does not sustain even an official economist forever. Within the older framework of fiscal and monetary policy, the choice is between severe inflation, loss to those on fixed incomes, distress and turmoil among public employees and, on the other hand, severe unemployment, severe discrimination against the industries that depend on borrowed money and serious strain in the financial markets — and along with all this, quite possibly, a good deal of inflation too. Whoever made respectable economic policy a choice between such repellent alternatives had a bad upbringing and is obviously a very mean man. But so it is. So the less reputable course of controlling the wage-price bargain obtrudes itself. And, since there is no escape, it will continue to obtrude itself. 142637

6

The Nixon Administration and the Great Socialist Revival

A note on the meaning of socialism

The term socialism suffers from ambiguity in part because (at least until the recent revival) conservatives often stigmatized as socialist any action by the state they did not happen to like. And liberals have glossed over unequivocally socialist actions by claiming them to be necessary for the functioning of free enterprise. In this article I use the word socialism in its technically precise meaning (as would the Wall Street Journal *or Professor Milton Friedman but in a much more restricted and less alarmist sense than does* National Review*) to denote a position by the state in the capital structure or plant of an industry or firm that is large enough to provide or portend major social influence or control. Such socialism is socialism.*

CERTAINLY the least predicted development under the Nixon Administration was this great new thrust to socialism. One encounters people who still aren't aware of it. Others must be rubbing their eyes for certainly the portents seemed all to the contrary. As an opponent of socialism, Mr. Nixon seemed steadfast — on this, even uniquely so. And ever since the end of the New Deal socialism itself had seemed clearly in decline. Conservatives still professed opposition but not much anxiety. Talk of socialist plots had largely disappeared among the followers of the Reverend Billy Graham and diminished among the followers of the Reverend Billie Hargis. In the twenty years following World War II, American businessmen proclaimed eloquently their confidence in the American system, their desire to stand on their own two feet, their ability to do so and their bold conviction that whatever the state could do, they could do better. "If every Communist knew the facts about capitalism, there wouldn't be any Communists," a big machinery manufacturer said in its advertising some years ago. Other entrepreneurs, if more restrained, agreed.

And this confidence had been, literally, infectious. The public took business at its word. Liberals, Eastern intellectuals, left-wing unions, professional malcontents — all the classic sponsors of socialism — were silent. They seemed to know when they were beaten. In time, young radicals came to denounce the system and on occasion put a brick through its windows. But they did not suggest that the government take over. That would be to put the Pentagon, the CIA, the Department of Justice, J. Edgar Hoover and the rest of that wicked crew even more in charge.

In an intelligently plural economy, a certain number of industries should be publicly owned. Elementary considerations of public convenience require it. For moving and housing people at moderate cost, private enterprise does not serve. But I had come reluctantly to the conclusion that socialism, even in this modest design, was something I would never see. Now I am being rescued by this new socialist upsurge promoted, of all things, by socialists not on the left but on the right. And they have the blessing, and conceivably much more, of a Republican administration.

The new socialism also shows an acute sense of strategy. In the years after World War II in Britain, where socialism had a fair run, British socialists developed the doctrine of the commanding heights. The state would not take over the entire economy. It would aim for that part which was so strategic that its loss destroyed capitalist power, shattered its morale and so secured social control over the rest. The new conservative socialism in the United States has taken over the strategy of the commanding heights with a vengeance.

Thus the first of the heights which the British socialists marked out for capture after World War II was the railroad system. It had great symbolic value. More than textiles, water transport or steel, this was the industry where modern large-scale capitalism began. So, pro tanto, it was where socialism should begin. To be astride the transportation system carried also the impression if not the reality of power.

The railroads were similarly marked out by the new American socialism for its first offensive. This was concentrated on the biggest of the systems, indeed the biggest transportation company in the United States, the Penn Central. The attack was not led by the passengers and shippers, the two groups which had been most aggressively abused by private capitalism in this industry. Nor did the workers, once the big battalions of socialism, react. The socialist thrust against the Penn Central was led by the executives of the railroad — by the agents and instruments of the capitalists themselves.

Under private capitalism, it is a commonplace occurrence that a company cannot pay its debts. That is because the system accepts the fact of loss as well as profit and enshrines the risk-taker. "The American competitive enterprise system is an acknowledged profit and loss system, the hope of profits being the incentive and the fear of loss being the spur," the U.S. Steel Corporation said in its annual report a few years ago. It was echoing one of the most articulate prophets of the capitalist faith, the late Clarence Randall, also a steel man, who had declared (in *A Creed for Free Enterprise*) that, "If we seek to keep government out of business, we must not ourselves invite it in . . . Free enterprise means private capital, and the man who does not risk is unworthy to share the rewards." Because risk is inherent in capitalism, there is, through bankruptcy proceedings, a well-recognized procedure for scaling down debts when a run of losses makes it impossible for the capitalist enterprise to pay.

But when the Penn Central found it couldn't pay its bills, its executives quickly revealed their deeper ideological commitment. The capitalist rules and procedures were summarily rejected. Urged on by what *Newsweek* called "a frantic consortium of 77 banks," the railroad executives turned to the state. The government was invited to take a $200 million participation in the capital structure of the railroad as a first step. Legislation was introduced to allow the government to stake out a $750 million capital position in American railroads in general. Once this was passed, the government was to be asked in to Penn Central for a lot more. This dramatic rush to socialism won the initial approval of the Republican Administration. Everything, indeed, seemed greased and ready to go.

There is, however, a dog-in-the-manger quality about people who are promoting social change. It is an old problem. Liberals, though themselves considered susceptible to socialism, evidently want it on their own terms or not at all. Though he is a liberal and the leading critic of American finance capitalism in the Congress, Representative Wright Patman blocked the socialist drive on the Penn Central.

His objection, he said, was to the helter-skelter character of the railroad's rush into the embrace of the state, and vice versa, and to the somewhat dubious legal authority provided for the initial steps by the Defense Production Act. (In the past the war power has been notoriously a cover for socialist experiment and, feeling that the end justifies the means, socialists have not hesitated, on occasion, to stretch the law.) But it seems likely that the setback is only temporary. Other railroads are known to want government participation in their capital structure. There is no chance that the Penn Central will get through receivership, much less escape from it, without public capital. Even if he feels strongly about defending private enterprise, Mr. Patman cannot stand up against this kind of pressure forever.

And, in any case, the sponsors of the new socialism have had a major moral success. For the first time since the Great Depression, perhaps even since their return to private ownership following World War I, private capitalism in the railroad industry is no longer assumed. Full nationalization of the railroads is being discussed. "Washington seems to be the only power that has the potential, at least, of building a rational, balanced, national rail system," *Time* magazine declared in a special editorial early in the summer of 1970, H. R. Luce's heavenly reaction being unreported. And the prospect for such Washington power is good. Once the government has a firm stake in Penn Central, the public will start demanding better and cleaner trains that also ar-

rive. And shippers will demand that their freight be delivered. The government, as those who fear socialism have
long warned, is extremely vulnerable to such pressure. Public
funds will be spent to improve service. And as things get
better on the Penn Central, people will want similar changes
on the other roads. There is no need to write any more of
the script. The new socialism has lost a battle but not a war.

II

The assault on Penn Central has been the most ambitious
effort of the new socialism to date but the forces back of it
are better revealed by what may perhaps be called its Lockheed caper. The Lockheed Corporation is also very big —
it is the largest defense firm and was forty-first among all
industrial corporations in 1969. As a candidate for socialism,
it has certain peculiarities: there are some who would insist
that it is already publicly owned. Much of its fixed plant
belongs to the Federal Government; it gets most of its working capital from the government; until recently, nearly all
of its business came from the government; its famous cost
overruns are fully socialized. Yet it has continued to describe
itself as a private corporation. Like the Penn Central, it
cannot pay its bills. An ill-timed venture into the civilian
market for planes; a contract for the C-5A military transport
plane that was so scandalous that bureaucrats and politicians
who would ordinarily have enriched it to save the company
scuttled instead for cover, along with the economic slow-
down, are all responsible for its difficulties. Like the Penn
Central, Lockheed wants the government even more in.

But much more clearly than in the case of Penn Central,
the inspiration to the new socialism is here shown to be
coming from the financial community. The banks have gone

to the foundations for their tactics, which is logical since the
foundations have often been accused of promoting socialism.
For some years, foundations have been using the so-called
incentive grant which means that the recipient gets money
only if he bestirs himself and does what the donor wants
him to do. In midsummer of 1970, a group of twenty-four of
the nation's major banks (as they were described by the
New York Times) agreed to make an $80 million incentive
grant to Lockheed. To qualify, Lockheed had to get the
government involved to the extent of (hopefully) $300
million in loans, guaranteed loans and gifts. Thus private
capitalism forced socialism in approximately a one-to-three
ratio. The fact that twenty-four large banks agreed on the
tactic does not leave much question as to how the financial
community feels about the new socialism.

As a device for socialist propagation, that of the banks in
the Lockheed case is almost certainly superior to the oratory,
agitation, strikes, demonstrations, sticks, stones and low-yield
explosives on which an earlier generation of socialists relied.
Along with others I have long felt that the specialized
weapons firms should be recognized as full public corporations — that, being extensively socialized already, they are
a natural for socialism. This effort has suddenly come to look
a lot more practical. Once the new socialism has made its
point at Lockheed and assuming the same help from the
banks, General Dynamics, North American Rockwell, LTV
Aerospace, Grumman and the rest should be easy.

As in the case of Penn Central, the new tory socialism faces
liberal opposition over Lockheed. But here instead of Congressman Patman, the Administration has two stalwart allies
on the two Armed Services Committees — F. Edward Hébert
of Louisiana in the House and John Stennis of Missis-

sippi in the Senate. With this kind of support, socialism is hard to stop. And, to repeat, socialism at Penn Central and Lockheed is not symbolic — a mere opening wedge. These are big companies — genuine peaks among the commanding heights.

III

President Nixon's third socialist front is the socialized SST. Here too the Administration is pressing hard and here too it has strong capitalist allies. The aircraft industry, like the banks to Lockheed, is giving valuable encouragement. The plane has the strong support of Transportation Secretary John A. Volpe. As a highway contractor in the public sector, a onetime Federal Highway Administrator and a road-building Governor of Massachusetts, Secretary Volpe has had an unparalleled association with the most purely indigenous branch of American socialism which is moving earth under public auspices and covering it with asphalt and concrete. (In total value of public resources deployed over a lifetime, it is doubtful if any member of the Central Committee of the CPUSSR can match Secretary Volpe's score.) Given his background, the Secretary is not likely to be deterred by any ideological, financial or ecological objections to spending a few hundred millions for a public airplane.

Important as they are, however, the railroads, the defense industries and the next generation of planes are not the ultimate goal of the new socialism. The ultimate target is Wall Street. This is as it should be and here it is making its greatest move — one that for drama and a kind of sanguinary gall would be appreciated even by such a master of these arts as the young Leon Trotsky himself.

The Wall Street objective is nothing less than the New

York Stock Exchange itself, the very heart of American, even of world, capitalism, the Everest of the commanding heights. The opportunity arises, as ever, from economic crisis. A known, appreciable but undisclosed number of members of the Stock Exchange have been hit by falling revenues, high costs and the slump in the stock market and thus in the value of the securities they own. In consequence of this and their own inefficiency, their capital is impaired, the chances for repair are poor and, a miracle apart, they cannot make good to their customers the money and securities left with them for speculative use. Moreover, when such stresses develop, as Walter Bagehot pointed out in the last century and Richard Whitney, lately President of the Exchange, proved anew in the thirties, a certain amount of thimblerigging, prestidigitation and pure larceny always comes to light. These will add to the loss.

Admittedly it is the money of speculators that is at risk. An ordinary investor who buys stock to keep and takes delivery doesn't get hurt when a broker goes broke. Only the man with a margin account who sells short or who leaves stock with his broker for trading purposes runs any appreciable risk. It is speculators who have margin accounts, sell short or maintain an active trading account.

A speculator, even more than a man who lends money to a railroad, is expected under capitalism to risk loss. Were there no losses, speculation would be altogether too attractive. Included among the traditional risks of capitalism is that of doing business with people who can't pay. However, the new socialism has not been deterred. Taking a leaf from the old socialists who never hesitated to weep over widows, orphans and helpless young women victimized by the capitalists, the new ones have converted the speculator into a trusting investor, a truly helpless figure, as much in need of protection as Sister Carrie.

The Wall Street vehicle of the new socialism is the Securities Investor Protection Corporation or SIPC, a fund created by the Stock Exchange which is to be guaranteed by the government to the extent of a billion dollars. This will pay off the customers, creditors and victims of the failed houses. Because of some residual opposition to socialism in Wall Street, SIPC is being billed, rather imaginatively, as an insurance fund. Since the firms to be rescued are already in deep trouble, it is the first insurance fund in some time to insure against accidents that have already occurred — to place a policy on barns which have already burned down. But this is a detail. As the new socialists see the prospect (one may assume), several of the larger stock exchange houses will eventually fail. The government will step in to conserve their assets against the claims it has paid. There will be strong pressure to minimize hardship and unemployment by keeping the firms going. The government will oblige — the familiar yielding to pressure again. Presently other firms will fail and the government will find itself in a dominant position on the Street and in the Exchange. It will rationalize the now hideously inefficient arrangements by which securities are exchanged, ban short selling and advise innocents who hope to get rich on glamour stocks and go-go funds to be more sensible. The SEC will be disbanded. Socialism will have been accomplished and in the seemly fashion that one would expect of the financial community.

This, of course, is only a sample scenario. It may not happen. In the last hundred years, the plans of socialists have gone often awry and the world is littered with the wreckage of their utopias. But no old-fashioned socialist ever had a better idea for getting a foothold on Wall Street. Their hats should be off to the new men. Friedrich Engels, a rich and gentlemanly businessman who loved fox-hunting, would, one senses, especially approve.

IV

An old tactic of socialists is the campaign designed systematically to discredit capitalism. Not only is capitalism exploitive but it is also billed as dishonest and incompetent. The new socialists with their inside, as distinct from old-fashioned outside, agitators have shown themselves especially adept in this tactic. By subjecting their customers to extensive delay in delivering their stock and arousing apprehension as to whether, in fact, any particular transaction would be accomplished, various brokerage houses have recently engendered doubts about capitalism even in the resistant minds of the relatively rich. According to Philip Loomis, the general counsel of the SEC, they also have "occasionally" allowed cash and securities to vanish from their customers' accounts to be used instead by the firm. This kind of behavior lends itself especially well to propaganda designed to discredit the system.

Within Lockheed the allies of the new socialism have withheld bad news from the public in order to enhance the value of the company's stock. Such action by insiders also encourages the critics of capitalism, especially if they happen to have bought at the wrong time. The $1.5 billion error in estimating the cost of the C-5A was helpful in conveying an impression of inefficiency. So were factory operations. A former Army colonel, who was employed by the company as an airlift expert, estimated that the company got six hours' work out of an eight-hour shift except when it went to overtime. Then it got five out of ten. From time to time, he told James Phillips, a *New Republic* writer, "since I had nothing better to do, I would walk through the plant." These trips were his major contribution to the company, "since workers seeing me without a badge and in a suit and white shirt went back to work, as they were not sure of who I was." It seems they took him not for a new socialist but an old-fashioned mean capitalist. In any case, the tactic of the new socialists at Lockheed was clear. They were out to make the Post Office look good and they succeeded.

For discrediting capitalism the socialist vanguard at Penn Central was, however, much the most effective and surprisingly, considering its showing on other matters, the most imaginative. That their method of operating the passenger trains and freight service encouraged a widespread interest in socialism has already been mentioned. But, additionally, dividends (about $100 million in 1968 and 1969) were paid with cash that was badly needed to prevent derailments or even to move the trains at a reasonable speed. More capital (about $19 million), similarly needed, was diverted to real estate promotion in Florida, California, Texas and other precincts. To waste capital is a good way to dramatize the shortcomings of capitalism. A number of high officials emphasized their conviction that the capitalism with which they were associated had no future by selling their own stock and Chairman Stuart T. Saunders, in an especially nice touch, emphasized his disinterest in having any knowledge of the enterprise he headed by buying more. With the assistance of some remarkably convenient accounting rules, the company converted impressive losses in 1968 and 1969 into decent but wholly ethereal profits. This has further significance. It means that if auditing can be nationalized too, no public corporation under the new socialism need have a serious deficit. Socialism will be protected on what, in the past, has been its weakest flank — the tendency for socialized firms to lose money.

v

It would be a mistake to ascribe too much to the campaign from within these companies to discredit capitalism. Economic recession has been important. In fact, without it nothing else would have been possible and here the question arises as to how deliberately the Nixon Administration paved the way for the new socialism.

It is a path that has been amply illuminated. A hundred and twenty-five years ago Marx noted that it was the capitalist crisis that gave socialism its chance: "It is enough," he said, "to mention the commercial crises that by their periodical return put on trial, each time more threateningly, the existence of the entire *bourgeois* society." Mr. Nixon is probably not a great reader of Marx but Drs. Burns, Schultz and McCracken are excellent scholars who knew him well and could have brought the President abreast. And it is beyond denying that the crisis that aided the rush into socialism was engineered by the Administration. Money was deliberately made tight. The budget was deliberately made restrictive. The effect of these actions in raising interest rates and depressing the economy was firmly acclaimed as the Nixon Game Plan. The difficulties of Penn Central, Lockheed and the member firms of the NYSE were part of the same game plan — and socialism, as we have seen, is the name of the game. Cause and consequence were never closer; cause could not have been more deliberately contrived.

And suspicion is deepened by the sensational silence of conservatives. As the new socialism has moved against the great corporations and Wall Street, there have, as noted, been protests from liberals. But nothing has been heard from Roman Hruska. Or Goldwater. Or Attorney General or Mrs. Mitchell. Or from Caspar Weinberger, the President's new budget man who took office with the announced intention of ending, in Washington, the only mildly socialist influence of John Maynard Keynes. Or from David Rockefeller. Or from James Buckley. Or from William F. Buckley, Jr., a man whose silence has never before been remarked. These are keen men — and women, alert defenders of an ancient faith. Not one of them could have overlooked so massive a movement to socialism. They cannot have been converted. They could not be part of the plot. Is it possible that they have been repressed into silence? Has Mr. Agnew got to them too? Are they taking cover like the networks and the really sensible publishers? It is plausible.

Yet things might not be as they seem. A conspiracy theory of history is always too tempting. Dr. Arthur Burns as the Kerensky of this revolution, the Federal Reserve Building as its Smolny, tight money rather than oratory as its weapon, forces unleashed which, as in the case of Kerensky, no man can control — these thoughts are almost irresistibly attractive.

But, in fact, we could be seeing not a deliberate and well-planned thrust toward socialism but one of the less dramatic tendencies of capitalism. That is the tendency to say to hell with principle when the prospect is for losing money and go for any port in the storm.

7

On the Grave and Frightening Perils
of Financial History

I WROTE *The Great Crash* during the summer and autumn of 1954. At the time I was engaged on the manuscript which eventually became *The Affluent Society*. Or, more precisely, after months of ineffective and frustrating labor which had produced a set of chapters so vapid in content and repulsive in style that I could not bear to read them, I was totally stalled. Suicide seemed a possible answer; unfortunately it was an exceptionally lovely summer in southern Vermont. My neighbor in Cambridge, Arthur M. Schlesinger, Jr., had once made the modest request that I do the definitive work on the Great Depression. It would be convenient, he thought, for his work on Roosevelt. I resolved to compromise and write a book on the days that ushered it in, concentrating more on the crash itself than the events that followed.

I never enjoyed writing a book more; indeed, it is the only one I remember in no sense as a labor but as a joy. I did the research in the Baker Library at Dartmouth College, working under the Orozco murals on the ground floor. They somehow supported the mood of unreality, gargantuan excess and hovering disaster of the months before the crash. And if this mood became too overpowering, as might happen toward the end of the morning or the end of the afternoon,

I could walk out into the sunshine, across the nicest village common in New England, and have a martini and a meal at the Hanover Inn. I scamped my teaching that autumn to work on the manuscript; when I left it with the publisher, I felt that I was saying goodbye to a close and valued companion.

II

My labors during the autumn had been made to seem rather more relevant by the contemporary boom in the stock market. This was small compared with 1929; it was very small compared with the insanity that subsequently broke out. But it was plain that an increasing number of people were coming to the conclusion — the conclusion that is the common denominator of all speculative episodes — that they were predestined by luck, an unbeatable system, divine favor, access to inside information or exceptional financial acumen to become rich without work.

In the winter the boom, or boomlet, continued. The Democrats had won the Congressional elections the previous November; the Republicans were continuing to enjoy the White House for the first time since Hoover. It seemed worth the while of the Senate Committee on Banking and Currency to see if the boom portended another bust. Chairman William Fulbright said it would be a quiet and friendly investigation. I was called to testify. This was not entirely by accident. While appearing a few weeks earlier on another matter before another committee, I had used the opportunity to tell Mr. Robert A. Wallace and Mr. Myer Feldman, two of the excellent men who serve the public by serving Congressmen and their committees and who were then staff members of the Banking and Currency Committee, of the book I had under way. An invitation to testify on the 1929 experience came promptly and was not an unbearable surprise.

I believe that everyone with experience enjoys testifying before a friendly Congressional committee or even a moderately censorious one. For the moment you are an oracle, a minor oracle to be sure, but possessed of knowledge important for the future of the Republic. Your words go down in an imperishable, if sadly unread, record. Newspapermen, one or two at least, are present to transmit your better thoughts to the world or, more frequently, your worst ones, for these, being improbable, have novelty and seem more likely to merit a minor headline. An audience is on hand. Except for an exceedingly dramatic investigation, this audience is always about the same. Apart from watchdogs from the Executive Departments and one's friends, it consists of connoisseurs of Congressional hearings who attend them every day. Quite a few are of advanced years, none has alternative employment, and if they are not our best, they must at least be our most widely informed citizenry. Consumer problems, missiles, cost overruns, the imminent demise of the environment, radicals young and old, the economic outlook are all grist for their highly diversified mill. They listen attentively and critically; any Congressional hearing has about it a touch of theater and this is helped by having such a competent and critical house.

The witness at the Congressional hearing is treated with courtesy and deference, which in politics is always a trifle more effusive and therefore a great deal more pleasant than in any other walk of life. He must, however, expect to be seduced into statements damaging to his case if that is beneficial to the political needs or beliefs of an interrogator. This adds interest, and the stakes are not very high. My academic colleagues occasionally complain of the time they spend in preparing for or attending these inquiries. This is strictly for the purpose of impressing the others at the Department meeting. They enjoy it and wouldn't dream of declining.

III

I testified at the morning session of the stock market hearings on Tuesday, March 8, 1955. Several witnesses from the financial world, including Mr. G. Keith Funston and a bevy of vice-commissars of the New York Stock Exchange, had preceded me. The market had reacted to their testimony with admirable equanimity perhaps because they had said nothing although they had said it very well. Nor was my testimony sensational. I had brought along the proofs of my book; I drew on them to tell what had happened more than twenty-five years before, in 1928 and 1929. Toward the end I suggested that history *could* repeat itself, although I successfully resisted all invitations to predict when. I did urge a stiff tightening of margin requirements as a precautionary step. Similar action to minimize the use of credit for speculation had been taken during World War II when the speculative enthusiasm was much less. Through it all, the newspapermen sat gazing with partly open mouths at the ceiling of the Senate Caucus Chamber or looking down briefly to scribble a random note. An aide appeared occasionally, sidling along the wall behind the Committee, to pass a note to one of the Senators. The audience, I knew from waiting my turn at earlier hearings, was following me closely and, on occasion, exchanging a critical aside on my facts, logic or diction. As the testimony gave way to questions, more Senators came in. This is perhaps the most trying time of any hearing. Each in his turn apologizes graciously for being late and then asks the question that has occurred to him on the way over. The question is always the same and the Senator does not know that it has been asked before. Here was the basic query that morning:

Senator Robertson (who had been there all along): Well, Professor, we have been told by all the witnesses so far that present stock prices are not too high. What is your view on that?

Senator Ives: You do not think we are faced with a bust, do you?

Senator Monroney: I am wondering if there is any substance to the oft-repeated reason for the new high levels . . . That the stock market is merely catching up with the inflationary boom . . .

Senator Payne: I am sorry I came in late . . . would you want to indicate whether or not some of these increases have perhaps more truly reflected the true value of stocks in relation to their earnings?

The experienced witness observes that the question, though it bears a resemblance to some already asked, has been formulated in a novel way. Then he gives an answer which is the same in substance but decently different in form from those offered before. The audience is especially appreciative of an able handling of such details.

Toward the end of the morning, interest appeared to increase. First one and then several photographers appeared. Then came a movie camera or two. Through the weariness that develops with even so modest a sojourn in the public eye, I thought I sensed a certain tension. I noticed that the normal attrition of the Committee — which on a subject such as economics can leave one in a matter of an hour or so with only the Chairman and a precautionary member of the opposition — was not taking place. All Senators were staying. And soon I was the only one in the room who did not know the reason. The stock market was taking a nasty plunge.

I still did not know the reason when the hearing recessed at 12:57 P.M., just as a harried man from CBS came dashing into the chamber followed by two beasts of burden carrying a vast poundage of electronic gear. He had been off in another room photographing Dulles. The real history had passed him by. In response to his almost tearful plea, I repeated several minutes of my testimony to an open window. The substitution of the glass for the Senators led to a considerable release from inhibition. I rather let myself go with the gestures — at times grave and statesmanlike, at others perhaps a trifle flamboyant. It was this that the world and my children saw.

I still did not realize what had happened until someone handed me a noon paper with a big headline. The *New York Times* industrials were off seven points that day. Stocks had lost $3 billion in value on the New York Stock Exchange.

IV

Back in Cambridge, the next few days were among the most interesting in my memory. The phone rang persistently — so persistently that my secretary went home in annoyance, leaving me to answer it myself. Some of the calls were from the very great like Ed Murrow, who wanted me to extend my remarks for an even larger audience. I declined. A few wanted to know if I was likely to say anything that would affect the market in the near future. I promised them silence. The rest merely wished to denounce me for destroying their dream.

The telephone calls were supplemented, beginning the morning after the testimony, by a mountain of mail. All was unfavorable. Some was denunciatory; more was belligerent; much was prayerful. The belligerent threatened various forms of physical violence. My wife professed particular concern over five successive communications from a man in Florida announcing that he was on his way north to kill me. Her alarm subsided when I pointed out (having thoughtfully checked the point myself) that all were postmarked Palm Beach. The prayerful all said they were beseeching their God to have me meet with a bad accident — some were asking that I be deprived of life, some of limb, and the minimum request was that I lose all ability to open my mouth. On Wednesday night, I crawled into bed reflecting on all of the prayers that were spiraling up at that moment petitioning my dismemberment or destruction. I thought of saying a word on my own behalf and then struggled with the shattering thought that these matters might be decided by majority vote.

The next morning dawned bright and clear, and my wife and I decided to take a day away from it all. We went to Mount Snow, Vermont, to ski. Toward the end of the afternoon I turned from shaded and hard snow to some that had been softened by the sun and had a bad spill and broke my leg. The papers carried a note about my mishap. I now heard from those whose belief in the existence of a just and omnipotent God had been deeply strengthened.

A few days later, the market started up again. My mail

fell off and stopped. A representative collection of the letters was posted in a seminar room and viewed admiringly by students for weeks. But there was more to come.

v

At the time, the state of Indiana was represented in the Senate of the United States by Homer E. Capehart. He was a Republican, conservative and wealthy. It is possible, as partisan Democrats, at least, believed, that the people of Indiana could have had a better representative. But he was not a wicked man. His colleagues found him pleasant. So had I on previous brief encounter. These were the diminuendo days of Senator Joseph McCarthy. Unlike his colleague, William Jenner, Capehart had never been much involved in McCarthy's crusades. The senior Republican on the Banking and Currency Committee, he had not been present on the day I testified. He did not seem to consider this a handicap.

On March 20, in the course of a network television program, Senator Capehart announced that I would be recalled before the Committee to answer for having written favorably of Communism and then, presumably, having advanced its cause by collapsing the market. I had had some warning. A gentleman from the Senator's office had called me a day or two before to see if I admitted to authorship of the offending encomium. The program had been filmed the day before its release. Also present on the program was a good and gallant friend, Senator A. S. Mike Monroney of Oklahoma. After extemporizing a brilliant defense of my dereliction, he called me up to tell me what was coming.

The praise of Communism had been extracted from a pamphlet I had written for the National Planning Association dealing with problems of postwar Europe. It noted that the Communists had a better reputation for sincerity and determination in attacking old social grievances and that they also had a solution to the problem of petty nationalism by asserting a higher loyalty to the workers' state. This sounded pretty bad. But Senator Capehart's case was not without flaw. My kind words were marred by a caveat, expressing suspicion and distaste of Communism on other grounds, which had been put into the very middle of the paragraph for the precise purpose of preventing any inconvenient use, a precaution normal in those days. The Senator had thought it necessary to delete this offending clause, a distinctly noticeable act. The pamphlet had been based on a lecture given originally at the University of Notre Dame in, of all states, Indiana. An earlier version had even been published by the University. The pamphlet had been endorsed in principle by Allen Dulles, the brother of the Secretary of State, and Milton Eisenhower, the brother of the President, an underwriting which could cause some doubts as to the vigor and originality of the ideas advanced. Even a brilliant improviser like Joe McCarthy might have wished for a better case.

A day or so later, the Senator made the further discovery that, at a meeting of the American Economic Association not long before, a somewhat conservative professional colleague had jeopardized any reputation for understatement he might have had by saying that I was, though perhaps unconsciously, "one of the most effective enemies of capitalism and democracy" in all the land. But this did not retrieve matters as much as might have been hoped. My friend thought me dangerous because I was too soft on industrial monopoly.

Like most other liberal academicians, I had been a thoughtful observer of the methods of the Wisconsin Titus Oates.
Two of them had always seemed to me worth adopting by
anyone attacked. The first was to avoid defense of one's
self and instead assault the accuser. The second was to
eschew any suspicion, however remote, of personal modesty.
I put these methods to the test when I heard of the charges.
I sent a telegram to the network carrying the program, to
key stations, to the wire services and to important papers,
indicting the Senator for incompetence. I identified incompetence with failure to know my views and these I
implied — indeed, I stated — were an imperishable chapter
in the intellectual history of our time. I followed the wire
a few days later with a press conference which, by a fortunate accident of travel, I was able to hold in Indiana.

The effect of my efforts, I am persuaded, was to convert
an attack that otherwise would have been largely ignored
into front-page news. The press dealt well with me though.
It concluded that I had been assailed for being unkind to the
stock market. This it refused to say was subversive.

The Senator then took the floor of the Senate for a further
denunciation. Some of this centered on my characterization
of Communism as a monolithic force (commonplace at the
time but sadly inaccurate as events proved). "Mr. President,
'monolithic' means like a monument, or a pillar of strength
. . . That is like describing Communism as a monument or
as a pillar of strength; or, as we used to say, like the Rock
of Gibraltar."

But by now he was losing power. He said, handsomely,
that there were things in the offending pamphlet with which
"we can all agree." It was unfair, he added, to suggest that
he had called me a Red. After some further bickering in

the Committee, he subsided. The Senator had no further reputation as a witch-hunter. I like to think that he himself was plucked as a brand from the burning. I filed a further and rather sanctimonious statement with the Committee but was not recalled.

VI

On April 21, 1955, my book was finally published. The publisher had some months before decided that the volume needed a good strong jacket. This turned out to be a bright and very visible red. With this color and all the excitement of the preceding weeks, it seemed certain that the interest in the book would be overwhelming. In the end, the response was admirable but the early market was very orderly. Indeed, depressingly so. One evening I was coming through the old La Guardia terminal on my way back to Boston and I paused, as usual, to eye the window of the little bookshop on the way to the ramp. As usual, there was no sign of the bright red jacket.

The saleslady asked me if I wanted something and I summoned all of my resources of courage and verisimilitude and said, "I seem to remember a lot of recent discussion about a book — I forget the name of the author, maybe Galbraith — but I think it was called *The Great Crash.*"

She replied, "That's certainly not a title you could sell in an airport."

8

Financial Genius Is Before the Fall

How Fools and Their Money Are
Still Being Parted

ONE DAY in the winter of 1969, I was in Los Angeles on a political errand that called for a press conference. With an air of obvious thoughtfulness, a reporter asked me if I expected another stock market crash. I replied, as I had a hundred times since I wrote a book on the 1929 experience, that of course there would be. The only difficulty was telling when. Because of some unnatural shortage of news, this was a headline the next morning without, of course, the qualification. The following summer, when the market was falling by large coarse steps, I got a number of calls congratulating me on my foresight and one from a Pittsburgh businessman telling me that I had made him, or anyhow saved him, a great deal of money. He offered a contribution to some good cause. I felt a little guilty about these compliments, though I accepted them gracefully, for I did not want to say whether market weakness in 1969 portended a new collapse.[1] The only thing certain forty-odd years after the 1929 debacle was that *some* day, without fail, there would be another such disaster.

The reason is that the stock market is inherently unstable, the instability being related to its superbly orchestrated abil-

[1] As, a year later, in the summer of 1970, it became clear, more or less, it did.

ity to attract people with a promise of effortless riches, give them a taste of such gains, give them the promise of a great deal more gain, persuade them that it is rewarding their financial acuity (of which they have none) or that of the people who are managing their money (which may be less) and then, usually after overcoming some preliminary setbacks which greatly add to the general state of confidence, destroy these illusions in one mortal thud. What is necessary for a new disaster is only for memories of the last one to fade, and no one knows how long that takes. This essay has primarily to do with what happened in the autumn of 1929 and it draws shamelessly on my earlier book on the subject.[2] But first I must say a word as to the way the stock market, in combination with the avarice so celebrated as an incentive of the free enterprise system, contributes to mass illusion, even insanity, and of some of the evidence of fading memory which encourages the conviction that, sooner or later, we will have another debacle.

II

The anatomy of the self-destroying speculative boom is simple. Over time with advancing technology, an increasing national product and a reliable tendency in the economy to inflation, most common stocks will rise in value. As this happens, people are attracted to the market and this causes the stocks to rise more. This further gain attracts yet more people and gradually, perhaps over a period of some years, the purchases of people looking for this increase in value come to determine what stocks are worth. Prospective earnings are still mentioned but as an afterthought — or to show that there is still some tie to reality. The knowledgeable

[2] *The Great Crash, 1929* (Boston: Houghton Mifflin, 1955).

man, as he unwisely considers himself, is now concerned with the way a stock is attracting buyer interest. That, rightly for the moment, determines its value.

Then, at some stage, the supply of buyers runs out — or dries up. Or there may be public action, e.g., a drastic tightening of bank lending, to dry up the spring. The increase falters. This causes the more nervous to get out. This in turn causes the market to falter still more. More decide to get out and the slow upward climb is replaced by a precipitate drop. As I have previously noted, there usually will be some preliminary episodes of nervousness before the climactic fright arrives. The greater the preceding buildup, the more stocks have come to depend on a continuing influx of buyers attracted by the prospect of capital gains, the more violent will be the eventual collapse.

III

This simple design is, on the whole, less interesting than the secondary insanity which it induces. Because the market is going up, almost everyone associated with the market makes money. Almost anyone can thus look like a financial genius and with little qualification or none at all. In the late twenties the nation was replete with instant Rothschilds. There have been even more in these last years. Then as now they were not engaged in a put-on. Most of them were perfectly sincere men who first fooled themselves as to their financial genius and then proceeded to fool other people.

The most common vehicle for manifesting this genius in the twenties was the investment trust of which there was an explosion. Instead of buying shares in the ultimate companies, the investor bought shares in a company managed by a man of genius who in turn did the investing. If these investment trusts in the late twenties sound suspiciously like a mutual fund, of which in these last years there has been an even more spectacular explosion, that suspicion is well founded. There is a technical difference between the closed-end trusts of those days and the modern fund. The former had an authorized capital which it sold and used to purchase common stocks. The investor who wanted out did not cash in his stock for its share pro rata in the current value of the stock held by the company, as in the case of a mutual fund. Up until the time of the Crash, he simply sold the stock on the open market. After the Crash, he practiced Christian (or some equivalent) forbearance, for the stock in most of the investment trusts became unsalable.[3]

One of the breathtaking discoveries of the late twenties was leverage. Nothing so marked a man of financial genius as his bold and knowledgeable use of this device. It meant that an individual or firm in one fashion or another bought common stocks with borrowed money or preferred stock. In consequence, the individual or firm could own much stock

[3] One of the greatest investment trust promotions of the twenties was by Goldman, Sachs and Company, since become more austere, under the auspices of Waddill Catchings, the most notable of the contemporary financial geniuses until the Crash. In 1929 Goldman, Sachs sold nearly half a billion dollars worth of securities in its investment trusts. In 1932, the following colloquy took place before a Senate Committee in Washington:

Senator Couzens: Did Goldman, Sachs and Company organize the Goldman, Sachs Trading Corporation? [One of the investment trusts.]

Mr. Sachs: Yes, sir.

Senator Couzens: And it sold its stock to the public?

Mr. Sachs: A portion of it. The firms invested originally in 10 percent of the entire issue for the sum of $10,000,000.

Senator Couzens: And the other 90 percent was sold to the public?

Mr. Sachs: Yes, sir.

Senator Couzens: At what price?

Mr. Sachs: At 104. That is the old stock . . . the stock was split two for one.

Senator Couzens: And what is the price of the stock now?

Mr. Sachs: Approximately 1¾.

for a little investment and when the stock went up in value, since the debt (or its equivalent) remained the same, all the gain accrued to that small stake. Margin buying, which means, of course, that the individual borrows money to buy stocks, is a manifestation of leverage. The big utility and railroad promoters, whom I will mention in a moment, bought control of their numerous companies with borrowed money. And the investment trusts sold bonds and preferred stock in large volume in order to buy common stocks and thus win the advantages of leverage for their own stockholders.

It was also learned, in the very late twenties, although no one had much thought of it before, that when stocks go down, leverage goes brutally into reverse. For now, since the claims of the bonds (or preferred stock) are undiminished, all of the fall is taken by the stock. For those who own the stock, it is a formula for becoming poor with remarkable celerity. Leverage has a similar reverse effect on reputations for financial genius.

In recent years leverage has been rediscovered. The gamier of the funds, the hedge funds in particular, have been operating on borrowed money in order to concentrate all of the gains on the stock. Heavy borrowing with resulting leverage has also been important in agglomerating the conglomerates, an outrage to which I will return. One lesson has, however, been learned. Margin trading, which was the most damaging way of getting leverage before 1929, has been circumscribed.

In 1928 and 1929, the investment trusts invested extensively in each other's securities. (If a leverage trust invested in a leverage trust, it got a terrific leverage.) Here again legislation enacted since then has been inconvenient; such financial incest is forbidden by the Securities Exchange Commission. Fortunately for genius, if not for the investors involved, the SEC's jurisdiction stops at the water's edge. So this manifestation of genius has reappeared among American entrepreneurs (notably Mr. Bernie Cornfeld) operating in Europe, and causing great hopes for enrichment among the deserving people there.

In the twenties there was particular interest in glamour stocks, among which an electronics firm, RCA, was far and away the speculative favorite. On September 3, 1929, it reached 505, up from 94.5 in the preceding year and a half. It had never paid a dividend. Glamour stocks have been greatly celebrated in these last years. Electronics have been among the favorites.

The late twenties were a period of Napoleonic mergers. These led in turn to much exchanging and reshuffling of securities, the rumors of which led to great action on the exchanges. Principally involved were the utilities and railroads — Samuel Insull, the Van Sweringen brothers and Howard C. Hopson then enjoyed an eminence that would be the envy more recently of James Ling or Charles Bludhorn. The basic technique was to issue bonds or preferred stocks with which to buy the common stocks of the companies being merged. Interest payments were then paid out of dividends. Some of the new creations were conglomerates, though not so called. Only days after the 1929 Crash, and adding appreciably to the gloom, one of these folded up. It was the Foshay enterprises of Minneapolis, owners of hotels, flour mills, banks and manufacturing and retail establishments at random sites in the United States and Canada. Its thirty-two-story obelisk in downtown Minneapolis had been dedicated only a few weeks before by Secretary of War James Good at a time when the firm was already at least technically insolvent. Secretary Wood had called the tower the "Washington Monument of the Northwest." Nothing has been so admired in these last years as the rediscovery of the conglomerates. Most of them, as noted, have been built by issuing debentures or other fixed income obligations. In the case of Ling-Temco-Vought the common stock equity in 1969 was estimated at around seven percent, the rest of the capital being long-term debt or the minority interest in the constituent firms. There was also a small amount of preferred stock. Around half of all net earnings were absorbed by fixed charges. Several other of the more admired conglomerates — Bangor Punta, General Host, Rapid-American — had a common stock equity of 12 percent or less. Some had even larger proportions of their earnings absorbed by fixed charges than LTV.

In the nineteen-twenties, the combines and conglomerates did well as long as they could acquire new companies — such expansion brings growth without going through the slow and tedious process of acquiring new customers. But such expansion proved to be possible only when the market was rising. That too has been the recent experience. When the market fell in 1929, reverse leverage went into effect. All earnings and more were needed to support the debt. No more money could be borrowed. A company that was busted itself was in no position to buy others, however Napoleonic its management. Reverse leverage has now again been operating and if the slide in the market continues and is combined with a reduction in earnings, a number of the new agglomerators will go the way of Foshay, Insull, the Van Sweringen brothers, Howard Hopson and the other men of earlier genius. Some of this earlier genius consisted less in earning money than in so keeping the books as to give this impression. That manifestation of genius has also been extensively rediscovered.

In 1929, money to borrow was scarce and interest rates were painfully high. That meant that a banker with his privileged access to funds could do a great deal for himself and his friends. The Chase National Bank was shortly to suffer painfully for the conflicting private operations of its president, the redoubtable Albert H. Wiggin. In 1929 he borrowed from the bank to sell the stock of the bank short and subsequently claimed that such operations heightened a man's interest in his business. The president of the National City Bank, Charles E. Mitchell, gave his bank an even worse name. In the last months of 1969, an officer of the Chase was explaining how he happened to give a loan to one of the sportier of the conglomerates, Gulf & Western, just before departing to join that firm.

In 1929 the brokerage houses had trouble keeping their paperwork abreast of the volume of trading. Back office problems were particularly oppressive at the time of the Crash. The paperwork problem has again become very serious in recent times.

In 1929, as I have observed, margin trading was far more important than of late. In contemplating a security, there may have been more of a tendency to lose sight entirely of the firm that had issued it. (One 1929 favorite was Seaboard Air Line, a railroad. Many thought it was an aviation firm with growth prospects.) But at a homier level the parallel between the two eras is sustained. In April of 1929, an article in the *North American Review* told how women had become players of "man's most exciting capitalistic game." It explained that the modern housewife now reads that,

"Wright Aero is going up . . . just as she does that fresh fish is now on the market . . ." In August of 1969, the *New York Times Book Review* carried an advertisement for a *Teenager's Guide to the Stock Market.* "Absolutely the first book to give young people who show the slightest interest in finance. Only $5.25. Worth millions . . ."

In the months before the 1929 Crash, men of academic reputation and substance looked at the market and the mergers and put their blessing on everything that was going on. This was very reassuring. Professor Irving Fisher of Yale, a few days before the Crash, told an audience that stocks had reached a new high plateau from which they could only go on up. Even more eloquent was Professor Charles Amos Dice of Ohio State University. Looking at the financial geniuses in 1929 (some of whom were soon to be broke and a few in bad trouble with the law), he was struck by their "vision for the future and boundless hope and optimism." He noted that "they did not come into the market hampered by the heavy armor of tradition." He described their market impact in a splendid sentence: "Led by these mighty knights of the automobile industry, the steel industry, the radio industry . . . and finally joined, in despair, by many professional traders who, after much sackcloth and ashes, had caught the vision of progress, the Coolidge market had gone forward like the phalanxes of Cyrus, parasang upon parasang and again parasang upon parasang . . ."

No academic figure in this prosaic age has matched Professor Dice's parasangs. But one, Dr. Neil H. Jacoby, on detached service from being Dean of Business Administration at UCLA to the Center for the Study of Democratic Institutions, recently held in an article of intolerable length, that the modern conglomerates, including the outrageous ones, attest, "in a broader perspective . . . to the flexibility and adaptability of the U.S. economy in response to underlying structural changes." Of their assaults on other corporate managements, he said encouragingly, "No institution of a democratic society should be above challenge." Such thoughts make one yearn for Professor Dice and his parasangs.

In 1929 any suggestion that anything was wrong was badly received. The principal offender was Paul M. Warburg, the banker and a founder of the Federal Reserve System. In March of 1929, he attacked the orgy of "unrestrained speculation" and said he feared it would "bring about a general depression involving the whole country." He was accused of "sandbagging" American prosperity. Some implied that he was short in the market. He described the experience as the most difficult of his life. It remains to be seen whether those who compare the present generation of geniuses with those of the earlier age can escape reproach.[4]

But my concern is not to find or even to suggest precise parallels between now and then any more than it is to predict when the present enthusiasm will have run its course. I am concerned with reminding everyone that financial genius consists almost entirely of avarice and a rising market. And I would like to do anything possible to keep bright the memory of the events of that first great crash. To the latter end, let me now turn back to the chronology of those days.

---

[4] Actually, from some personal experience, I think the financial community and the country in general has become more tolerant of criticism. In this connection, modesty barely allows the mention of another parallel. On his death, Paul Warburg's family endowed a chair in economics at Harvard in his honor and for many years I have been the Paul M. Warburg Professor of Economics.

IV

The speculative market which ended in the Crash of October 1929 was some five to six years in the making. For a long while the movement was far from violent. At the beginning of 1924, the *New York Times* averages of the prices of twenty-five representative industrial stocks stood at 110. They had eased up to 135 at the beginning of 1925. At the close of trading on January 2, 1929, they were at 338.35. Apart from mild setbacks, notably in early 1926 and early 1928, the advance was steady. By the beginning of 1929, the speculative phase to which I adverted in the early pages of this essay had fully arrived. People were wholly preoccupied with capital gains; this being so, stocks were being bought extensively on margin. This was an added source of market instability. If the value of the stock dropped, there were calls for more margin, i.e., for more cash, or collateral security. If the owner of the stock could not provide these, he was of course forced to sell his shares. Forced sales of this kind could greatly accelerate any downward movement of the market, and did.

There was nervousness in the early months of 1929 caused by some highly diffident warnings about speculation from the Federal Reserve. The Federal Reserve was made even more nervous by its own warnings and soon became silent. In June, stock prices started on their last great surge. Almost every day that summer the market went on to new highs. By the end of August, the *Times* averages were at 449, up 110 points since the beginning of the year. Margin accounts expanded enormously, and from all over the country — indeed, from all over the world — money poured into New York to finance these transactions. During the summer,

brokers' loans to carry the margined stocks increased at the
rate of $400 million a month.

Not everyone was playing the market as legend holds —
the great majority of Americans were then as innocent of
knowledge of how to buy stocks as they are today. Subsequent estimates have suggested that as many as a million
people were involved in the speculation. During that summer, almost all of them made money — at least on paper.

v

In September of 1929, the market faltered. The first break
was blamed on Roger Babson, a notable economic prophet
who in early September said with stunning accuracy, "Sooner
or later a crash is coming, and it may be terrific." In consequence, he added, "factories will shut down . . . men will
be thrown out of work . . . the vicious circle will get in full
swing and the result will be a serious business depression."
Babson, like Warburg, was roundly denounced. His reputation was damaged by this premature pessimism. And for
a while the market was steady. Then things went bad again.
On October 18, there were heavy declines on late trading
and the *New York Times* industrial averages dropped about
seven points. And on the 19th, things were worse. In the
second heaviest Saturday's trading in history, 3,488,100
shares changed hands. At the close of the day the *Times*
industrial index was down twelve points.

On Sunday, October 20, the break was front-page news —
the *New York Times* headline read: "Stocks driven down as
wave of selling engulfs market." Its financial editor, who
along with the editor of the *Commercial and Financial
Chronicle* was one of the few financial journalists who had
never wavered in his conviction that people had gone mad,

said that for the moment at least, "Wall Street seemed to see the reality of things." The news stories also made two points which the papers were to make wonderfully familiar in the next fortnight. They reported that, at the end of Saturday's trading, an exceptionally large number of margin calls went out. And they said that if the decline continued, the men of genius would do something about it. The market would have "organized support."

Things got worse on Monday, October 21. Sales totaled 6,091,870, the third greatest volume in history. There was a further and disturbing phenomenon. The anxious men and women who were watching the market throughout the country had no way of telling what was happening. Previously on big days of the bull market, the ticker had often fallen behind, and one didn't discover until well after the market closed how much richer one had become. That, however, was information for which one could wait with safety if not with patience. Now with a falling market one might be totally ruined, and not know it. Such information one needed to have. Also, even if one were not going to be ruined, there was a strong tendency to imagine it so a late ticker added to the rush to sell. From the opening on October 21, the ticker lagged and by noon it was an hour late. Not until an hour and forty minutes after the close of the market did it record the last transaction. Every ten minutes prices of selected stocks were printed on the bond ticker, but the wide divergence between these and the prices on the tape only added to the uneasiness — and to the conviction that it might be best to sell.

However, this was not yet disaster. The Monday market closed well above its low for the day — the net loss on the *Times* industrial averages was about six points — and on

Tuesday there was a rather shaky gain. Some credit for this improvement goes to Wall Street's academic prophets. Thus on Monday in New York, Professor Fisher said that the declines had represented only a "shaking out of the lunatic fringe." He went on to argue that the prices of stocks during the boom had not yet caught up with their real value. Among other things, the market had not yet reflected the beneficent effects of Prohibition, which had made the American worker "more productive and dependable." Others echoed his optimism.

By Wednesday, October 23, the effect of this cheer had been dissipated. Instead of further gains, there were now heavy losses. The opening was quiet enough, but toward mid-morning automobile accessory stocks were sold heavily, and volume began to increase throughout the list. The last hour was quite phenomenal — 2,600,000 shares changed hands at rapidly declining prices. The *Times* industrials for the day dropped from 415 to 384, giving up all of their gains since the end of the previous June. Again the ticker was far behind, and to add to the uncertainty an ice storm in the Middle West caused widespread disruption of communications. That afternoon and evening thousands of speculators decided to get out while — as they mistakenly supposed — the getting was good. For many, it was too late. Other thousands were told they would have no choice but to get out unless they provided more collateral, for, as the day's business came to an end, a flood of margin calls went out.

Speaking in Washington, even Professor Fisher was somewhat less optimistic. He told a meeting of bankers that "security values in *most instances* were not inflated." Almost desperately it was predicted that, on the morrow, the market would receive "organized support."

VI

Thursday, October 24, is the day history designates as the beginning of the Crash of 1929. The designation is deserved. On that day, 12,894,650 shares changed hands, most of them at prices which shattered the dreams and the hopes of those who had owned them. Of all the mysteries of the stock exchange, there is none so impenetrable as why there should be a buyer for everyone who seeks to sell. October 24, 1929, showed that what is mysterious is not inevitable. Often there were no buyers, and only after wide vertical declines could anyone be induced to bid.

The morning was the bad time. The opening was unspectacular, and for a little while prices were firm. Volume, however, was large and soon prices began to sag. Once again the ticker dropped behind the market. Prices fell faster and farther, and the ticker lagged more and more. By eleven o'clock what had been a market was only a wild scramble to sell. In the crowded boardrooms across the country the ticker told of a frightful collapse. But the selected quotations coming in over the bond ticker also showed that current values were far below the ancient history of the tape. The uncertainty led more and more people to try to sell. Others, no longer able to respond to margin calls, were sold out. By 11:30 A.M., panic, pure and unqualified, had taken over.

Outside the New York Stock Exchange on Broad Street, a weird roar could be heard. A crowd gathered. Police Commissioner Grover Whalen, though a man of limited perception, sensed that something might be wrong and dispatched a special police detail to Wall Street to protect the peace. A workman appeared to accomplish some routine repairs atop one of the high buildings. The multitude, assuming he was a would-be suicide, waited impatiently for him to jump. At 12:30 P.M., the visitors' gallery of the Exchange was closed on the wild scenes below. One of the visitors, oddly enough, was the former British Chancellor of the Exchequer, Winston Churchill. He had never better revealed his instinct for being on hand for history.

At noon, however, things had taken a turn for the better. The long-awaited organized support materialized. The heads of the National City Bank, Chase, Guaranty Trust and Bankers Trust met with Thomas W. Lamont, the senior Morgan partner, at 23 Wall Street, the Morgan citadel. Bankers in those days were men of prestige — indeed, they were the folk heroes of the age. These were the greatest bankers of all. They quickly agreed to come to the support of the market and to pool resources for this purpose. Lamont then met with reporters to offer what achieved fame as one of the more remarkable understatements of history. He said, "There has been a little distress selling on the Stock Exchange." He added that this passing inconvenience was "due to a technical situation rather than any fundamental cause," and he told the newsmen the situation was "susceptible to betterment."

Meanwhile, word had reached the Exchange floor that the bankers were meeting and salvation was in sight. Prices promptly firmed and rose. Then at 1:30 P.M., Richard Whitney, known to be a floor broker for Morgan's, walked to the post where Steel was traded and left with the specialist an order for 10,000 shares at several points above the current bids. He continued the rounds with this largesse. Confidence was wonderfully revived, and the market now boomed upward. In the last hour the selling orders which were still flooding in from afar turned it soft again. But the net loss for the day — about twelve points on the *New York Times* industrial averages — was far less than the day before. Some issues, Steel among them, were actually higher on the day's trading.

However, this recovery was of distant interest to the tens of thousands who had sold or been sold out during the decline and whose dreams of affluence had gone glimmering. It was eight and a half minutes past seven that night before the ticker finished recording the day's terrible misfortunes. In the boardrooms, speculators who had been sold out since early morning sat silently watching the tape. The habit of months or years, however idle it had now become, could not be broken at once. Then the final trades were registered and they made their way out into the gathering darkness.

In Wall Street itself lights blazed from every office as clerks struggled to come abreast of the day's business. Messengers and boardroom boys, caught up in the excitement and untroubled by losses, went skylarking through the streets until the police arrived to quell them. Representatives of thirty-five of the largest stock market houses assembled at the offices of Hornblower and Weeks and told the press on departing that the market was "fundamentally sound," adding, by way of emphasis, that it was "technically in better condition than it has been in months." The host firm dispatched a market letter which stated that "commencing with today's trading the market should start laying the foundation for the constructive advance which we believe will characterize 1930." In a small corner of heaven those financial men who are saved are required nonetheless to assemble each morning and read aloud these predictions.

VII

On Friday and Saturday following the Thursday debacle, trading continued heavy — just under six million on Friday and over two million at the short session on Saturday. Prices, on the whole, were steady — the averages were a trifle up on Friday but slid off on Saturday. Not only were things better but everyone knew it was the bankers who had made them so. They had shown their courage and their power, and the people applauded — warmly and generously. The *Times* observed that the financial community was "secure in the knowledge that the most powerful banks in the country stood ready to prevent a recurrence."

But security in knowledge notwithstanding, nothing was left to chance. Not only were financial resources mobilized, so were those of public bamboozlement. Colonel Leonard Ayres of Cleveland, another well-regarded prophet of the time, assured people that no other country could have survived such a crash so well. Eugene M. Stevens, the president of the Continental Illinois Bank, said: "There is nothing in the business situation to justify any nervousness"; Walter Teagle, the oil magnate, said there had been no "fundamental change" in the oil business to justify concern; Charles M. Schwab, the steel tycoon, said that the steel business had been making "fundamental progress" toward stability and added that this "fundamentally sound condition" was responsible for the prosperity of the industry; Samuel Vauclain, chairman of the Baldwin Locomotive Works, declared that "fundamentals are sound"; President Hoover said that "the fundamental business of the country, that is production and distribution of commodities, is on a sound and prosperous basis." A Boston investment trust took space in the *Wall*

Street Journal to say, "S-T-E-A-D-Y Everybody! Calm thinking is in order. Heed the words of America's greatest
bankers." Only Governor Franklin D. Roosevelt, one day to
become the scourge of Wall Street and the bankers (as they
saw it), criticized the "fever of speculation." No one paid
any attention to *him*.

On Sunday in the New York churches there were sermons
suggesting that a certain measure of divine retribution had
been visited on the Republic, and there were hints that it
had not been entirely unmerited. It was evident, however,
that almost everyone believed that this heavenly knuckle-
rapping was over and that speculation could now be re-
sumed in earnest. The newspapers on the Sabbath were full
of the prospects for next week's market. Stocks, it was
agreed, were again cheap and, accordingly, there would be
a heavy rush to buy. Stories from the brokerage houses told
of a fabulous volume of buying orders piling up in anticipa-
tion of the opening of the next day's market. In a concerted
advertising campaign in Monday's papers, stock market firms
urged the wisdom of buying stocks promptly. On Monday,
October 28, the real disaster began.

Trading on Monday, though in great volume, was smaller
than on the previous Thursday — 9,212,800 as compared
with the nearly thirteen million. But the sustained drop
in prices was far more severe. The *Times* industrials
were down 49 points for the day. General Electric was off
47½; Westinghouse, 34½; Tel. & Tel., 34. Indeed, the decline
on this one day was greater than that of all the preceding
week of panic. Once again a late ticker left everyone in
ignorance of what was happening save that it was very
bad.

At 1:10 P.M., there was a momentary respite; Charles

E. Mitchell of the National City Bank — with the Chase National Bank, then one of the two largest — was detected going into Morgan's and the news ticker carried the magic word. Steel rallied and went from 193½ to 198. But this time Richard Whitney did not appear; "organized support" was not forthcoming. Mitchell, on the strength of later evidence, was almost certainly negotiating a much-needed personal loan. He too had been caught by the market, and for the next ten years he would be defending himself in various courts in consequence. The market weakened again and in the last hour three million shares changed hands at rapidly declining prices.

The bankers also assembled that day at Morgan's and remained in session from 4:30 P.M. to 6:30 P.M. They were described only as having a "philosophical attitude," and they told the press that the situation "retained hopeful features." But, alas, it was also explained at the conclusion that it was no part of the bankers' purpose to maintain any particular level of prices on the market. Their operations were confined to seeing that the market was orderly — that offers would be met by bids at some price, and that "air holes," as Mr. Lamont dubbed them, would not be allowed to appear in the market. In other words, the bankers had decided to go short on promises and this was chilling news. To the man who held stock on margin, disaster wore only one face and that was falling prices. He wanted to be saved from disaster. It was poor comfort that his ruin would be accomplished in an orderly and becoming manner.

Tuesday, October 29, was the most devastating day in the history of the New York stock market, and it may have been the most devastating in the history of markets. Selling began at once and in huge volume. The air holes, which the bankers had promised to close, opened wide. Repeatedly and in many issues there was a plethora of selling orders and no buyers at all. Once again, of course, the ticker lagged — at the close it was two and a half hours behind. By then 16,410,030 shares had been known to have been traded — more than three times the number that had once been considered a fabulously big day. Despite a closing rally on dividend news, the losses were again appalling. The *Times* industrials were down forty-three points, thus finally canceling all of the huge gains of the preceding twelve months. Losses on individual issues were far greater. By the end of the trading, members were near collapse from strain and fatigue. Office staffs, already near the breaking point, now had to tackle the greatest volume of paperwork yet. By now, also, there was no longer any certainty that things would get better. Perhaps they would go on getting worse.

During the first week of the Crash, it seems likely, the slaughter had been of the innocents. Now the well-to-do and the wealthy — the men of affairs — were suffering. During the first week the boardrooms were crowded; now they were nearly empty for the new victims had facilities for suffering in private. On this day at noon the bankers met again and they met once more in the evening but there was no suggestion that they were even philosophical. In truth, their prestige had been falling even more disconcertingly than the market. During the day the rumor had swept the Exchange that, of all things, the "organized support" was busy selling stocks. Lamont met the press after the evening session with the trying assignment of denying that this was so. Nor for the moment was there much effort at reassurance from other quarters. James J. Walker, then the remarkably indolent Mayor of New York, offered the only constructive proposal of the day. Addressing an audience of motion picture exhibitors, he asked them to "show pictures that will reinstate courage and hope in the hearts of the people."

On the Exchange itself it was felt that courage and hope might best be reinstated if the market were simply closed and everyone given a breathing spell. This forthright thought derived impressive further support from the fact that everyone was badly in need of sleep. The difficulty was that the announcement of the closing of the Exchange might simply worsen the panic. At noon on October 29, the issue came to a head. So as not to attract attention and add to the panic, the members of the governing committee left the floor in twos and threes to attend a meeting; for reasons of secrecy the meeting itself was held not in the regular room but in the office of the Stock Clearing Corporation below the trading floor. The panic roared on a few feet above. Richard Whitney, who besides being the instrument of salvation the previous Thursday was also Vice President of the Exchange, later described the session. (Later still, and no longer a financial genius, Whitney would go to jail for covering his losses in applejack, peat and other products with stolen money.) Nervous brokers lit cigarettes, stubbed them out and lit fresh ones. The air soon became blue. Everyone wanted a respite from the agony. Quite a few firms needed a few hours to ascertain whether they were still solvent.

But caution was on the side of keeping the market open until it could be closed on some note of strength and optimism. So the reluctant decision was to carry on. Again in the financial district the lights glowed all night. In one brokerage house an employee fainted from exhaustion, was revived and promptly put back to work again.

Next day, just when salvation seemed impossible, salvation came. Volume was still enormous, but prices were much better — the *Times* industrials rose thirty-one points. No one knew why; maybe it was because all the available prophets had again gone all out with optimism. On the evening of the 29th, Julius Klein, a leading figure in the national administration, took to the radio to remind the country that President Hoover had said that the "fundamental business of the country" was sound and prosperous. To be certain that no one missed the fundamental point, he added: "The main point I want to make is the fundamental soundness of [the] great mass of economic activities." On Wednesday, Waddill Catchings, the financial genius hitherto mentioned, announced on returning from a Western trip that general business conditions were "unquestionably fundamentally sound." (The same could not be said for the stock of the great investment trusts he had launched — Blue Ridge, Shenandoah, Goldman, Sachs Trading Corporation. Reverse leverage was reducing their value to next to nothing.) Of more importance, perhaps, from Pocantico Hills the aged John D. Rockefeller issued his first public statement in many years: "Believing that fundamental conditions of the country are sound . . . my son and I have for some days been purchasing sound common stock." Eddie Cantor, describing himself as "Comedian, Author, Statistician and Victim," said later, "Sure, who else had any money left?"

Just before the Rockefeller statement arrived, things looked good enough on the Exchange so that Richard Whitney felt safe in announcing that the market would not open until noon the following day (Thursday) and that on Friday and Saturday it would stay shut. The announcement was greeted by cheers. Nerves were everywhere past the breaking point. On LaSalle Street in Chicago, a boy exploded a firecracker. The rumor spread that gangsters whose margin accounts had been closed out were shooting up the street. Several squads of police arrived to make them take their losses like honest men. In New York the body of a commission merchant was fished out of the Hudson River. His pockets contained $9.40 in change and some margin calls.

IX

No feature of the Great Crash was more remarkable than the way it passed from climax to anticlimax to destroy again and again the hope that the worst had passed. Even on the 30th when the Crash was over, the worst was still to come. It was only that it came more slowly. Day after day during the next two weeks prices fell with monotonous regularity. At the close of trading on October 29, the *Times* industrials stood at 275. In the rally of the next two days they gained more than fifty points. By November 13 they were down to 224 for a further net loss of fifty points. By then the stock of investment trusts was largely unsalable. Their creators had, by now, ceased to be men of genius. A similar demotion will come one day to the men of genius who now command the mutual funds — or to some of them. So also to the men who made the conglomerates — or some of them.

The levels of late 1929 were wonderful compared with what was to follow. On July 8, 1932, the average of the closing levels of the *Times* industrials was 58.46. This was not much more than the amount by which they dropped on the single day of October 28, and considerably less than a quarter of the closing values on October 29. But by then, of course, business conditions were no longer sound, fundamentally or otherwise. The United States, indeed the industrial world, was in a terrible depression.

x

In later years, when considering the causes of the Great Depression, economists were inclined to exculpate the market. Looking back at the summer before the Crash, evidence was found that production of consumer goods was outrunning demand. Business investment was thus due for curtailment. The stock market, it was held, was only reflecting this change in underlying factors, i.e., in those fundamentals. None of this is so. If the economy was in recession in the late summer of 1929, it had certainly gone unnoticed. Unnoticed it couldn't have affected the market. And if there was weakness, the current doctrine and view held that it would be self-correcting. The stock market crash was the consequence of the preceding speculation. And the collapse itself had an immediate, powerful and unmistakable effect on the economy.

In the weeks following the Crash, spending for automobiles, radios and other durable goods fell off sharply as people reacted to their own misfortunes or those of their neighbors. Business investment plans were scaled down as firms found themselves pressed for cash, worried about existing debt and unable to raise new money. As security values fell, business and bank failures increased, forcing further contraction of spending and investment by those affected.

The Crash of 1929, along with the speculation that preceded it, was, in short, a prime cause of the depression that ensued. My own guess is that the further consequences of the next speculative episode will be less alarming. There is a better knowledge now of what the government might do to offset the deflation in consumer and investment spending that would follow such a collapse. The danger could thus be contained. But it would be better not to have the speculation and crash in the first place.

9

Some Reflections on Public
Architecture and Public Works

WRITING IN 1776 in *Wealth of Nations*, Adam Smith concluded that the building and maintenance of "public institutions" and "public works" as a function of the state was surpassed in importance only by provision for the common defense and the administration of justice. Public builders and architects were thus ranked immediately after the warriors and lawyers, definitely ahead of revenue agents, the ceremonial officers of the crown and the bishops of the established church. So presumably it had been from the earliest times. Since then the position of the public builder has declined. I would like to argue that this is unfortunate for, in consequence, we fail to encourage good trends in public building and favor bad ones. The changes in attitudes that have brought these bad results are worth examining in the hope they may soon be reversed.

II

Toward the end of the eighteenth century, when Smith wrote his famous chapters on the financing of public works, these structures had a dual function. In part, of course, they were useful and were so judged. Public works facilitated the administration of the realm; they promoted the safety, health, education or convenience of the people; and in such fields as canal-building, road-building and the provision of aids to navigation, they nurtured commerce and industry. They accomplished their useful purpose when they served these practical ends.

But public structures had always been something more. A castle had always been more than a defense facility, to use the modern term. A palace had always been more than a shelter. By their magnificence, these structures proclaimed the power, wealth, ability to confiscate wealth and, on frequent occasions, the good taste of the occupant. They visibly associated man and state and thus helped to ensure that both would be held in proper respect or fear. As with residences, so with other public edifices — houses of parliament, courts of law, hôtels de ville, hunting lodges, parks, plazas, promenades, fortresses and jails. (It is only in comparatively recent times that artillery has been made with the simple undecorated purpose of popular annihilation. For many centuries royal armorers were as much concerned to decorate their ordnance in a becoming manner as to make it efficiently lethal.) And the citizenry which looked on the buildings, often from a considerable distance, could at least reflect that it was no mean and miserly authority by which they were exploited. Purely functional buildings would have done nothing or, in any case, much less for the prince and nation. Though Versailles was, in practical function, a vast dormitory for the French nobility, to have calculated closely the cost per square foot of housing the various grades and categories of occupants would have sadly defeated its purpose. It would have ceased to be a testament to the greatness of Louis XIV and to the glories of France, the latter purpose being, quite accurately, the one proclaimed to all who entered the gates.

All this makes clear that where the public building is involved, usefulness is an elusive concept. The plain functional structure may not be the most useful. Elegance and even extravagance may serve a larger purpose. They may even be more economical. Each summer a great migration of American tourists embarks to visit the prime achievements in princely and ecclesiastical architecture. It is not the buildings of the sensible rulers and the austere prelates that they visit. Rather it is to the monuments of the profligate princes and the openhanded, power-hungry and even somewhat sinister bishops that they go. As a consequence, the commercially fortunate countries and towns nowadays are those who had the least conservative builders in the past.

This remains true even in the extremes. In the last century, Ludwig II of Bavaria became afflicted, in violent form, with the hereditary disease of the Wittelsbachs which was an uncontrollable desire to build. And so on the mountains and in the valleys and amid the dark forests of southern Bavaria, palaces began to appear — a rococo residence in a mountain glade, a Wagnerian picture-book castle on a mountaintop, a very decent replica of Versailles on an island in a lake. Eventually it became known in Munich that the king had completed plans for still another Wagnerian castle, was contemplating a Byzantine palace and intended recreating the Forbidden City of Peking on another outlandish stretch of Bavarian terrain. He was taken into custody and committed as insane to yet another of his palaces where in 1886 he committed suicide. This was economically a misfortune for, as it turned out, this was the last moment in the world's history when palaces could be built at a reasonable price. Those he had completed now draw tourists by the thousands. No investment of the sensible Munich burghers who held Ludwig to be off his rocker ever paid off so well for so long.

III

The monarchial building was partly for use and partly for display. This duality was not immediately altered with the rise of representative government in the last century. The feeling that the public building should be a little larger than life — certainly a lot larger than necessary — remained. It was still part of its function to proclaim the dignity and majesty of the state.

Instead of the vanity of princes expressing itself in the splendor of their buildings and giving the people a vicarious if costly participation, there was now the useful phenomenon of national and civic pride. A new nation could not be sure that it was a nation until it had built a capital of some magnificence, preferably, as in the case of Washington, Ottawa and Canberra, by converting to such use a rather inconvenient stretch of wilderness. The tangible manifestation of statehood in early America was a state capitol with a dome. A courthouse showed, as nothing else, that the frontier had come and gone. Buildings, in brief, were the best proof of nationhood, sovereignty and progress. And, on the whole, the more expensive the building, the stronger the proof.

But of late all this has changed. Public buildings have ceased to be a manifestation of public achievement, a source of public pride. We no longer build impressive courthouses or city halls (the nearly exceptional and wholly commendable case of Boston apart). It is only rarely that we build unimpressive ones. We associate local government with moth-eaten surroundings. If space is needed, it is encased in the most economical glass, steel and aluminum. Justice is now administered in shabby, oaken interiors where dignity is in a losing battle with grime. The Federal Government continues to build but its new office buildings are square, functional, antiseptic and anonymous. They serve their purpose but, unlike the Department of Commerce or the Pentagon, no one any longer knows what they house. Only in our airports and occasionally in our schools do we show signs of wanting something that flatters the eye or nourishes the public pride. Why this compulsion to austerity at precisely the point in our history when, by all outward evidence, we could best afford more?

IV

No doubt fear plays a part. The extravagance of one period is, on occasion, the eyesore of the next. In consequence, the Moorish revival courthouses in California, the skyscraper capitols in Louisiana and Nebraska and the heavy grandeur of the Greek revival in Washington became, in a mere forty or fifty years, not the wonders of the new world they were meant to be but merely aberrations in architectural taste. This being the fate of the last generation of builders, the present one made a virtue out of careful self-effacement. But, more important, in recent times there have been two changes in social attitudes toward public works which have significantly affected their position.

In the years of the Great Depression, public buildings ceased for a time to be things that were needed and enjoyed and became, instead, a solution to the unemployment problem. Anything that is deprived of its primary function risks losing its character and quality. The automobile began to deteriorate when it ceased to be (as William Knudsen once described it) a device for moving people from one place to another sitting down and became, instead, a solution to a sales problem. Once public works became the answer to unemployment, excellence in design was less important than ability to get the project quickly under contract or the employment provided. I once spent the better part of two years studying the public works experience of the thirties without ever reflecting on the quality and design of the resulting structures. These were a by-product; the contribution to employment and economic recovery was what was wanted.

The second and much more important change occurred in the years following World War II. Partly as a reaction to the enlarged role of government under the New Deal and during the war, the state became for many an object of antipathy and suspicion. A doctrine was developed to support this antagonism which identified liberty with private consumption from one's personal means. Public consumption required the coercive collection of taxes and was thus morally inferior. The state, in this view, had a personality that was separate and distinct from the people it comprised. It was an ambitious and aggressive personality and sought to extend the scope of public consumption regardless of the wishes of the constituent citizenry. In consequence, all activities of the state — specifically, all nonmilitary activities — were to be regarded with suspicion. This doctrine was persuasive, and continues to give a superior moral tone to the arguments of all who find taxes inconvenient. To save money on taxes is one thing. To do it in the name of liberty is something much more and far better.

Given this change in attitudes nothing could have been more perilously situated than the public architecture and public works. These had once been used to advertise the power, ambition, grandeur and even the capacity for extravagance of the state. These things had all become wicked. So, among all objects of public expenditure, public works needed most to be reduced in profile. From being ostentatious it was now important that they be ostentatiously efficient. As in no other great country at any time in the past, a narrow notion of physical efficiency came to be the rule when contemplating public architecture. In office buildings it became important only to enclose the greatest number of bureaucrats at the lowest cost. In building highways the aim, a slightly different one, was to move the greatest possible number of people in the least time. And in the maintenance of public structures — cleaning, painting, mowing and removal of litter — the aim was only to get by. Brazil could take her architects into the back country and from her relatively meager resources build a brand-new capital. Pakistan, which is even poorer, might do likewise. They were still proving something as regards the state. Not so the United States.

v

This era of false austerity will, I am sure, one day come to a close. The ideology that supports it is spurious. Public consumption is not inferior. One hopeful indication of change has been our building in foreign capitals. There, of course, we had to put our best foot forward. So there some years ago we began commissioning our most imaginative architects to do new embassies. The results were so interesting and rewarding that American magazines often carried pictures of the buildings in New Delhi, Brussels, Dublin and elsewhere so that Americans could have a glimpse of them too. But this will not always be sufficient. Someone is certain to suggest that if beauty and elegance are good for foreigners, they may be good for Americans too.

I urge it. There is no case for purely pointless extravagance in public construction. Even though insanity paid off handsomely in Bavaria, it probably need not be encouraged here, and we have our native forms. But beauty and elegance in public construction are worth having and they are not cheap. It is my distinct impression that a good building almost always costs more than a bad one and that an architect who promises something both better and cheaper is a fraud.

The cost of good building is something which we should now view accurately. The return on a public structure is not merely the task that it facilitates. It is the whole pleasure that it provides the community. Accordingly, a building can be very expensive but a rare bargain for the pleasure it provides. A modest structure at modest cost would have provided durable and hygienic protection for the mortal remains of Mumtaz Mahal and Shah Jahan. But by spending more — by some estimates about three million pounds in all — Shah Jahan got the Taj Mahal. It has rejoiced the whole world ever since. Surely this was sound economy. Our test should be similar. The most economical building is the one that promises to give the greatest total pleasure for the price.

A good building should naturally invite the question, not what it cost but who was the architect. And it is bound to be controversial. There need be no debate over what building will do its job at the lowest price. This can be calculated. But there is bound to be debate over what building gives the most pleasure to the public. I think it unwise, incidentally, to worry too much about what the next generation will say about the building. It may well be lofty and contemptuous. It is enough that we like it.

Roughly the same rules should hold for maintenance. This for a public building should not be merely sufficient; the standards of cleanliness, paint and polish should arouse positive pride and also be an example for the citizen in his own housekeeping. We may also remind ourselves that beauty and elegance do not exist apart from environment. No building can transcend empty cigarette packages, discarded newspapers and gently wafted Kleenex.

In all public construction, we must seek not only to create beauty but to protect it. This brings up the case of highway and traffic engineering. Here, as I have noted, we have not been excessively concerned with keeping down costs. We look at public buildings and wonder at their cost. We rarely so reflect on viewing a new cloverleaf. But highway construction has been far too much concerned with moving the maximum number of vehicles in the minimum of time with the greatest commercial advantage to all in a position to seize it. This has meant that our concrete trade routes march relentlessly over countryside and city with little concern for what they preserve and what they destroy. And after the highway engineers and the contractors come the billboard artists, the motel builders, the sellers of countless nutrients and artifacts all advertised by neon, to turn the road into an efficient instrument of commerce. Unless their hands are firmly arrested, these entrepreneurs add to the traffic hazard for one cannot drive slowly. It is simply too hideous.

The time has also come on our roads when charm and

beauty must be considered as important as commercial efficiency. Wherever travel is for enjoyment or even where enjoyment is an important byproduct of travel, protection of beauty must take precedence over efficiency. It is not imperative that the road which winds pleasantly along the lake or which accepts the contours of the valley be widened and straightened today or even tomorrow. Those who use it can take a little more time in getting to their destination. Efficiency has no overriding claim to oppose to aesthetics in urban traffic planning or the design of superhighways. And the purgatory inhabited by the architect who emphasizes only function at low cost must be enlarged to include the highway planners and builders who still believe that their job is done when they complete the roads and who do not work for protection against the locust blight of the hucksters which follows in their path.

VI

I have said that efficiency has no overriding claim against beauty. To be more precise, I am arguing for a more adequate concept of efficiency. We are acting efficiently when we maximize the product for the given expenditure or when we adopt the expenditure which maximizes product. Beauty and elegance, and the pleasure that they provide, must be counted as part of the product. We are being inefficient if by false economy we deny the community pleasure and pride in its achievement or if we fail to see, as in the case of the highways, that part of our return is in the form of agreeable and uncluttered countryside.

Those who are unwilling to pay for beauty and some elegance, and those who profit from commercial squalor, will be quick to say that these standards are too subjective, too precious. Americans, in their frequently proclaimed masculinity, cannot be concerned with them. There is certainly no absolute standard of beauty. That precisely is what makes its pursuit so interesting.

Peace
and the Rest of
the World

1

Foreign Policy: The Plain Lessons
of a Bad Decade

THE DECADE OF THE SIXTIES, in the absence of a massively
successful revisionist exercise, will be counted a very dismal
period in American foreign policy. Indeed, next only to the
cities, foreign policy will be considered the prime disaster area
of the American polity and it will be accorded much of the
blame for the misuse of energies and resources that caused
the trouble in urban ghettos and the alienation and eruption
in the universities. The result was very dim in contrast with
the promise.

The promise was bright — "Let the word go forth . . . to
friend and foe alike," President Kennedy said in his Inaugural
Address and no one doubted the power and not many the
wisdom of the word. The prestige of foreign policy in 1961
was enormous. No one much cared about who was to run the
Treasury. It mattered greatly who was to be the Secretary,
or Undersecretary, or even an Assistant Secretary of State,
although there were enough of the latter to form a small
union. In the early months of the new administration, numerous quite marvelous ideas were spawned for strengthening or improving or revising our overseas affairs. There was
to be an expanded and reorganized aid program, a Grand
Design for Europe (subject to some uncertainty as to what

that design might be), the Alliance for Progress, the Kennedy Round, a Multilateral Force, the Peace Corps, counterinsurgency, an expanded recognition of the role of the new Africa, a dozen other enterprises which did not achieve the dignity of a decently notorious rejection.

Now ten years later one looks back on a seemingly uninterrupted series of disasters. The comic opera affair at the Bay of Pigs; the invasion of the Dominican Republic to abort a Communist revolution that had to be invented after the fact; severe alienation throughout Latin America; broken windows, burned libraries and more or less virulent anti-Americanism elsewhere in the world; over everything else, the brooding, frustrating, endlessly bloody, infinitely expensive and now widely rejected involvement in Indochina.

So it seems in retrospect. And at least one of the successes of these years seems a good deal less compelling when one looks back on it. In the Cuban missile crisis President Kennedy had to balance the danger of blowing up the planet against the risk of political attack at home for appeasing the Communists. This was not an irresponsible choice; to ignore the domestic opposition was to risk losing initiative or office to men who wanted an even more dangerous policy. There is something more than a little wrong with a system that poses a choice between survival and domestic political compulsion. The missile crisis did not show the strength of our policy; it showed the catastrophic visions and the resulting pressures to which it was subject. We were in luck but success in a lottery is no argument for lotteries.

II

Yet not everything in these years went wrong. Our relations with Western Europe and Japan caused no particular pain; these had been the theaters of ultimate misfortune in the twentieth century, always assuming war to be such. And, during the nineteen-sixties, relations with the Communist countries improved both in the vision and in the reality.

When the decade began, the official vision of the Communist world was still that of a political monolith — the word was still much used — relentlessly bent on the destruction of what few were embarrassed to call the Free World. If there were divisions within the Communist world, they were presumably on how best to pursue the revolution. Foreign policy vis-à-vis the Sino-Soviet bloc, as it was still called, was accordingly a facilitating instrument for a larger conflict. During his long tenure as Secretary of State, Dean Rusk was criticized for his conviction that foreign policy was subordinate to military convenience. But if conflict with the Communist world was the great and inevitable fact, the Rusk view was at least consistent. Diplomacy, like truth, is an early casualty of war.

But that vision has now dissolved. True believers are still to be found in the more airless recesses of the Pentagon. Retired Chairmen of the Joint Chiefs; Joseph Alsop, Kenneth Crawford, one or two other aging sages; Cold War diplomats solemnly contemplating the world over their martinis in the Metropolitan Club still evoke the Communist conspiracy on which their fame and fortune were founded. They rejoice in anything that seems to suggest a revival of the conflict; they try to warn a generation that does not share their wisdom. But their audience dwindles; and amusement replaces even nostalgia in what remains. The terrible fact obtrudes. The Communist world is as relentlessly plural as the non-Communist world; China and the Soviet Union are much farther from coordinated action than France and the United States. On the record, too, the Communist powers are cautious — rather more cautious perhaps than the government of the United States — about risking disaster in pursuit of an idea. One must sympathize with those whose lives were predicated on the theory of a more unified and heroic Communism. They are the walking wounded of the Cold War.

The Cold War vision of Communism always owed much to men whose place in the American pantheon and whose self-confidence of outlook substantially exceeded their information. But there has also been change in the substance of world affairs. When the decade began, the United States and the USSR were each equipped with weapons capable, even at the lowest levels of military expectation (then more sanguine than now), of destroying each other and most of the world between. At the end of the decade, each was capable of destroying the other from five to fifteen times over. The difference to a population already dead is not decisive. Meantime — and here one can speak with certainty only of the United States — there has been a considerable accretion of knowledge both about the insecurity inherent in the weapons race and the unwisdom of leaving the contest under the control of the Armed Services and the affiliated weapons industries. It would be optimistic to suggest that this control has yet been broken. But the emergence of the Pentagon and its power as a political issue is one of the major developments of the late sixties. It is something for which one could hardly have hoped at the beginning of the decade.

Meanwhile tension between the two superpowers has diminished in other respects. In the United States there is not quite the same conviction of total economic and social success that there was in 1960 — at the crest of the Keynesian revolution. One senses similar doubts in the Soviet Union. In our case, at least, self-doubt is a valuable antidote to evangelism — with its capacity both to offend and endanger. At the beginning of the decade, to accept coexistence with world Communism suggested a slightly defective moral stance. Among the custodians of the current foreign policy cliché, gathering for the ritual discussion at the Council on Foreign Relations, a suggestion along such lines induced a raised eyebrow. Perhaps Khrushchev was coming through a bit too well. That existence and coexistence are identical, few now doubt. That the great industrial societies have common requirements in planning, industrial discipline and organization and common disasters in environmental effects is at least being discussed. Richard Nixon in the fifties spoke the lines of a militant Cold Warrior; it was on this theme and its domestic repercussions that he founded his political career. John F. Kennedy was at least moderately in the opposition camp. Yet enough has changed in the last ten years so that Nixon's expressions as President on the Communist menace are both fewer and more pacific than were those of Kennedy. No one will argue, where Mr. Nixon is concerned, that he is responding to anything so simple as a change in conviction.

Difficult problems remain between the United States and the Soviet Union. No bilateral relationship that depends on or is associated with capacity for reciprocal destruction can be regarded with equanimity — or considered stable. Circumstances and politics have given us different and relentlessly hostile friends and clients in the Middle East — a problem area which I am deliberately passing over in this article. Still, the larger fact remains. It was not our relations with the Soviet Union that made our foreign policy in the sixties the mess that we have come, not incorrectly, to consider it.

III

The disaster area of our foreign policy has been in what the knowing unite in calling the Third World. It was here — in Cuba, the Dominican Republic, in minor degree in the Congo and most of all in Indochina — that the mistakes were made or the disasters occurred. Had it not been for the policy in these parts of the world, Lyndon Johnson would still be President of the United States, the wishes of his wife notwithstanding; and Dean Rusk would still be Secretary of State or, at a minimum, in honorable retirement as president of a college well on the Establishment side of the Mason-Dixon Line. The Third World has been their and our foreign policy trap. On the visible evidence, this has been also true of the Soviet Union. If from the Soviet Foreign Office anyone has recently been assigned to Ulan Bator, it has not been for his handling of relations with France, Germany, Britain or the United States. Indonesia, North Korea and, above all, China were where Soviet policy went off the rails. Again the Third World.

Foreign policy is a gentlemanly profession which sets much store by tradition and continuity, even in error. Far better, one knows, to continue error than to lower the prestige of a great nation (or its servants) by changing course and thus confessing the mistake. Accordingly, introspection, and even thought, are held in low esteem in the diplomatic estate. However, even brief reflection on the recent history of our relations with the Third World suggests that we have made policy on the basis of a startling succession of wrong assumptions. That this is so will even be conceded. The assumptions being wrong, the results caused deep trouble. What remains to be recognized is that a shift in assumptions, from wrong to right, would produce better results. Such recognition does not come easily, as I shall presently argue. A bureaucracy defends, even with righteousness, the wrong assumptions if they are the ones on which it is operating. But first let me list what we have learned from dealing with the Third World in the last decade. Four lessons seem clear:

1. We have learned, first of all, the limits on our power in this part of the world. Following World War II in Western Europe we developed a Marshall Plan syndrome. This view held that the United States could always work wonders in other countries. Our capital, our energy, our economic system, our idealism, our business statesmen, our special standing with a benign God, all combined to produce such capacity. It seemed so in Europe after World War II. There economic organization or the capacity for such organization, industrial skills, technical competence, highly developed public administration and services already existed. The only missing ingredients were capital and people with the special blessings of Providence. When these were supplied by the United States, the miracles predictably followed.

Elsewhere, we have now learned in the hardest of schools, things are different. Where the pre-existing European ingredients of success are missing, the power to work miracles is, not surprisingly, nonexistent. Governments can be influenced but where governments are weak and their power negligible, the power implicit in so influencing them is also predictably negligible. Where organizational, administrative and technical capacity and skills are lacking — where, in short, there is no industrial base or experience — the economy does not respond to an infusion of capital. For capital is not the missing ingredient. In the colonial era, European powers had a substantial influence on the inner life and development of the Third World countries. This they obtained by *creating* a structure for colonial administration and having done so, they did not influence, they governed. Given this public framework, industrial, railroad and modern agricultural development could be induced in reasonably predictable fashion if policy so prescribed. Such a solution is no longer allowed. Thus it has come about that the superpower which seeks to intervene in the Third World remains the victim of the organizational, administrative and technical vacuum which, after all, is what tends most to distinguish this World.

2. The next lesson that we have learned, or more precisely are relearning, is that Communism and capitalism are concepts of practical significance only at an advanced stage in industrial development. In poor rural societies they have only a rhetorical relevance. Capitalism is not an issue in a country that has yet to experience capitalism, and neither is Communism as an alternative. The Third World consists by definition of poor rural societies — that is what undeveloped or underdeveloped countries are. It follows that whether such countries call themselves free, free enterprise, capitalist, socialist or Communist has, at the lowest levels of development, only terminological significance. They are poor and rural, however they describe themselves. For the appreciable future, they will so remain. Even by the crudest power calculus, military or economic, such nations have no vital relation to the economic or strategic position of the developed

countries. They do supply raw materials. But even here the typical observation concerns not their power as sources of such supply but their weakness as competitive hewers of wood in the markets of the industrially advanced countries.

It is hard to see now why so much tension developed in the fifties and early sixties over whether such countries would follow the Communist or non-Communist pattern of development. That alternatives to capitalism only become interesting after there is capitalism (and associated industrialization) was eloquently affirmed by Marx more than a century ago. That capitalism is only an issue if there is capitalism is a proposition not, in its essentials, difficult to grasp. In part, no doubt, our error was the result of a fantastic overestimate (as it now seems) of the speed of economic development in the Third World. Latin American, African and Asian countries would soon be industrialized. Therewith they would become military powers. To global strategists, a relentlessly amateur calling which the United States nurtured in alarming numbers after World War II, it seemed important, accordingly, that ideological affiliation be not with Moscow but with Washington and lower Manhattan. We now know — a few special cases such as Formosa and Israel apart — that the process of development is infinitely slow, that the ultimate organization of these societies is far too academic a question to influence the policy-making even of the most passionate ideologue. By the time India, sub-Sahara Africa and most of Central or South America are industrialized to anything approaching present Western European levels, even greater changes will have occurred in the United States and the Soviet Union.

But it is a mistake to look for complex reasons for the error when simpler ones avail. American foreign policy in

the fifties and sixties was made by men to whom a difference between capitalism and Communism was the only social
truth to which they had access. That the difference is one
thing in Europe or the United States and something very
different in the Congo, Vietnam, even Cuba, was well beyond their reach. Often there was even a measure of pride
— tough-mindedness it was called — in rejecting such com-
plications.

3. Next we have learned that although the inner life and
development of the Third World is beyond the reach of the
power of a superpower, and equally beyond its visible self-
concern, the effort to influence that development brings into
being a very large civilian and military bureaucracy. Colonial power was exercised rather simply through a line of
command which, in general, gave orders. Working indirectly
by way of the hearts and minds of a people requires a much
more massive table of organization. This is partly because
such influence is disappointing in effect and the normal
bureaucratic answer to frustration and noneffect is to get
more money and more men and build a bigger organization.
Military missions, military advisers, active military formations
in the more tragic instances, counterinsurgency teams, pacifi-
cation teams, technical assistance teams, advisers on aid uti-
lization, auditors and inspectors and other instruments against
indigenous larceny, information officers, intelligence officers,
spooks — the list extends indefinitely. Where, as in Vietnam
and Laos, the frustration has been nearly total, the bureaucratic input has been all but infinite. But elsewhere as well,
in Asia and Latin America and in lesser degree in Africa, the
sixties saw the deployment of a huge American military, counterinsurgency, intelligence, diplomatic, public information

and aid establishment designed to influence potentially erring governments and people away from Communism.

4. Next we have learned that an overseas bureaucracy, once in existence, develops a life and purpose of its own. Control by Washington is exiguous. Control by the Congress is for practical purposes nonexistent.

This is partly because of the nature of its task. A government that is being seduced by a superpower wishes, at a minimum, to have the deed done in private. So also a foreign politician. Decency has its claims. Surveillance of Communists, or more active military operations to put down subversion, also requires public reticence. It is axiomatic that in such matters one does not show one's hand to the enemy. Secrecy is also occasioned by the intrinsically high failure rate in these operations. Much of the work of our intelligence and military missions abroad is only possible because no one is aware of how little is obtained for the outlay involved. But secrecy is not the only protection from public scrutiny. The sheer number and variety of such overseas operations in all their different national settings, coupled with the revolving-door nature of higher Washington officialdom, also foster anonymity. Few men in the executive branch remain in office long enough to have knowledge of the affairs of which, nominally, they are in charge. Legislators who must rely on such men for knowledge have even less. This autonomy is combined, in turn, with the tendency for any bureaucracy, military or civilian, in the absence of the strongest of leadership, to continue to do whatever it is doing. This is a matter of the highest importance, one that explains the most basic tendencies of our foreign policy. It calls for special attention.

IV

The tendency of bureaucracy to find purpose in whatever it is doing is superbly revealed by the experience of the past decade in Vietnam. Without exception every reason originally offered for our intervention there has dissolved. Some have now become ludicrous. This is not the parochial view of an opponent of the war; not even the defenders of the conflict affirm the original reasons for the venture. None now say, though it was doctrine in the early sixties, that our action in Vietnam is in response to a probe deliberately directed from Moscow against a weak point on the perimeter and to be resisted, accordingly, as a matter of global strategy. That the NLF carries the banners of Vietnamese nationalism is now generally (if not quite universally) accepted. Once it was asserted that vital American strategic interests were involved — that, quite literally, if we did not fight in the jungles of Vietnam we would soon be assaulted in the Philippines or even on the beaches of Hawaii. Now that contention is offered only as an exercise in irony. Once it was held that we were saving the fledgling democracy of General Thieu and Marshal Ky. An election was cited in support of the pretense. This vision too has become comic. In the late summer of 1970 much energy was expended on keeping Marshall Ky from coming to Washington for a political rally lest he remind Americans of the repressive, obscene and incompetent dictatorship with which they are aligned. Once there were the dominoes. Now to cite the domino doctrine is to remind people that it was the war itself that tumbled the first domino (or most of it) in Cambodia. Once it was held in its defense that, purpose aside, the war could readily be resolved by military means. Now the suggestion that the Pentagon is pursuing the

chimera of military victory in Vietnam provokes an indig-
nant denial. Once it was a defense of the war that it was
a marginal exercise which the American economy could take
in stride. That guns could be had with butter was the not
excessively novel formulation. Now it is sound doctrine that
the war caused the inflation of the latter sixties that still
frustrates good economic management. And its conflict with
sensible priority in resources use has become a cliché.

It is impossible to think of a case more intellectually inert
than that for the Vietnam war. Yet the war continues. This
is because the bureaucracy, the military and intelligence
bureaucracy in particular, operates not in response to national need but in response to its own need. The national
need can dissolve and become ludicrous as in the case of
Vietnam. But this does not affect the need of an army for
the occupation, prestige, promotions that go with active military operations; the need of the CIA for the interest, personal
drama, excitement and outlet for money that go with its
Laotian adventures; or the need of the Air Force for bombing
as a raison d'être. Since Korea we have been learning and
relearning the lesson that strategic air power is ineffective
against primitive agriculture or men moving at night along
jungle roads. This has had little effect on Air Force doctrine
for it happens not to be what the Air Force needs to believe.

But it would be a mistake to picture bureaucratic need in
terms of a too specific bureaucratic self-interest. A more important factor is pure organizational momentum. Bureaucracy can always continue to do what it is doing. It is inca-
pable, on its own, of a drastic change of course. And the
process by which it ensures its continuity — in the case of
the Pentagon by which it prepares budgets, persuades the
Bureau of the Budget, instructs its Congressional sycophants

— is itself highly organized. Thus the momentum. So it has come about that after all national purpose in Vietnam has dissolved, and this is extensively conceded, bureaucratic purpose and momentum still serve. The change in direction that is involved in stopping military operations, bureaucracy cannot accomplish. Dozens of other activities — military support to Latin American countries, staff services to SEATO and CENTO, bases in Spain, the radar watch in the Arctic, ABM, nuclear carriers, any number of Cold War intelligence and countersubversive activities — owe much or all of their existence to the same momentum. Innocents imagine that when they have shown that purpose has evaporated, function will end. It is not so. Purpose is among the least of bureaucratic needs.

v

I do not, of course, suggest that a military and foreign policy bureaucracy, once launched on course, can never be diverted. The sixties were particularly favorable to its exercise of inertial power. The prestige of the military and foreign policy establishment, following the successes of World War II and the Marshall Plan, was high — far higher than now. The Cold War panic led to a large delegation of power over the fearsome technology and clandestine maneuvering which seemed the only answer to the Communist menace. And this was the age of the Establishment in foreign policy — of the New York and Washington *genro* which had come to prominence in World War II, under the Marshall Plan, in the German occupation and under John Foster Dulles. Although the impression was to the contrary, these statesmen had given little independent thought to foreign policy — it was their natural assumption that given their experience and high position in the community they already knew. In consequence, men such as Dean Rusk as Secretary of State, Allen Dulles and John McCone as heads of CIA, John J. McCloy and Dean Acheson as advisers at large were strongly and even uniquely compliant with the bureaucratic view. It added to their confidence and resulting acquiescence that the bureaucratic case was always couched in the resonant Cold War platitudes which, as experienced men, they associated with sound policy. In the Johnson years it helped also to have a President who, though not lacking in either intelligence or will, was least experienced in the field of foreign policy and (from his Congressional experience) had also a habit of acquiescence on military matters. But the inertial dynamic of the bureaucracy is the major explanation of the disasters of the decade. At the Bay of Pigs, in the Dominican Republic, in Vietnam, Laos, Thailand (as again in Cambodia), the bureaucracy showed its power to sweep the leadership into disaster and against all the counsels of common sense.

VI

The lessons of the sixties, as regards foreign policy, are then both specific and self-reinforcing. What remains, as noted, is to act on them. The area where our course most needs correction is not Western Europe or Japan. Doubtless there are improvements to be made in both places but the past has not been intolerable. Relations with the Soviet Union, including the indirect encounters in the Middle East and Germany, include a terrible component of latent risk. But it was not here in the last decade that we stumbled.

We stumbled in the Third World. In this World we cannot intervene, need not intervene and we have intervened. The effort has required a large bureaucracy, military and civilian. This by its nature cannot be controlled. Acting where action is both impossible of effect and unnecessary, it has produced disaster. Given the nature of bureaucracy, there is great persistence in disaster. None of this, given the underlying circumstances, is altogether surprising.

The remedial action is also clear. It is greatly and promptly to contract our policy in Latin America, Africa and Asia. This means specifically that we no longer stand guard against what is called Communism in this part of the world. It means that we no longer distinguish between governments that we like and those of which we disapprove. It means even more specifically that over the generality of Latin America, Africa and Asia, military missions are withdrawn and military aid comes to an end. So also in all three continents do counter-insurgency, countersubversive and intelligence operations. Remaining bases related to the defense of these areas are given up. It means that henceforth the raison d'être of aid and information programs is to assist economic development and inform countries as regards the United States, not to fight Communism. (I set very great and particular store by the continuing importance of foreign aid.) It means that in these countries we will return to orthodox diplomatic relations and the assistance in capital, technique or volunteer manpower that an economically and technically advanced country finds it morally rewarding or economically advantageous to render to its less equipped neighbors. Not distinguishing between good and bad governments, we recognize all. We also trade with all. Our commercial relations, it is worth noting, will thus be freed from the incubus of suspicion that they reflect some larger imperial ambition.

Foreign policy, especially of the more belligerent sort, is regularly formulated with a view to rejoicing its author and audience with its therapeutic simplicity. But that is not my present intention. This is what must be done. It follows that, although the broad rule of nonintervention and nonpresence applies to all of the Third World, differing history will dictate a differing time schedule. Withdrawal from the Philippines and Korea will have to be negotiated. In the case of Korea withdrawal could be very slow. The SEATO treaty need not be denounced; it is sufficient that the Asian members know that it is being allowed to wither on the vine. Even the liquidation of the Indochina disaster will take time —although, in principle, no more than is needed to negotiate an amnesty for those who have served us and to move the men to the ports and airports. Bureaucratic momentum being the only reason for continuing the war, there is no case for a more gradual procedure.

VII

The strength of the nations of the Third World, in relation to the superpowers, lies in the absence of levers by which they can be controlled and the absence of power at the end of the levers. Without public administration there can be no control; there is no industrial society to be controlled. This accords immunity equally to effective intervention by the Communist powers and by the United States. Although one guesses that the Soviets have seen the impracticality of socialism without previous preparation, one cannot guarantee that such intervention will not be attempted. One can only be certain that Soviet and Chinese efforts to dominate these countries will encounter the same obdurate circumstances as have we. They will end, accordingly, in frustration not different from that of the United States in Vietnam or their own experience in Indonesia.

The course here urged does not mean that all will be well in the Third World. This World has no monopoly on peaceful behavior, occasional doctrine to the contrary notwithstanding. The possibility of struggle within and between nations and peoples remains. American withdrawal does not ensure good international behavior. Nor will it ensure greater reliance on collective reaction to attacks by one country on another, although that might be hoped. It accepts only the lesson of the last decade, which is that our intervention does us no good and, for the people involved, can make everything much worse.

In recent months considerable movement along these lines has been implicit — though with an inconsistent commitment to earlier Cold War rhetoric — in the so-called Nixon Doctrine. This is much to be welcomed. But it will now be clear that what is here proposed is no mere matter of announcing a change in policy. The present policy sustains and empowers a large bureaucracy which reacts to its own needs. The needed policy disestablishes this bureaucracy — indeed, one of the constraints on foreign policy in the future is that it must be of a nature that it is subject to political as distinct from bureaucratic control. (We cannot guide affairs in Laos; we do not need to do so; and we cannot, in any case, have a policy that requires that much delegation to the CIA.) None will doubt the extent of the exercise of Presidential and other political authority that will be needed. It is not easy to associate the prospect with the passive tendencies of President Nixon. The proper policy toward the Third World requires not only new doctrine but also elimination of the need for a large part of the military, intelligence and civilian bureaucracy that conducts the present policy. The survival of that bureaucracy depends on making policy on the wrong assumptions. It would be naïve to imagine that these organizations will acquiesce easily in the change, however effectively they are proven in error and however ghastly the resulting experience. Not wickedness but the dynamics of big organization is involved. It is a far greater factor in our foreign policy than we have even begun to realize.

2

The American Ambassador

WHATEVER the noteworthy aspects of the American system of diplomatic representation, it produces an exceptionally large number of men who are qualified, in their own view, to comment on its shortcomings. Other advanced countries have, predominantly, a career service. This means that it is only after retirement that a man can sit down and reflect on the eccentricities of the organization in which he has spent his life. By then the habit of careful speech, and even more of careful thought, is likely to be well ingrained. That is why diplomatic memoirs may lack even the modest exuberance of the *State Department Bulletin* which in general style they otherwise resemble.

Our system, by contrast, absorbs with each new administration a considerable number of political ambassadors and in due course extrudes them to law firms, teaching jobs, corporation vice-presidencies, punditry, mutual funds or research projects of the Council on Foreign Relations, often well in advance of tabular senility. All feel qualified to report in depth, and with the confidence born of grave practical experience, on the Foreign Service of the United States. That is my situation.

However, I do not wish entirely to disparage my credentials. India, where I served from 1961 to mid-1963, presents a large and complex problem in diplomatic representation. The Chinese attack of 1962 increased by perhaps twentyfold the responsibilities of the post. This was also my second tour with the Department of State. Immediately following World War II, I was nominally in charge of economic policy in Germany and Japan. (I say nominally for our two pro-consuls in the field, General Lucius Clay in Germany and General Douglas MacArthur in Japan, prevented anyone in Washington from having a damaging sense of personal power. We often discussed what we would do if MacArthur completely severed relations. One idea was to cut him off from the press.) So I had some grounds for comparison. Finally, of the seven ambassadors who had represented the President of the United States in India from the time of that country's independence until my tenure, my tour of roughly two and a half years was the second longest. It will be suggested that this was not unduly long and that the others were too short. I think that is right.

II

With quite a few of the problems that are commonly held to afflict American ambassadors I had no experience. That is partly because some are imaginary and others can be eliminated with a little effort by the ambassador. But India is, in important particulars, a special case. I would be doing a disservice to less fortunate envoys in other capitals were I to suggest that my experience was in all respects typical.

Thus, in India, we had no personal financial problems. We did not quite live on our salary of $27,500[1] but we could have done so. Our entertainment allowance was not quite suffi-

[1] In 1970 it would be $42,500.

cient but only because I absorbed the small deficits of the less well paid officers. However, by the standards of Paris or London, the social life of New Delhi is austere. Most politicians avoid alcohol; one or two will not come to parties where it is served. There is a good deal of entertaining around among members of the diplomatic community but this is a waste of time. Although often good public servants, many are not closely in touch either with Indian affairs or their own governments. The American ambassador is commonly believed to be one of the most relentlessly driven people in India. This pressure of work served admirably as an excuse for not going to diplomatic dinners. The loss was nil.

I am not entirely decrying the social life that is so intimately associated with diplomacy. No doubt with the Russians, French or even Arabs, it, along with alcohol, mellows what otherwise might be an acid relationship. But its importance is much exaggerated. Deft entertaining is greatly stressed by the man who is no good for anything else. Also, most people enjoy giving or attending parties and human vanity is served in a uniquely undemanding way by the rites of the reception line. What is so much enjoyed is canonized as high official duty. During my time in New Delhi, while we extensively entertained and were entertained by Indians, I never transacted any business at a party that wouldn't have been accomplished in due course at the office. And I never picked up any information which, in the by no means certain event that it was true, wouldn't have reached me through regular channels. An ambassador is meant to be a spokesman, negotiator and administrator, and a guide to his own government on policy toward the country to which he is assigned. If he is preeminently a social figure, he is either neglecting his job or in a capital where the job is unimportant.

As I have said, ambassadors in Paris, Tokyo, London or Bonn may well feel the wind financially, and trying to save money on their allowances is something that appeals only to legislators with a queer sense of financial proportion. But it was in Washington that people in the Kennedy years needed more pay. Unlike an ambassador, a man accepting a Cabinet or sub-Cabinet position and moving to the capital must pay for his house and for household staff if he can find any. He receives no educational allowances for his children and he must stand the cost of his entertaining, official and otherwise, except in the rare case where he looks after an overseas visitor. And his salary is less than that of an ambassador in a leading capital.

III

It is also commonly imagined that the American ambassador has become a rather pathetic ceremonial figure who is treated with amused tolerance by his AID mission, the CIA, the military mission, the United States Information Service, the Department of Agriculture, the Library of Congress and the Peace Corps. These agencies possess and on frequent occasion fight over the real power. Nothing of this sort happened in India. My predecessors in office had taken for granted that they were in charge of all American activities in the country. They had not assumed that this was for the purpose either of nourishing their own egos or bolstering the jurisdictional position of the State Department. I found no real problem in continuing and, where necessary, strengthening this tradition.[2]

Where the ambassador is not in charge, it is usually his own fault. He regards himself not as the representative of the President of the United States but as the partisan of the State Department. The representatives of the other agencies then feel that they must fight for their independence from a bureaucratically partisan figure. Or, in the more common case, the ambassador does not want to take responsibility for the AID organization, the military, the information services or the CIA. That is because he is too lazy or dignified to get his back into the difficult and unglamorous problems of agricultural education, new fertilizer plants, military procurement, or how to get better space for the USIA libraries. And when something goes wrong, he wants to be able to tell Washington (and maybe with suitable discretion the local American correspondents) that the CIA men were acting with their usual fecklessness or recklessness. If an ambassador is to be in charge, he must be prepared to take the rap for his people when something blows.

I am persuaded that the local staffs of the various overseas agencies — AID, the military, USIA, the others — very much prefer an ambassador who does take charge and who fights their battles in Washington. The Washington agencies do not like it so well — Agriculture, Commerce, the Pentagon and the CIA each wants to direct its own people, run its own foreign policy. But they will not quarrel with a determined ambassador for they know he can be a very awkward enemy.

[2] I have been most frequently asked about the CIA. I dispensed with most of its activities on taking over, they being unnecessary and possibly embarrassing. The rest were fully under my control. Its members were, in general, effective, sensible and disciplined men.

IV

American missions abroad are believed also to be sadly over-staffed and with people who are neither very responsible nor very smart. Our public activities are perhaps more extensive in India than in any other country at peace. Including food, we were, during my years, providing about $800 million worth of economic assistance, much the most to any country. Our information program, which cost just under six million, was also the biggest. There was a military mission and the usual diplomatic presence. When I left in the summer of 1963, the AID organization had 106 Americans in New Delhi, the State Department, 40, and the United States Information Service, 33. The military mission numbered about 100. Other agencies had about 70, including the staffs of the military attachés, and the men who flew the Embassy Convair, the twelve Marines who guarded the Chancery, the two employees of the Treasury and the four who ran the Peace Corps. In the country as a whole, about five hundred Americans manned the Embassy and three Consulates, provided a wide range of technical services, ran libraries, reading rooms, newspapers and magazines, and supervised civilian and military expenditures totaling around a billion dollars. Harvard uses a somewhat larger number of people to run its student dining halls.

Again, however, India is not typical. A large number of highly educated and extremely diligent Indians are available at (by our standards) very modest pay for tasks for which in other countries Americans would have to be exported. Moreover the social life in New Delhi — and other Indian cities — is pedestrian, the food does not appeal to all tastes, the opportunities for social drunkenness are circumscribed, the women are sexually restrained, there are no winter sports, and for six months of the year the weather is insufferable. So India does not appeal to the professional expatriate — to the bureaucrat, military or civilian, who finds Paris, Rome or Wiesbaden far more agreeable than Falls Church. Some are now so settled that they would not move for the Red Army and could not be dislodged by Alaric. It must also be said that our numbers were kept down only by eternal vigilance. During the Chinese border attack of 1962, India was much in the news and it came to dozens of people in Washington that New Delhi might be their rendezvous with destiny. My deputy and I met every morning to turn down the offers of help that had come in overnight.

As compared with those of twenty years ago, the younger State Department Officers with whom I worked struck me as impressively better educated, in far more sympathetic touch with the people of the country, more imaginative and just as hard-working and disciplined. The staff of the United States Information Agency is almost as good. Since it has a suspiciously intellectual and artistic preoccupation, this agency naturally arouses the antipathy of those statesmen who stopped with the McGuffey Readers. I found it a hard-working organization of exceedingly competent people. In the early sixties, it underwent a rejuvenation of spirit under Edward R. Murrow. He showed as did no other Kennedy appointee what intellectual courage, good leadership and a kind of sanguinary enthusiasm to get things done can still accomplish on matters of foreign policy.

The military staff which launched the military aid program following the Chinese attack was alert and professional and these men quickly won the confidence of their Indian colleagues. The AID organization, in its technical ranks, left a good deal to be desired. In principle, all Americans agree that our best talent should go abroad to work on the great tasks of economic development. In practice, the best can't be budged. Men in mid-career are held at home by laboratories, professional colleagues, salaries, their children's schools and their own prospect for promotion. A large source of technical talent for AID has come to be men who have passed retirement age in the United States. Some are very good; some are not good in 120-degree heat. Some should have retired. The only solution, I fear, is to tailor our efforts to the manpower available. In India and Pakistan which are moderately well-supplied with technicians, I would cut back sharply on our technical assistance program and use the best of the talent so saved in Africa or other areas of greater need. This would not, of course, affect our loans in support of industrial, transport and agricultural development. These loans represent overwhelmingly the largest part of our aid program and the part that really counts.

The American community in New Delhi was exceedingly responsible and well-behaved. During my time there I did not have to deal with a single instance of pugnacity, intoxication, reckless driving or other public misbehavior and only one case of seduction by a Marine. Doubtless there were more lapses than I knew about but they achieved no notoriety. The officers, NCO's and airmen of the 322nd Air Division, who were based in New Delhi to fly support for the Indian forces in Ladakh for some nine months, were not charged in all that time with a single act of public impropriety or indiscipline. *Blitz*, the Indian left-wing paper, which kept them under thoughtful surveillance, once complained that a beer can had been tossed from a window of Kotah House, the

princely palace where an appreciative Indian government
had billeted them. That was all and the charge was not sub-
stantiated.

v

Finally, we were not especially bothered by Congressional
visitors who, according to the folklore, are the bane of an
ambassador's existence. A number came but they applied
themselves rather diligently to their investigations and, I
think, went away better informed as a result. Businessmen,
real and bogus, were more of a problem. They swarmed into
the Chancery in the travel season to consult the economic
staff and the Commercial Counsellor about markets or investment prospects. All this was with a view not to increased
American commerce and industry but to making their junket
tax-deductible. Most asked for a business card to take home
so they could prove they had done business. This annoyance
diminished perceptibly when the Treasury, at my behest,
began looking into the racket and especially at entrepreneurs
who were deducting the cost of business travel on cruise
ships.

The major offender on travel is, in fact, the State Department. When no one in the Department knows what to do
about a problem or whether anything can be done, this
failure of imagination can always be covered by dispatching
some official of suitable rank to the scene. This could, on
occasion, be the result of a plot by subordinates against their
superior. "This is a very difficult situation, sir. There's no
use sending just anyone. It must be somebody they'll listen
to." The great man agrees to go. He fails. But he does learn
why his subordinates haven't succeeded. And the exercise
also helps the world to understand the first principle of Amer-

ican diplomacy which is that while we may not have policies, we do have airplanes.

Although our man has not accomplished anything, he is allowed to say that the talks have been useful. There are few ironclad rules of diplomacy but to one there is no exception. When an official reports that talks were useful, it can safely be concluded that nothing was accomplished. Admirers of Secretary of State Dean Rusk stressed his penchant for having useful talks.

VI

Our tendency to substitute mobility for thought may be taken to be a criticism of the way we conduct our foreign policy and, lest I be thought to be giving too perfect a bill of health to the State Department, there are others I would offer. The standards of promotion of the career service are ambiguous. In principle, the system favors the clear-headed, determined operator who knows what should be done and has a strong desire to do it. In practice, such a man has usually been involved in controversy. As a result, preference goes to the well-honed, socially graceful and politically emasculated figure who is efficient only as a telegraphic conduit for clichés. He seems safe right up to the moment when strong political judgment is required and then, of course, he is a disaster. Our troubles in the Congo and Laos, to cite two examples of my period, were made greatly worse because, initially, we had the wrong men on the job. When useful men were sent, things took a marked turn for the better.

The most persistent error of American foreign policy is the tendency to identify our fortunes with dictators in their brief moments of glory. Thus we manage, time after time and in place after place, to share in the animosity which these men arouse in their own people. The political innocence of the diplomatic clotheshorse is one cause. To his superficial eye the road company Caesar always seems more popular and more powerful than he really is. So he reacts as amateur politicians once reacted to Carmine DeSapio. They believed what he said about his power in New York.

VII

But while it is the fashion of those who are discussing the State Department to dwell on the shortcomings of the career service, more needs to be said of those of us who serve for shorter periods. If the political or expert appointee, either in Washington or in the field, has any function, it is to assume risks that the career man, whose life is committed to the service, cannot afford. Anyone who concedes the continued existence of the Chinese, believes the future of Africa is not with Portugal, deals with Congressman John Rooney not as a minor god but as a Brooklyn hack of negative attainments, allows that other countries can be as devoted to socialism as we are ostensibly to capitalism, thinks the rich countries can live more comfortably with the poor countries by providing aid, takes the same calm view of trade with the Communist countries as do the Western Europeans, and fights the more gruesome military designs of the Pentagon or the American right, is sure to induce a certain amount of political static. The noncareer man, since he is not placing his whole life on the line, should absorb this animosity.

Alas, quite a few political appointees persuade themselves that it is their function to set the career service an example in political caution or cowardice. They greatly enjoy their jobs; they do not relish the rough and tumble of political controversy; they wish to avoid trouble. A very large part of the cable traffic to New Delhi during my tenure was devoted to warning me that this or that action, admittedly meritorious, would cause criticism in Congress. Much of it came from Phillips Talbot, my Assistant Secretary and a Kennedy appointee, who later brought even greater caution to the cause of the Greek colonels.[3] George Kennan, one of the wisest and certainly the most literate foreign policy operative in our time, has taken the Congress to task for its failure to accept informed guidance on foreign policy. In fact, Congress on these matters is what we make it. If State Department officials, in their desire to avoid trouble, yield to Congressional prejudices, Congress will be bad. Fight and it will be better. There would have been no test ban agreement if Averell Harriman, who is notably exempt from my criticism, had yielded in advance to the prejudices of Richard Russell. And there would have been fewer votes for the treaty if he hadn't fought like a lion for its ratification. Kennan suggests that our foreign policy is conducted for the convenience of the Congress. I would argue that more often it is designed to keep State Department officials out of trouble. The modern foreign policy expert is a man who knows what should be done but has exceptionally sophisticated reasons for not wishing to risk criticism.

In passing, I might say that the function of the modern liberal when he assumes State Department responsibilities is especially interesting. Partly he gives a new and sophisticated sanction to the more moth-eaten foreign policy positions which he previously criticized. For the rest, by the

---

[3] As Ambassador in Athens. Helen Vlachos, the brilliant, independent and conservative Greek publisher, tells a hilarious story of calling Talbot for help when she wanted to leave the country. He bravely told her to try a smaller embassy.

ingenious intransigence with which he reacts on all matters which concern the Communist countries, he proves that the suspicions of the American right, growing out of his earlier advocacy of a more conciliatory policy, are really quite groundless.

VIII

The State Department is also slow in its responses. This is especially so on smaller matters which, however, have the capacity of becoming serious. On important problems, by resorting, as necessary, to crude and even vulgar language, one can always get attention and usually the answer one wants. I found it worked wonders on occasion to end a cable with the injunction, "Now will someone back there kindly get off his ass." But Ceylon, Nepal or Canada cannot claim the attention of the top officials of the Department. So their concerns get lost in endless meetings in the office of the Assistant Secretary or some other subordinate official. The inability of the Department to respond does mean that in time of crisis it is good to be the man on the spot. You can do what is necessary without interference.

Many of the diplomatic techniques on which we rely are archaic. The most precious conviction of the State Department is that an ambassador can call on the foreign minister of the government to which he is accredited and with great benefit tell him the facts of life as these are seen by Washington. The comparatively rare Washington meeting that does not break up with a decision to travel invariably agrees on instructing the relevant ambassador to seek an appropriate official and inform him firmly of the wishes of the United States. The telegram is duly dispatched: ". . . you should leave the Government in no doubt . . ." On receipt of the cable, the ambassador makes an appointment, mounts his Cadillac and delivers the message. Then he telegraphs back that the mission is accomplished, adding routinely that he did not mince words. Otherwise when nothing happens, it will be assumed that he did not speak with sufficient force.

Thus we influence the course of policy of other nations in our favor. Mostly it is a terrible waste of time. For it assumes that highly placed officials in other governments are both uninformed and omnipotent. Learning through forceful words of the wishes of the United States, they will use their power and act accordingly. That officials have such power is a fiction in which the State Department rejoices even as regards Laos.

In fact, if the Indian government is a fair example, officials usually know exactly what we want before we ask. And whether they act in accordance with our wishes depends not at all on the rank or eloquence of those making the appeal but on the consequences to the official of doing so. Whether one's plea is successful — trivial matters of course excluded — depends on whether the action is in accordance with Indian self-interest and on whether it will be so interpreted by the politicians, press and the public. It follows that one's success depends not on whether one persuades some bureaucrat but whether one can persuade political leaders, newspapermen and the public at large. These hold the power to which the official is beholden.

So what counts is one's ability to get through to the public. In India, at least, this was vital. In 1963 we worked out with the Indians a proposal for joint air exercises as a protective measure in the event of a new Chinese attack. It warned the Chinese were they considering a new adventure and, more important, it postponed, for the time being, the need for the

Indians to build up a force of high-performance aircraft that would have been formidably expensive both for them and for us. In light of the Indian policy of nonalignment, it was also an action that could easily have been misunderstood. I spent hours urging the merits and economies of the arrangement on Indian political leaders and the press. There was similar effort on the Indian side. Without this explanation, the step would have been bitterly attacked, as also our motives; there would have been much talk of our tying India to our war chariot. In the end, even the left was only formally critical. Partly because of the time devoted to this, I gave little thought to a minor agreement we had made for joint use of some radio facilities to reach Southeast Asia. This encountered bitter criticism as an impairment of the nonalignment policy and a suspected Yankee trick. It had to be abandoned.

IX

One must be selective about efforts such as the above. One cannot see political leaders or the press on everything. One must explain, but not seem to be mounting a campaign. And if something is obviously bogus, one had better leave it alone. At the time of the Bay of Pigs, Washington dispatched reams of guidance, all of it palpably fraudulent, on how to explain this action to the local politicians and press. I decided that silence was best. Our friends could then overlook the error; explanation would require them, as a matter of self-respect, to debate it. Eventually a cable from the State Department came in urging this course. Each summer the Department gets out a tortured and spectacularly unpersuasive telegram on reasons and strategy for keeping the Chinese out of the United Nations. The ultimate reason, which is that the

Department fears not Mao but the American right wing, is thoughtfully omitted. Once my neighbor, Mr. Henry Stebbins, our Ambassador in Khatmandu, simply wired back in response that the only man in the Royal Government of Nepal capable of following the Department's logic was in Calcutta having his teeth fixed.

Pamphlets, speeches and official magazines and newspapers are, no doubt, of some importance for persuasion. Ours, in the past, have lost credibility because they were written to impress not foreigners but Congressional illiterates. They have been great on free enterprise and the sins of the Russians but have contained little that one would willingly read.

Speeches by the ambassador may serve to explain things but this requires far more restraint than is commonly imagined. One can elucidate the American position on, say, control of nuclear weapons and, if it is well-stated and interesting, the audience will listen and the papers will report what you have said to their much larger readership. But if you make the same speech to other audiences the press will begin to ignore you. Pretty soon it will reach the sensible conclusion that it should ignore everything you say. If, fearing this, you say something new and interesting, a rocket will arrive from the State Department. It may be slow about making policy but it doesn't want you doing it.

Speeches on the need for international goodwill, the importance of common understanding, the unity of the free world, the future of the free world, our common commitment to liberty, the need to resist Communist aggression, the importance of ideals and the need to avoid impractical idealism are even more dangerous. They not only lose the audience and the press but they establish even more quickly your reputation as a man with nothing to say. Quite a few American ambassadors have the reputation of being inarticulate. It is far, far better than being thought a vacuous windbag. That too is a common view of our men.

One of my hardest jobs in India was to limit the number of my public appearances to the occasions when I could — by some reasonable stretch of the imagination — say something. This couldn't, in practice, be more than once a month. To help out, I worked up a set of addresses on economic development based on my old lectures at Harvard. The subject was not sufficiently lofty so that the State Department would worry about my making policy or the AID organization would dare to disagree. The Indians were naturally interested in the whole field or professed to be. The subject was fresh in my mind when I returned to Harvard. It was an excellent arrangement and conserved thought.

3

The Proper Purpose
of Economic Development

ONE OF THE GENERALLY AMIABLE idiosyncrasies of man is
his ability to expend a great deal of effort without much in-
quiry as to why. Most of the descriptions and pictures of the
moon I have seen make it out to be a rather questionable
piece of property. The absence of atmosphere would seem to
be a real handicap. Likewise of water. The climate is predictable, if poor. In northern Canada and Alaska, agriculture suffers from a very short growing season. The moon
presents the limiting case of none. Settlement will almost
certainly be slow. Yet these and similar shortcomings show
no signs of deterring man in his enthusiasm to get there. Nor
can one be completely sorry. Though not an inexpensive
adventure, it may be worth pursuing for no particular reason.
Evelyn Waugh in *Decline and Fall* tells of a modern church-
man who, while reflecting deeply on the sins of the world,
came suddenly to wonder why God made it in the first place.
Thenceforth he could think of nothing else. He had to give
up his church; the only further employment he could find
was as chaplain in a progressive penitentiary where he was
soon murdered by another deeply thoughtful man. It is a
warning against excessive introspection.

But it may still be useful on occasion to ask about the goals of any costly effort and such, I am persuaded, is the case with economic development. For some twenty-five years the world — East and West, capitalist and Communist, democratic and more democratic (no country since Hitler has described itself as undemocratic or antidemocratic) — has been pursuing such development. Development, semantically if not always practically, is in active voice; it implies movement toward some result. What should be the result? There is always danger that, in the absence of such specification, we will triumphantly achieve some unwanted end. Or we will act less efficiently than we might to get what we really want.

ɪɪ

One reason for specifying the goals of development for the poor country is that the special circumstances of the economically advanced countries have allowed them, in very considerable measure, to remain unaware of the need for choice. So their economists do not much discuss the matter. In these countries the purpose of the economy is to produce goods. And the particular mix — the distribution of capital and manpower to different products and services — is given or is assumed to be given by the distribution of income, the efficiency of markets and popular political decision. If the distribution of resources between necessaries and luxuries — between products for the masses and the more esoteric delights of the few — seems wrong, the thing to change is the distribution of income. An increase of taxes on the incomes of the well-to-do or the products they consume is the appropriate remedy.

Given the income distribution, the only need is to make production as efficient as possible. Since efficiency is assumed to have its own reward, that too is taken care of. What one gets, accordingly, is the best one can have — or such is the commonly accepted view. At least in peacetime there has been little tendency to think further about the desirability of what is being produced. And there has been a further measure of concurrence from the Soviet-type economies. The Soviet Union has repeatedly proclaimed that its industrial goal is to "catch up" with the United States. This means that it seeks a broadly similar industrial apparatus in the service of similar ends. It has been easy to go to the further and final assumption which is that the industrial apparatus of the United States, Western Europe and the USSR are the natural and indeed the only model for the newer countries. These newer countries need only recreate in some rough form what the more developed countries already have. Development is and should be the faithful imitation of the developed.

III

In fact, this is not a proper procedure. In the less developed lands the simple goal of an expanding production, the assortment reflecting the demand given by the income pyramid, is not a satisfactory guide. There is, first, a very large population which is very near or sometimes below the margin of subsistence. Those who are hungry have a special claim on resources. So do the measures which remedy this privation. For the same reason there is a special case against the luxury consumption of the well-to-do. Certain claims of the state also take on an added or seemingly added urgency in the poor country — a point to which I will return. The question of how much should be consumed now and how much should be invested for larger production and consumption later on is also vastly more urgent in the poor country, for the necessary saving, or some of it, will come from people who are insufficiently supplied. A decision in favor of present starvation in order to secure the consumption of a subsequent generation is one that no rich country has to make. And it has a decided poignancy for the country that does have to make it.

Faced with the special problem of goals that grows out of their poverty, one sees the poor countries coming up with a variety of solutions. Three in particular can be identified. They are as follows:

1. *Symbolic modernization.* This goal gives development the purpose of according the country the aspect of progress. There are certain things the modern state must have. These include a decently glittering airport, suitably impressive buildings of state, one or more multilane highways, an economic plan, a considerable hydroelectric project, at least the intention of creating a steel industry and a balance of payments deficit. No one should be lofty or patronizing about these symbols; leaders have always known the importance of the concrete and visible expressions of national being. Abraham Lincoln insisted during the Civil War that work on the then unfinished Capitol go on. If that continued, people would feel that the Union would continue. In the last century, American settlers had no sooner redeemed some forest or prairie than they bonded themselves to build an impressive courthouse. Perhaps they needed other things more. But nothing else so proved they were civilized people with whom others should reckon.

Yet economic well-being as such is not much advanced by symbolic modernization. More often it is retarded for those who must pay the bill. And much symbolic modernization is a political stratagem for fooling people into believing something is being done. Or it is a form of monument-building by which politicians commemorate their existence and also their inadequacy at public cost. As it would be unwise to deny a role for symbolic modernization, so it would be unwise to accord it much approval.

2. *Maximized Economic Growth.* I come now to a more respectable formulation of the goal of development and the one which reflects most strongly the influence of Western economic thought. This proclaims it to be, over some period of time, the greatest possible increase in total and per capita product. Import restrictions and duties and domestic taxes may discourage the production of some less essential goods. But the composition of the product is secondary. The goal is to get more. At the extreme, investment outlays are favored in accordance with their capital-output ratios. This means that the test of an investment is the amount by which it increases total product.

Not only will investment be so tested but there will be emphasis on increasing investment. The more of this over time, the greater the increase in output. This means, in turn, that there will be effort, in principle at least, to increase the savings from which comes the investment. Since voluntary savings are scarce in the poor country, there will be a case for involuntary savings through taxation or inflation.

Questions of priority that cannot be resolved by resort to statistical tests — and these in the poor country tend to be both exiguous and flexible as to outcome — will also be decided in accordance with assumed contribution to expansion of output. The position to be accorded education or other social overhead investment, the balance between industry and agriculture, between light industry and heavy industry will be so resolved.

As compared with symbolic modernization, this test of in-

creased income and product obviously has much to commend
it. The reality of economic advance — the production of
goods and services — replaces the mere image. These are
solid and objective tests of performance.

Yet this goal too is not without dangers. Considerable
extremes of wealth and income continue to exist in nearly all
of the less developed lands. These create a strong drag of
consumer demand in the direction of higher-priced or luxury
products. And this tendency is especially insidious, for many
of these products are commonplace in the more advanced
countries and equally so in the consumption habits of the
upper income minority of the poorer country. To the extent
that the high incomes of the minority draw development resources into privileged consumption, social differences are
widened and to the strains associated with poverty may be
added those associated with obvious differences in well-
being. People soon come to sense that economic development
is not for the many but for the few.

There are further dangers. As just noted, in this development goal, taxation — what has come to be called fiscal
savings — plays a considerable role. In the poor country
there is a particular likelihood that taxation will be regressive — that it will fall most heavily on the poor who are
available in the most abundant supply and have the fewest
facilities for escaping the tax collector. And since the underdeveloped country is, pro tanto, an agricultural community, there may be a traditional tendency for this taxation to
fall upon the farmer or his land. Thus not only does un-
differentiated growth tend to support higher income consumption, it may do so partly as the result of saving from
lower income consumption.

Moreover, the process of development itself both requires

and justifies a substantial increase in the number of people earning higher incomes. Administrators, managers, engineers, technicians, accountants, clerks and other civil servants are all required, and all at rates of pay that will seem high to the poorer taxpayer. The political consequences of this may be discomforting in any case. If these jobholders are engaged in forms of development that do not benefit the poor taxpayer, it will obviously be worse. The latter soon comes to think of development as something which rewards not him but some official.

Finally, there are serious dangers in the heavy investment. The saving that this requires can easily reflect the preferences of the planner, not the people. In a number of countries since World War II — Yugoslavia, Poland and China — there have been revolts against rates of saving and investment in excess of what the community would endure.

3. *Selective Growth.* The foregoing problems have not gone unrecognized although the recognition has been less explicit than might be wished. Much development planning has been based on the belief that benefits must accrue as a matter of priority to the more needy sectors of the population. Resources so painfully conscripted from the people must return benefit to the same people.

Unhappily this politically salutary principle has led to highly contradictory conclusions as to its application. To some, agriculture, agricultural extension, community development and local primary education have seemed the obvious answer. The poor are in the villages. It is to these that the investment should go. But to others this, at best, is only a palliative. People are poor not because of insufficient agricultural investment but because they are in agriculture. The real answer is industrial employment. This argues for investment

in manufacturing, power, transportation and the other components of an industrial base. The progressive solution is to
rescue people, if not from the idiocy, at least from the inevitable poverty of rural life.

In some countries, notably in India, there is further disagreement between those who defend modern machine methods and those who contend that, since employment is the
goal, labor-intensive enterprises, including rural and cottage
industries of various kinds, should be favored.

Thus, although there may be wide agreement on a policy
of selective economic growth, there can be very little agreement on what should be selected.

IV

There is a further, and I think preferable, development goal
which I believe resolves the foregoing difficulties. It is one,
incidentally, that has been implicit in a good deal of past
Indian thinking — and in the best planning in other countries.
This anchors economic development to the consumption requirements, present and prospective, of the typical citizen
— of statistically speaking, the modal consumer. It organizes
development around the protection and increase of the living
standard of this consumer. By way of illustration, if, as in
India, the annual income of 80 percent of all family units
is less than R.1200 (at the time of writing, about $250), de-
velopment resources will be concentrated on consumption
that is purchasable by people with such income. The number
of goods and services is not large. Obviously it means a major
emphasis on food, clothing, shelter and education since these
are the dominant items in the economy of the low-income
family. The same rule operates equally against automobiles,
any but the most inexpensive housing, luxury consumer

goods and conspicuous public goods. This is not a decision for agriculture or for industry or for light industry as opposed to heavy industry. It is a choice for the industrial structure which supplies the typical or modal citizen. That person wants, perhaps first of all, an abundant supply of inexpensive food. But back of an improved agriculture lie fertilizer plants and a chemical industry and well-designed agricultural implements and an efficient transportation system and hence a source of steel. Back of textiles, bicycles and other low-budget consumer goods is a similar supporting capital investment. To gear investment to the present and prospective requirements of the modal income family will decisively influence the pattern of development, but in a positive and not a negative way.

The goal I am here describing — I have called it the Popular Consumption Criterion — will be seen to resolve the political problems which arise in connection with other criteria. The attention of those who tax, plan or otherwise influence economic resources is kept concentrated on the needs of the typical consumer. The test of development is the reward that accrues to him. The test warns against extracting too much saving from him for a too distant reward. It provides a firm criterion for discouraging luxury imports, production and consumption. It is also a useful barrier to outlays for symbolic modernization. The required taxes for airports and new buildings of state reduce popular consumption or sacrifice investment opportunities that might increase it.

The application of the Popular Consumption Criterion cannot be total. By an odd arrangement of things, poor countries, such as India in the past, have produced luxuries for the affluent lands. Exports are still necessary and export and domestic markets are never wholly separate. What is supplied to one will leak over to the other. And development that is firmly geared to the income of the modal consumer means higher incomes for some people. Evidently there is no economic arrangement — capitalist, socialist or communist — which does not give more money to those who manage, invent, devise, instruct or punish. Goods will then be produced to meet this demand — and must be. The Popular Consumption Criterion is a criterion and not a straitjacket.

It is not less important for this reason. For it fixes objectives and establishes the priorities in the distribution of investment. If investment is distributed in accordance with some plan, it guides the plan. If investment is subject to the influence of taxation or import duties, it guides this influence. It provides no final decision. But it does establish the line between what is favored and what is subject to the burden of proof.

4

Poverty and the Way People Behave

*(This article and the following two, which were written orig-
inally to be given as the Massey Lectures for the Canadian
Broadcasting Corporation, are meant to be read consecu-
tively.)*

A VISITOR from another planet in these last twenty years
would have been inclined to divide this one into two plausibly
different halves. On the one hand would be the poor countries of Latin America, Africa and Asia where, he would
observe, poverty is combined with the circumstances that
tend to make it self-perpetuating and where — as the recent
history of Peru, Bolivia, Guatemala, Indochina, India, Pakistan, China, the Arab lands, the Congo and Nigeria would
persuade him — there is also a good deal of contentiousness
and even combat. And to the other half he would assign the
Soviet Union, all of Europe, the United States and a few
other scattered jurisdictions where comparative affluence is
combined with comparative ease in getting more income and
where social contention is either relatively slight or, as in the
case of the United States, is combined with domestic poverty
and deprivation or follows from a deep difference of opinion
over intervention in the quarrels of the poor countries of the
world.

Any such division the visitor would soon enough discover to be wrong. After being accorded a surreptitious look at the staff papers of the National Security Council, reading a book by a retired Air Force General or, with suitable assistance, rendering into English an article by an erstwhile bureaucrat in *Foreign Affairs*, he would come to know that the only acceptable distinction is between the Communist countries and what, with some flexibility of phrase, is called the Free World.

Nevertheless, the first instinct of the man from outer space has a great deal to commend it; poverty has more to do with determining social and political behavior than the ideological differences of the comparatively well-to-do. With this even Marx might not disagree. The distinction between the Communist and the non-Communist world is firmly grounded in bureaucratic and military truth, in the wounding recollection of Joseph Stalin and in the desire to show a negative reaction in the event of any future saliva test for loyalty. There are, certainly, differences between the Communist and non-Communist states, and it seems certain that these are emphasized according to one's position in the particular society. High Communist officeholders are more likely to emphasize the unique blessings of socialism than the average toiler in a factory or on a collective farm. Whatever the system, he ends up working eight hours a day. And no one celebrates the values of capitalism so eloquently as the oil millionaire who has his taxes reduced by depletion allowances and capital gains, unless it be his daughter who lives effortlessly on the dividends. The soundest of political rules is always to mistrust the political perceptions of the comfortable.

II

The first and most elementary effect of poverty is to enforce the very attitudes and behavior that make it self-perpetuating. Similarly the first effect of wealth is to allow the freedom that permits of the creation of more wealth. It is regularly observed, often with some surprise, that very poor communities are conservative — that, more than the more fortunate, their people resist the change that is in their own interest. Illiteracy, and the limited horizons it implies, is a partial cause of this; so is the inertia resulting from poor health and malnutrition. But poverty is an even more direct cause of conservatism. If there is no margin to spare, there is no margin for risk. One cannot try a new variety of wheat or rice that promises an additional twenty percent yield if there is any chance that it is vulnerable to insect pests, disease or drought and thus in an occasional year might fail altogether. However welcome the extra twenty percent, it is not worth the risk of not eating for a whole season, the consequences of which tend to be both painful and irreversible. Since there is a measure of risk in anything that is untried, it is better to stick with the proven methods — the methods that have justified themselves by the survival of the family to this time. The well-to-do, by contrast, can accept some risk of loss if the prospect is for a greater gain. They are in no danger of starving, whatever happens. Within India the comparatively well-to-do Punjabis in the north have been far more inclined to try new crops and new methods, notably the new high-yielding varieties of wheat, than the villagers in the poorer regions who live closer to subsistence. Needless to say, in the firm tradition of the fortunate, they attribute their progressiveness not to higher income but to higher intelligence.

But fear of loss is not the only cause of conservatism among the very poor. Any change is regarded with uneasiness or dread — and also with reason. In the rich countries, change is identified with new and better ways of producing things or of organizing production; it is an article of faith that the whole community benefits from the advance. If someone loses his job, he is told with much unction and some truth that his sacrifice is for the greater good of the greater number. As a result, to be against change is like being against God and perhaps worse for, generally speaking, we are more tolerant of religious than of economic heresy.

The experience of the poor community is with a very different kind of change. Benign technical innovation is unknown. Change, when it has occurred, has usually meant that some rascal more powerful, more ruthless or more devious than the rest has succeeded in enriching himself at community expense. Change is associated with someone seizing land, collecting rents, levying taxes, provisioning an army or exacting tribute. In the language of my colleague, Professor A. O. Hirschman, the image of change is "ego-focused."[1] This being the view of change, the instinct of the community is to suspect all change.

III

These are the psychological effects of poverty; the biological consequences are equally profound. In all well-to-do communities, there is a strong tendency to limit the number of children in order to protect the given standard of living.

[1] Albert O. Hirschman, *The Strategy of Economic Development* (New Haven: Yale University Press, 1958), pp. 11 ff.

Population may increase with increasing well-being but never so rapidly as to threaten the improvement itself. Education, emancipation of women, the knowledge of birth control methods and the widespread availability of contraceptives all contribute to this controlled birthrate. In such communities, moreover, the available knowledge on infant care, epidemiology and public health is extensively applied. The life span may gradually lengthen from the development of new knowledge. It is unlikely to increase suddenly from the rapid application of existing knowledge.

In the poor country, things are almost exactly in reverse. If the standard of living seems already as low as it can go, there is no reason to protect it from further decline. Children share and eventually take over the burden of manual toil (a more important matter than sedentary workers suppose) and, since old age pensions cannot be afforded, they are also a man's only hope for care in old age or infirmity. It is prudent to have as many babies as possible for, infant mortality being high, not many will survive. Neither contraceptive knowledge nor contraceptives are available and — a neglected point — sexual intercourse plays a larger recreational role in the poor community than in the rich. For the couple who come from the field to a hut devoid of newspapers, radio, light, even a comfortable chair, it is all there is.

But not only is poverty a strong inducement to procreation, modern medical science and public health research have provided a large reservoir of measures that reduce the death rate. Their application means a further sharp increase in population. This is one of the earliest effects of modernization. And in many, though by no means all, of the poor countries this addition is to a population that is already massive. The industrial development of the United States and Western Europe was launched in countries of — by modern standards — almost negligible population. In 1770, on the eve of the Industrial Revolution, the population of England and Wales was not much over seven million. The United States seventy years later had fewer than twenty million. India in 1960 had 433 million and was adding eight and a half million — many more than the pre-industrial population of Britain — every year. Indonesia and Pakistan had 97 million and 93 million respectively. Poverty applies the greatest population pressure to those countries least able to absorb it.

IV

I turn now to the effect of poverty on economics — on what all right-thinking people recognize as the queen of the social disciplines. One fact of economic life is common to capitalist, socialist and communist societies, as also to Catholic, Presbyterian, Pentecostal, Buddhist and Animist, and is not subject to controversy as between economists of any shade of color or opinion. It is that any purposeful increase in future production requires saving from current consumption. Only from such saving can the people be supported who are making the machines, building the factories, constructing the dams, digging the canals or otherwise elaborating the capital which makes possible the increased future output. Saving may be by the highly regarded men of thrift who put something by for their children or their own rainy day, or by the rich who are under no great pressure to spend all they receive, or by corporations which plow back revenue before it ever gets into the hot and eager hands of those who might spend it or by governments which, by a variety of devices of which taxes are the most important, can restrict consumption and thus enforce saving by their otherwise profligate citizens.

But while there must be savings in all societies if there is to be economic advance, the difference in the degree of difficulty in getting savings as between the rich countries and the poor is so great as to be a difference in kind.

In the rich country, to refrain from consumption may be inconvenient, difficult or well beyond one's power of will. It rarely involves physical deprivation — hunger, exposure, pain. And a great deal of saving is automatic or a byproduct of motives and preoccupations that have little to do with national progress. Thus, concern for personal security puts income into life insurance, pension funds and the social security trust funds of governments. The business prestige that comes from heading a growing corporation pours earnings back into expansion. Recurrently our problem is to offset by sufficient investment (or by public or private spending) all that we are disposed to save from high levels of income; for if we fail to offset savings, income and output will decline and unemployment will rise.

Thus, saving in the rich country not only comes easily; it may be excessive. The country must invest these savings (or offset them with increased consumption) if it is to avoid unemployment. Economic progress, it follows, is something it gets more or less automatically in the course of preventing unemployment. Unemployment is the ogre which stalks the politician and which he bends every effort to exorcise.

Here is the explanation of the remarkable course of economic events in North America and Western Europe in the twenty years or so since World War II. Although there were variations in detail, in all countries there was a large and well-sustained increase in output. This far exceeded anything in earlier experience. Faithful to the vanity of politicians, and the economists who advise them, this excellent showing was attributed in each case to the remarkably astute economic policies being followed. This was so even though the policies avowed in different countries differed by at least 180 degrees. West Germany brought off her economic miracle by (it is alleged) rigid adherence to free private enterprise. Norway did almost equally well by an intelligent application of the principles of socialist planning. France did yet better in some years by, it was said, intelligently eschewing any known principles. In fact, in all of these countries, as in the United States, comparative wealth made saving easy. Given this, and a policy of maintaining full employment, growth came with comparative ease. It would have required more determination to have failed.

The situation of the poor countries was sadly different. Here to forgo consumption, as I have said, is to suffer pain, and the pain is not eased if the government enforces the saving through taxation. In the rich countries, the poor do little saving; in the United States only a negligible amount comes from those in the lower half of the income brackets. In the poor countries, nearly everyone is poor. And the few who are rich are not a very good source of savings. The landed feudal tradition of the well-to-do minority in South America and the Middle East is one of easygoing and often lavish expenditure. And in the poor country there is also the exceptional visibility of the rich man. This, and his resulting insecurity, may cause him to invest his savings not in farms, factories and power plants, but in a numbered account in a Zurich bank.

Though the picture is not altogether grim (sometimes there

is oil), it can thus be seen that savings in the poor countries are painful to obtain and the amounts obtained, even painfully, are meager. As a result, the economic advance which comes easily and automatically in the rich countries comes at great cost and is wretchedly slow.

v

The obvious question, it follows, is whether savings cannot be transferred from the countries where they are abundant to those where they are so scarce. In the last century there was a substantial flow of savings from the relatively rich countries of Western Europe to the Americas and later on to parts of Africa and the Far East. This was largely under private auspices; the United States, Canada and Argentina were among the major beneficiaries. Canals and railroads and much else were so provided. All prophets of the commonplace, a remarkably numerous group whenever economic development is discussed, continue to call for a new flow of private capital from the rich countries to the poor. The chances that it will take place are very slight.

Where there is a prospect for developing petroleum, bauxite, iron ore or other resources for supply to the United States or Europe, private capital continues to go abroad. This is related to the profits to be made in the United States, Canada or Europe. A little capital also goes to develop additional markets — trucks, tires, soap, pharmaceuticals — for American or European firms. But almost none goes to build the power plants, railroads or factories which are designed to serve the people of the poor countries, as British capital in the last century built railroads in the United States, Canada and the Argentine to serve Americans, Canadians or Argentineans. This is partly because the poor countries, being poor, are an unattractive market as compared with the rich countries. Capital goes where people have incomes and money to spend and where, accordingly, money can be made. And, as I shall suggest, there are other problems. Some of the poor countries lack the social institutions and manpower which enable them to make effective use of capital and hold out a reasonable promise of repayment. In others the social system is unfavorable to effective capital use; power lies with those for whom government is not an instrument of economic progress but a means to personal enrichment or political aggrandizement. But even the countries which can make effective and secure use of capital for power, irrigation, transportation and basic manufacturing are unlikely to get it from private sources. They compete badly for funds with the developed and high-income countries. They must, therefore, have the help of other governments or such international organizations as the World Bank. Failing this, we in the rich countries will leave them in a painful and perhaps losing struggle for progress. We will go forward, meanwhile, with increasing ease. It takes a certain effort of mind to suppose that this will be the basis for an easy relationship between the rich and the poor lands.

VI

A scarcity of economic resources, in turn, deeply affects the economic policy of a country. We think of ideology as having a controlling influence on the way governments manage their economy. It is not without importance. But the availability of capital, and the associated poverty or affluence, exerts a much greater influence than we imagine.

Thus, in the United States where capital is abundant and privately mobilized through the capital markets, no one need give thought as to how it is used. We recognize that there is some waste — manufacturing of useless products, backing of Las Vegas deadfalls — but we do not worry and certainly not if our own money is not involved.

The poor country has no such easygoing options. It must use its resources for the right things; if it fails to do so — if funds go into fancy housing, a glittering airport or official Cadillacs — the cries of outrage and horror will come first of all from the most rugged American free enterprisers. If it is getting aid, such wasteful expenditure shows it is unworthy of help; if it is not getting aid, this proves it is wholly undeserving. It must, in short, exercise firm control on the nature of its growth. It must use its capital in accordance with a well-considered plan. And conservative critics are among the first to insist on such planning. If private entrepreneurs are not around to undertake the investment, the government will be urged to take the initiative itself.

So we come to the fairly remarkable result that free enterprise — the practice of letting the market decide where we invest and what we produce — is in part the product of well-being. Planning, by contrast, is compelled by poverty. This, of course, is not the whole story. Many of the governments of the new countries have embraced socialism and planning as a matter of conviction — capitalism has come to mean the British, French, Dutch or American companies that were associated with colonial rule. Or, as in Africa, it denotes the merchants and traders — also usually foreigners. These are firmly identified in people's minds with high prices, high profits and a good deal of sanguinary swindling. Students from such backgrounds learned eagerly about socialism at the Sorbonne, Oxford and the University of London, though almost never in Moscow. They now are cabinet officers.

None of this, I might add, is the good fortune of the poor countries. Socialism and planning are demanding in the administrative apparatus that they require. An unplanned economy is infinitely easier to run than a partially planned one. And the rich countries that are not obliged to plan have the most highly developed systems of public administration. The United States or the United Kingdom could go in for fairly complete planning without undue difficulty — and did during World War II. But they have no great need to do so. In Asia and Africa, where both the desire and the need for planning are far greater, the administrative structure is weaker and in some cases almost nonexistent. Whoever arranged matters in this way is open to criticism.

It follows further that we must be tolerant of different and far less efficient economic performance in the poor countries than in our own. Their task is both different and far more difficult. We are right to press for sensible use of funds that we supply and for economic policies that ensure that they will be effective. But we cannot press for a carbon copy of Western capitalism and we cannot hold others even to our sometimes imperfect standards of performance.

I turn now to the effect of wealth and poverty on national policy.

VII

In Europe in the last several decades, governments have been stable and secure because their people have been contented and secure. International cooperation, and most notably the creation of the Common Market, has been possible for the same reason. If unemployment is minimal and unfeared, then governments have freedom to reduce tariffs, lift quotas and arrange migration. Even now a bad depres-

sion in Europe would cause governments to concern themselves with their own people, if necessary at the expense of
their neighbors. If things got bad enough, politicians would
be tempted to divert attention from economic problems to
national concerns and grievances.

In the poor countries, on the other hand, things are always
bad. There is little to lose from change. The prerogatives
and spoils of office also look attractive to those on the outside — not only is it good to throw the rascals out but you
get a Mercedes as a reward. Meanwhile, the man who is
clinging to office and who finds economic development hard
going looks for a scapegoat for his failures — for some object
of popular antipathy which will engage passions and thus
divert attention. The British, French or Dutch are at fault.
Or the Yankees. Or the Indians, Pakistanis or Malaysians
next door. Or the Muslims, Hindus, Christians or Jews. As
well-being is a solvent for tensions, so poverty is a principal
cause. The poor countries are the focus of internal disturb-
ance, insecurity, interracial friction and international conflict
because these are intimately a part of the politics of privation.

We often have a simpler explanation for disorder in these
lands. It is the Communists. There is a fine, simple, hard-
boiled quality about this explanation which economizes
thought and for this and other reasons appeals to the American conservative. An official never arouses the intellectual
boondocks by blaming things on the Bolsheviks. George
Kennan once said that in the making of American foreign
policy, it is not the American interest that is consulted but the
American right. It is an elementary mark of sophistication
always to mistrust the man who blames on revolutionaries
what should be attributed to deprivation.

Obviously poverty has a penetrating effect on behavior. It affects attitudes toward technical change. It has a controlling effect on the ease or difficulty of economic progress and affects the nature of the country's economic organization. It determines political behavior and international attitudes. It has a profound effect on human reproduction and demography.

We have only to look a little further to see why its effect is more comprehensive than the differences associated with ideological preference or commitment. I have spoken of the effect of privation on the behavior of the countries of the non-Communist world. As between China and the Soviets there is an almost exact parallel. China, under the pressure of need, has tried forms of economic organization different from and more radical (although not for that reason more successful) than those of the Soviet Union. These the Soviets have thought wrong. The Chinese have taken this ill. They have accused the Soviets of being unfaithful to Marx and his prophets. But clearly what served in a comparatively affluent country such as Russia could hardly be expected to serve in a poor one such as China.

The Soviets once also used economic aid as a political lever. When the Chinese failed to follow their lead, it was withdrawn. The Chinese have bitterly resented this and, given the pride of the poor country and the importance of aid, one can see how this could be a source of contention. Finally, the Soviets have criticized the Chinese for chauvinism and adventurist foreign policy. Chinese foreign policy seems to be only verbally incautious. But chauvinism is also at least partly the product of poverty — of the need to fix people's eyes on noneconomic goals and to divert them from domestic difficulty. Thus the main points of contention between the two Communist countries are immediately explicable in terms of the conflicting interests of rich and poor. However, we may perhaps better reflect for a moment on some of the lessons for our own relations with the poor countries.

There are several. We must, for example, be braced for the resistance to change and react to it with sympathy and understanding. It is not the irrational stubbornness of backward people; rather it reflects an experience different from our own. We must, more than parenthetically, be scrupulously careful that the change we advocate is sufficiently riskless to be acceptable to people who cannot afford risk. More than one eloquent American agricultural specialist in these last fifteen years has converted villagers to techniques which, however impeccable in Michigan or Missouri, did not pay off in a distant clime. The price was paid by the villagers after our man was back home.

We must be aware of the difficulty which the poor countries have in finding savings and resulting capital. We must be exceedingly cautious about urging expenditure for anything but the highest priority. On occasion we have allowed our much more easygoing standards of spending to influence our recommendations as to what the poor countries should do. Our educators on occasion have sold curricular luxuries to the poor countries that we ourselves could not afford until this century. The land grant colleges and extension services have successfully urged the adoption of agricultural services which we have, not out of need but out of ability to pay. Worst of all has been military extravagance. The military alliances of Mr. Dulles, as endorsed and carried forward by Mr. Rusk, and the concomitant military expenditure and burden, may well have done more for the Communists than any support from the Soviet Union. In a just world both men, one day, would have a small plaque on the Kremlin wall.

Most important, we must not waver on the importance of aid. It is not a luxury of modern foreign policy. It is, in fact, the obvious accommodation between countries where saving is easy and automatic and those where it is difficult and painful. It is the principal basis for harmonious coexistence between the rich countries and the poor. We do need to adjust the form of aid much more closely to the circumstances of the poor lands — as I will soon argue. But we must also bear in mind that it is our most distinctive contribution to the comity of nations.

Next, we must be cautious about urging forms of organization that are commonplace in the rich countries upon the poor. The imperatives of the poor country, as regards economic organization, are very different from our own. The notion that a moderately well-to-do country and a poor one can have a common economic policy has been, as I have said, a prime source of friction between the Soviets and China. It could equally well be a source of friction between the United States and India. We should not be above imitating the accomplishments of the Communist countries but we need not imitate their errors.

It is also evident that relations between the rich and the poor countries are likely to be touchy — as also the relations between the poor lands themselves. We must bear in mind that the governments of these countries are subject to pressures, growing out of their poverty, from which we are exempt. Our occasionally more tranquil reactions are not the mark of superior patience but of superior fortune. To realize this is to be more tolerant and more painstaking in the never-finished tasks of mediation, negotiation and compromise.

There are other lessons, ranging from those that grow out of the relation of poverty to the birthrate and the bearing of this on birth control techniques to the prospects, given the difficulties I have cited, for development itself. But I must postpone further discussion of remedies pending a closer look at the poor lands. We have seen that poverty produces much that is common in behavior. We must now see that poverty has deep differences as to cause.

5

The Causes of Poverty:
A Classification

As CONCERN with the problem of economic development increased in the years following World War II, and especially as it became a subject for research, for what is called research and of instruction in the universities, there appeared also a tendency to divide the world according to the state of well-being. The rich countries were the developed countries. The poor were the underdeveloped or — where tact was thought more important than accuracy — the developing countries. (Many of them were not, in fact, developing very much and none of the developing countries was developing as rapidly as the developed countries.) It became the habit, both in looser political discussion and prescription as well as in ostensibly more precise pedagogy, to speak of the needs and problems of *the* underdeveloped country. They were assumed to have enough in common so that as "the descriptive literature on such countries suggests . . . we may confidently describe 'a representative underdeveloped country.' " [1]

This tendency to speak of a typical underdeveloped coun-

[1] Henry J. Bruton, "Growth Models and Underdeveloped Economies," *Journal of Political Economy*, August 1955. Reprinted in A. N. Agarwala and S. P. Singh, *The Economics of Underdevelopoment* (Bombay: Oxford University Press, 1958), pp. 219–220.

try, and to prescribe for it, has, with some modifications, continued. The corollary is the supposition that there is a roughly common therapy applicable to such countries as a class. Men will devise policies that are meant to be applicable generally to underdeveloped countries; they will continue to say, as they often do now, "This is what an underdeveloped country should do."

Or this will be the tendency. But, in fact, there has long been a considerable differentiation in the prescription for the poor countries. India, in per capita income, is almost as poor as any country in Africa. Yet we recognize that her capacity to use capital is much greater than most of them enjoy. In the years since World War II, she has absorbed, in the main usefully, somewhere between a third and a half of the capital assistance available through public channels to the poor countries. And with mention of India, the problem of population comes almost immediately to mind.

The African countries, for their part, have been strongly interested in education. And gradually a design for development is emerging which places primary emphasis on this. And this is in contrast, in turn, with the seeming requirements of many of the Latin American countries where social reform occupies a place of particular urgency. Though in analysis we still speak of the underdeveloped country, for purposes of prescription we make important distinctions. There is need, evidently, for bringing the analysis abreast of the differentiation that practical judgment requires.

II

Some years ago at Harvard, we began experimenting with a classification of underdeveloped countries that is based on the obstacle or combination of obstacles which, in the given case, is the decisive barrier to economic advance.[2] The classification is a fourfold one. Three classes are important for present purposes; the fourth embraces the countries where there is no strongly operative obstacle to development and where, accordingly, it proceeds more or less reliably. It is useful for fixing thought to give each of the classes or models not only a number but an identification with the part of the world to which it is most applicable. Its application is not, however, confined to the geographical or other area in the designation. The three models of underdevelopment are:

> Model I. The Sub-Sahara African Model
> Model II. The Latin American Model
> Model III. The South Asian Model

There are also, as might be expected, intermediate or mixed cases. And the geographical designations do not include all of the countries of the area. Ceylon is not typical of the South Asian Model; Ghana, Nigeria and Kenya are not fully characteristic of the Sub-Sahara African Model; Mexico, Costa Rica and Cuba do not conform to the Latin American Model; and Brazil, a notably difficult case, conforms more closely to that model in the northern than in the southern states.

III

In the Model I or Sub-Sahara countries, the principal barrier to development is the absence of what I shall call a minimum cultural base. It is important, both for reasons of tact and

---

[2] I have drawn heavily, and gratefully, on seminar and class discussion of this classification. I first presented it at the Third Rehovot Conference in Israel in August, 1965.

precision, that this not be misinterpreted; the problem is not absence of aptitude but absence of opportunity. Most of the countries that are described by this model have recently emerged from colonialism, sometimes of the more regressive sort. More fortunate countries have had decades and centuries of preparation for the tasks of economic development. These have had only a few years. "To an extent unmatched in most of the underdeveloped world, positions of skill and responsibility [in Africa] were until recently in the hands of non-Africans . . . As late as 1958 there were only about 8,000 Africans graduated from all the academic secondary schools below the Sahara, and only about 10,000 others were studying in universities — more than half of these in Ghana and Nigeria . . . in 1962 there were still few African countries where more than two hundred Africans received full secondary diplomas." [3] When the Republic of the Congo gained independence, there were fewer than 25,000 Congolese with any secondary education and only about thirty Congolese university graduates. The first university, Lovanium, had opened only in 1954 and only thirteen Africans had graduated by 1960. [4]

The consequences of an inadequate cultural base are comprehensive — on government, the economy, internal security, communications, even foreign policy. But the most visible manifestation is on the apparatus of government. People

[3] Elliot J. Berg, "Socialism and Economic Development in Tropical Africa," *Quarterly Journal of Economics*, November 1964, p. 561. (Mr. Berg argues with much effect that this shortage of qualified talent has not prevented — and has possibly encouraged — a number of these countries to commit scarce administrative resources to demanding experiments in socialism and planning at heavy cost to themselves.)

[4] Ernest Lefever, *Crisis in the Congo* (Washington: The Brookings Institution, 1965), p. 9.

with the requisite education, training and honesty for performing public tasks are unavailable. As a consequence, taxes are collected in haphazard or arbitrary fashion and public funds are spent inefficiently or for no particular purpose except the reward of the recipients. Where this is the case, government will ordinarily be unstable; those who do not have access to public income will have a strong incentive to seek the ouster of those who do. As a further consequence, law enforcement is unreliable; and so, at a minimum, are essential public services. In this context, in turn, there can be no economic development that involves any sophistication in technique or organization.[5] Primitive and local trade will flourish under almost any handicaps. But larger scale commerce and industry — the modern, large, technically advanced corporate enterprise — are more demanding in their environment; their persons and property must be reasonably secure; their property cannot be hidden and if taxed merely because it is visible, it soon becomes inoperative; their business cannot be transacted in the absence of posts, telephones and common carrier transportation. In the colonial era, firms were allowed to provide for their own security and establish the services essential to their existence. With independence, such extraterritorial administration ceased, in most cases, to be admissible.

The inadequacy of government reflects the absence of schools, colleges and cultural environment for producing or preparing people for public tasks. All discussion of economic development involves difficult problems of sequence and circularity. This is an example: How does a country get an

[5] Cf. George H. Kimble, *Tropical Africa*, Volume II, "Society and Policy" (New York: Doubleday, 1962), pp. 469 ff.

educational system without an adequate government? How does it get a government without the qualified people that an educational system provides? There is no obvious answer. But it helps to have narrowed the problem to this point. For we then recognize that little is accomplished by action that does not break into this particular circle. Assistance in the form of capital funds will not be useful if there is no one with the technical competence to employ it, and if the environment is hostile to the resulting enterprises. Technical assistance will not be useful if there is no one to advise or assist. In the next model, progress waits on reforms which reduce the power of a vested ruling elite. Here there is no such elite.

There is a measure of overstatement in any attempt to establish categories. No country is without some small group of honest and competent people in some area of economic activity or government. But in those countries where colonialism was exploitive and regressive — where there was no liberalizing urge that sought to prepare people for some role other than that of primitive agriculture — this group is very small. As a result, this model — as in the classic case of Haiti — can readily become one not of advance but of disintegration with eventual reversion to tribalism or anarchy. All that is needed is for the perilously small group of competent and honest people to be overwhelmed by those who see government in predatory and personal terms. Once the latter are in possession of the available instruments of power — the army, government payroll, police — it is not clear when (or even whether) the process of disintegration can be reversed by internal influences. This disintegration, not Communism for which these countries are as little prepared as for capitalism, is the form of failure in this model.

IV

I come now to Model II — what I have called the Latin American case. The great mass of the people in these countries is also very poor. But there is a sizable minority that is well-to-do. And associated with this well-to-do minority is a rather larger number of people with a diverse assortment of qualifications and skills — lawyers, physicians, accountants, engineers, scientists, economists and managers. As compared with the Model I countries, the cultural base is quite wide. And supporting it is a limited, undemocratic and otherwise imperfect, but still substantial, educational system. Peru, Ecuador and Guatemala are, by any calculation of per capita income, very poor countries. Argentina, Brazil and Chile are well below North American and European levels. But all have trained and educated people and facilities for their replacement that are more adequate than in the new African states. As a further aspect, they have a strong intellectual tradition. As is also true of the United States, they could use more people of the highest caliber and training. Public servants of high competence are rarely in surplus. But in these countries — as also in the Arab states where the pattern is similar — the absence of trained and educated people is not the obvious barrier to development.

The far more evident barrier is the social structure and the way it tends to subvert economic incentive and production. The elite, though sizable, depends for its economic and social position on land ownership, or on a comprador role in the port or capital cities, or on government employment or sinecure, or on position in the armed forces. Beneath this elite is a large rural mass and, in some cases, an unskilled and often semi-employed urban proletariat. The rural worker, in the characteristic Latin American situation, either earns the right to cultivate a small plot of land by giving service to the estate on which he resides or he is part of the minifundia — a cultivator of a small plot on which he has some form of permanent tenure. In either case he has no effective economic incentive. He thoughtfully renders the landlord the minimum service that will earn him the right to cultivate his own plot. The latter plot was anciently arranged to be of the minimum size consistent with more or less temporary survival. The same tends to be true of any holding to which he has title. So any possibility that he might improve his position by increasing output is excluded by what amounts to a systematic denial of incentives. In a number of countries — Peru, Guatemala and Ecuador, for example — the fact that most of the rural mass is Indian adds a sense of racial exclusion to this denial.

But the elimination of economic incentives is not confined to the rural masses. Beginning with them, it tends to become comprehensive. The landlord, since he has a labor force that is devoid of incentive, cannot do much himself to increase production. Often he lives in the capital city and does not try. Instead of the revenues of a small area farmed efficiently, he enjoys those of a large area that is farmed with extreme incompetence. (It is strongly characteristic of this model that agriculture, some plantation operations apart, is technologically stagnant.)

Income derived from government position or the armed forces is also unrelated to economic service. It depends, rather, on distribution of political or military power, and this leads to the further likelihood of struggle over the division of power. Feudal agriculture is so constituted as to survive unstable or avaricious government. Modern industry — again unless under external protection — is much more vulnerable. So instability in government and its use as a source of personal income has a further adverse effect on industrial incentives. In this model, substantial rewards accrue to traders. But this is more dependent on a strong monopoly position — the franchise for the sale of a North American or European branded product (cigarettes, radios, motor vehicles, pharmaceuticals) or a similar control over the financing, procurement and export of some local product — than on efficient economic service.

It is the normal assumption of economists in advanced communities that income rewards economic effort. Since it induces that effort, it is functional. There has been ample dispute over whether particular functions are over- or under-rewarded, and this is the foundation of the ancient quarrel between Marxians and non-Marxians. But the adequacy of reward for service is not the central issue in this model; the problem is that numerous claimants — landlords, members of the armed services, government functionaries, pensioners — render no economic service at all.[6] And the best rewarded businessman is not the one who performs the best service but the one whose political position or franchise accords him the most secure monopoly. It is useful to have a term for the income which is so divorced from economic function, and one is readily at hand. It may be called nonfunctional income.

---

[6] In certain philosophical or political contexts, this may be held to be true of the armed forces of any country. They are said to serve the wrong foreign policy, be part of the wrong defense strategy, serve only the arms race, or what not. But the armed forces are committed to the service of the disapproved philosophical or political goals. In Latin America no serious observer supposes that the armed services are seriously important for national defense, territorial integrity or any other military or foreign policy objective. Their role is exclusively related to domestic politics and income.

Not only is the nonfunctional income large but strong forces act to limit the amount of functional income. The rural worker gets the maximum established by custom; greater endeavor brings him no more. The landlord, as noted, is confined by a labor force that is without incentive. He cannot be more functional. The efficient urban entrepreneur risks being regarded as a better milch cow by those who live on the state. He can protect himself only by developing the requisite political power; this means that his income comes to depend not alone on economic performance but also on political power. His return, or that part of it which derives from political influence, thus also becomes economically nonfunctional.

The power of the controlling elite is commonly thought to result from the ownership of land — from the control of wealth and access to livelihood that this provides. Traditionally this has been the case. But it is a mistake to identify land in this model as the exclusive or even the primary source of power. Membership in the armed forces, control of hierarchical wealth from sources other than land, possession of trading monopoly, even bureaucratic position can all be sources of power over the state. And government in the interest of those who have such power, since they are nonfunctional, will be unrelated and unconducive to economic development.[7]

[7] This is a matter of much practical importance, especially as regards the armed forces. Generally in the United States there has been recognition of the bearing of a regressive or feudal land system on economic development. That caudillo government, either by itself or in association with other nonfunctional groups, can be equally inimical has not been so readily seen. As a consequence, conservative, or more often simplistically traditionalist, officials regularly turn up defending army dictatorships in Latin America. And, in the past, military aid funds have regularly gone to support armies, which were a source of political power, at the same time that economic assistance was being given to development or even (hopefully) to land re-

In a number of countries of this model, most notably Argentina, Brazil and Chile, the nonfunctional groups are in competition with each other and with more recently franchised economic groups for the available income. (In each of these countries an incomplete revolution accorded political power to urban white collar and working classes without disestablishing the old nonfunctional groups.) The total of these claims bears no necessary relationship to the income that is available. Since productivity is low, the tendency is for claims to exceed what is available, and invariably they do. The easiest way of reconciling competing claims is to meet that of each group in money terms and allow them to bid against each other for real product in the market. As a result, in these countries inflation is endemic. In countries such as Ecuador and the Central American countries, where the urban white collar and working classes are weak, inflationary pressures are much less strong. This, however, reflects the weakness of these classes, not their better position under noninflationary conditions.

v

With variations as to the composition of the nonfunctional elite, and its source of power, Model II has general application in Central and South America and in Iraq, Syria and elsewhere in the Middle East. In few if any of these countries — two or three Central American and Caribbean countries are possible exceptions — is the cultural base the decisive factor; economic advance is not barred by the absence

---

form. It would be difficult to find a policy with a greater element of self-contradiction and this is not lessened by the tendency of those who espouse support to the Latin American military to assume that pragmatism, professionalism and even an element of righteousness are on their side.

of trained and educated people. A shortage of capital is assumed almost intuitively by economists to be the normal barrier to advance. Iraq and other Arab states have rich sources of income from oil and Peru from oil and minerals. This has not rescued them from backwardness and some of the oil-rich countries are among the poorest in the world.[8]

In Latin America three countries break decisively with this pattern — Mexico, Costa Rica and Cuba. Mexico, by revolution, destroyed its old power structure based on land ownership. Costa Rica was always, in the main, a country of modest land holdings. Costa Rica has no army; the Mexican army is insignificant in size and cost. Neither country has any other strongly vested nonfunctional group which uses its power to exercise a major claim on income. In consequence, income in both countries is — by all outward evidences — far more closely related to economic performance than in the remainder of Latin America. They are the two countries which enjoy the most favorable rate of economic development. The case of Cuba is so far less clear. Its land system before the revolution, somewhat exceptionally, was socially regressive but technically proficient. Since the revolution it has lost markets and suffered the costs of much social experiment, not all of it successful. In the longer run, it is impossible to suppose that the Cuban revolution will be regarded as less to the advantage of economic development than the Mexican revolution.

[8] Venezuela also has rich income from oil but may gradually be breaking the hold of a regressive social structure which for a long time led to the dissipation and waste of this revenue.

VI

For purposes of identification, I have associated Model III with South Asia. The clearest prototypes are, indeed, India and Pakistan, although it has application to the United Arab Republic, in limited measure to Indonesia, and, since its characteristics transcend political organization, to China.

In this model, the cultural base is very wide. India and Pakistan have systems of primary and secondary education that are far superior to those of Latin America. There are at least as many full-time professors in the University of Delhi alone as in all Latin America. Both countries tend to a surplus rather than a shortage of teachers,[9] administrators, scientists and entrepreneurs. In recent years, these countries have been substantial, if inadvertent, exporters of medical and scientific talent to the United States and the United Kingdom. Without the doctors provided by this informal educational exchange, the hospitals of both countries would be even more inimical to health.

In both India and Pakistan, there is a substantial volume of nonfunctional income. But it is not, as in Latin America, associated with political power. In India the political power and nonfunctional claims on land revenues of the princes, jagirdars, zamindars and large landlords were terminated or greatly curtailed at the time of independence or in the ensuing land reforms. The armed forces, though costly, do not have decisive political power.[10] In consequence, in agricul-

[9] Although not in all categories of teachers or those with a sufficient willingness to serve in rural villages.

[10] The army has political power in Pakistan. However, it is not a recognized avenue to political power and economic advantage as in Latin America. The armed coup which brought President Ayub Khan to power in 1959 (like his subsequent administration) bore little or no resemblance to the Latin American phenomenon.

ture there is a rough and imperfect but still real relation between effort and return. Economic incentive is thus reasonably operative. The endemic inflation which characterizes many of the Model II countries is absent. The social structure in these countries is not at the highest level of compatibility with economic advance. But it is clearly not the operative barrier.

The barrier in this model is drastically bad proportioning of the factors of production. Demographic history, still imperfectly explained, has given these countries a large and dense population. The supply of arable land in India, Pakistan and Egypt has been subject to repeated and very great increases through irrigation. But this increase has been followed, as harvest follows planting, by a relentless increase in population. As a result, per capita agricultural production and incomes have remained small and, as a further consequence, savings are limited and so consequently is the supply of capital. Capital shortage, in turn, has retarded and continues to retard industrial development. The small land and capital base provides effective employment for only part of the available labor force. People who live close to the margin of subsistence, as I have noted, cannot afford any risk that they might fall below subsistence levels. This is a further inducement to backwardness.

The Model III countries are, in some respects, the most comprehensible in their lack of development. They conform most closely to the standard explanations of the economists; because of their education and cultural sophistication, their people tend to speak for all of the underdeveloped lands. (At any conference on economic development the most persuasive speaker is usually an Indian.) Their case, in consequence, is frequently and erroneously generalized to all instances of underdevelopment.

VII

It is now evident, I think, how dangerous it is to treat the poor countries as a class. The poverty that produces so many common tendencies in behavior — and which also gives such stark uniformity to the village hut or urban slum — proceeds from very different causes. For purposes of prescribing economic policy, it is at least as unwise to associate sub-Sahara African countries with India as to prescribe a common policy for India and the United States. There is at least equal error in associating for purposes of policy countries with a regressive social structure such as Ecuador, Iran or Peru with the African countries where social structure is not a primary obstacle to advance.

In recent years, economists have prided themselves on the progress that they have made in refining the concept of economic growth and in developing the theory that explains it and the policies that promote it. We are inclined to believe that we are becoming much more scientific about the whole business, although in an established tradition of the discipline there is some tendency to identify scientific precision with mechanical elegance rather than reality. But the claim to progress in these matters is not above reproach so long as underdeveloped countries are treated as a class and one theory is assumed to cover all. Science must be a trifle suspect if it involves unscientific generalization.

6

A Differential Prescription

I COME NOW to the question of policy — to what, given the various obstacles to advance, is called for by way of action. It is evident that if the obstacles to advance are different, the measures designed to remove these obstacles will also be different. Any line of policy appropriate for one model will, most likely, be inappropriate for another.

II

In the Model I countries, if the barrier to progress is the shortage of trained and educated people, the obvious first step is to widen the cultural base. Internal effort and external assistance must center on the provision of the trained and educated people without whom advance is impossible. It seems likely that this core must be substantial — large enough to dominate an adverse environment. Presumably, also, it must be pyramidal in shape — a small number with the highest administrative and technical skills, a larger number with the equivalent of secondary education, a yet larger number with basic literacy and companion preparation.

External training of teachers, administrators and specialists on a generous scale is important for these countries. So are organizations, such as the Peace Corps, which supply not money but the teachers that money may not by itself be able to buy. So is the need to supply administrators and specialists at a more advanced level than those provided by the Peace Corps. In all instances, it should be noted, emphasis must be on active or primary participants as distinct from advice. Advisers are of little value when there are no effective institutions to advise, and real resources are more important than money. Pecuniary assistance, where provided, will often need to be combined with the organization — provision of administrative and engineering skills, training of local people — that ensures its effective use.

Along with the requirements of the Model I countries, it is equally important to see what they do not need. Capital, by itself, may not be of great value. It must be supplied in conjunction with the companion institutions that allow of its effective use. Otherwise it will be wasted and, additionally, it can have a corrupting influence on the society.[1,2]

If administrative resources are not sufficient for the basic tasks of government, they clearly should not be taxed with these further and more demanding responsibilities. Social ownership of industry and elaborate planning of capital use are a drain on scarce talent. Social reform is not central to the problem of development in this model.

All discussion of Model I countries must reckon with the possibility that in limiting cases development will be impossible. Predatory and anarchic influence will overwhelm and

[1] The idea of a Teachers Corps in the United States, a proposal with which I have been identified, has similar provenance. The poor school districts need not money, which they often spend incompetently, but highly qualified and motivated talent which they cannot buy.

[2] Cf. Elliot J. Berg, "Socialism and Economic Development in Tropical Africa," *Quarterly Journal of Economics*, November 1964, pp. 549–573.

submerge the small cultural legacy of the colonial period. Thereafter there will be disintegration without foreseeable end. The Republic of Haiti, where social fabric, political structure and living standards have deteriorated with slight interruption in the century and a half since the French were expelled, is a case in point. Instead of the technically efficient slavery of the plantations, there is the incompetence and arbitrary despotism of Dr. Duvalier. This is defended in the name of national sovereignty. One wonders if some form of internationally sponsored administration, designed to develop the requisites of self-sustaining political development, should not be available for countries caught by such self-perpetuating misfortune. Whatever the virtues of national sovereignty, they are not so absolute as to justify the degradation of a whole people for an indefinite period.

In most of the Model I countries, given ample assistance in widening the cultural base, the prospect is much better. It is part of man's experience that the cultural base can be widened. And it is easier of accomplishment than the elimination of a regressive social structure or the management of an excessive population. But it is important that all have an ample view of this task and of the aid that helps accomplish it. Because such aid does not go into dams, airports, steel mills and other physical monuments, it is not, for that reason, less important and should not, for that reason, be less in amount.

III

Coming to the Model II countries — the Latin American case — we may begin by discarding, or assigning a low priority to, what is least important.

These countries already have an educated elite. However desirable it might be to have more educated people, this shortage is not the decisive obstacle.

Nor is capital as such the decisive requirement for change. Many of the countries of this model have considerable earnings from oil or — less frequently — other natural resources. These resources are now misused. The power structure, pursuing its own goals, channels them into nonfunctional employments. There is some danger that this will happen to pecuniary aid; it will further enrich the functionless rich and further strengthen, or at least rigidify, the power structure which is the obstacle to progress.

Inflation is not the operative barrier to economic advance. As noted, it is the product of much more deeply seated social and political factors — in particular, the political power of the nonfunctional groups, the low productivity which returns income to political power rather than economic performance, and the bidding between groups for the product that is available. But inflation has high visibility. And regularly in Latin America, it has been regarded not as the consequence of these deeper disorders, but as the disorder itself. As a result, men of self-admitted soundness of view, on coming into touch with Latin American problems, have regularly prescribed not for the disorder but for the symptom and countries have been urged to treat whatever such symptom they were displaying at the moment. If prices are rising rapidly, policies are urged that will arrest the inflation. These will include budget curtailment, restraint on wage and salary increases, efforts to reduce government employment and restrictions on government and private investment. The nonfunctional income, as in the particularly clear case of the army, has political power. Thus, it can protect itself from such curtailment. Or, as in the case of landed income, it is beyond the reach of any effective restriction. The burden of stabilization is thus borne by the urban proletariat, white collar workers or other vulnerable groups. Comprador or trading enterprises, or old and static industries which have no need for funds for expansion, are unaffected. Developing industries which do need funds are vulnerable. So, as a broad rule, functional incomes and outlays are vulnerable to an anti-inflation policy; nonfunctional income is protected.

In consequence of this disparate effect, a stabilization policy is borne by the weakest groups and strikes at the expanding sectors of the economy. It becomes a source of social tension, possibly even social disorder, and a cause of economic stagnation. Those who arrive to advise the country at this stage are certain to urge relaxation. And, in the more common case, this is forced by political necessity — to continue the stabilization would be to jeopardize the position of those in power and also give further ammunition to the Communists and Fidelistos. The result of the relaxation is a greater rate of inflation. This policy rhythm dealing with symptoms not causes has now continued for many years in Brazil, Chile and Argentina.[3]

There can be no effective design for economic development in the Model II countries which does not disestablish

---

[3] Professor A. O. Hirschman has drawn attention to other such policy rhythms, derived from a tendency to look with favor on any alternative to what is presently being done, in the field of exchange control, fiscal policy and development administration. *Economic Development and Cultural Change* (Chicago: University of Chicago Press, 1957). I have been impressed by the same tendency and attribute much of it to optimistic newcomers, both indigenous and foreign, in the field of economic development. Along with extremely important enthusiasm they bring a strong tendency, on seeing something wrong, to assume that any change must be for the better. They cannot easily be persuaded that present policy is the result of similar previous convictions or that the alternative policy had an earlier and equally unsatisfactory incarnation.

the nonfunctional groups — which does not separate them from political power and, pari passu, reduce or eliminate their claim on income. This solution applies equally whether power derives from land, other hierarchical wealth, the army, the nonfunctional bureaucracy or some coalition of these. There can be no a priori judgment that a particular nonfunctional group, for example landlords or the army, is more regressive than another. Any nonfunctional group which governs in its own interest will govern at the expense of economic incentives.

The inconvenient fact is that the disestablishment of nonfunctional groups is a task not of reform but of revolution. A country does not redistribute land or eliminate an army by passing a law. Certainly it will not do so if landowners or the military are in control of the government. Nor is compensation an answer; men will sell property but they will not sell power. Such change in recent times has usually involved some violence except where it has been under the force majeure of military occupation. General Douglas MacArthur's land reforms in Japan and Korea — one of the more remarkable achievements of an occupying army and one that would have provoked fascinating comment in conservative circles in the United States had anyone but MacArthur been responsible — were peaceful because any protest was futile. The disestablishment of the princes and other feudatories in India was peaceful (except for the police action in Hyderabad) only because those affected recognized that vast shifts in the power structure had made opposition futile. Bolivia and Cuba, the other two recent examples of land reform, did not escape violence.

Yet there must be change in the social structure if there is to be economic advance. And the pressures for advance,

in a world where the demonstration effect of economic development is persuasive, are unlikely to abate. The choice
may well be between earlier and later revolutionary change.

All who react adversely to the advocates of violence or
who find it intrinsically disagreeable, as do I, must urge the
liberal reforms that would forestall it. There is also merit in
the notion, more or less explicit in the Alliance for Progress,
that money paid to landlords may serve, if not as a substitute
for power, at least as an analgesic for the pain from its loss.
Countries have managed to accomplish revolutionary change
without great violence in the past. It would be unduly pessi-
mistic to imagine that it cannot happen again. But in this
model, economic development of any efficiency does require
revolutionary change. One of the more discreditable devices
of scholarship, borrowed no doubt from politics, is to predict
that for which one can only hope. Alone among the several
models, this one has a strong revolutionary potential for the
reason that it is the one in which a revolutionary change in
social structure can make a major difference. It may not be
the task of the United States to encourage such revolution.
It must not be its task to prevent it.

Where United States policy is concerned, it goes without
saying that not only moral but material support should be
denied to nonfunctional ruling groups. Support to Latin
American armed forces has been the most symmetrically self-
defeating exercise in American foreign policy in the last half
century. In the belief that power was being built up for
resistance to Communism, a power was created that was
strongly inimical to orderly political development and to
economic progress. It helped make Communism increasingly
attractive as a solution. Like most moderately well-paid and
sedentary groups, members of these armies are averse to per-

sonal risk. So, as in Cuba, they are not certain even to interpose much physical opposition to the Communists. By surrender and possibly even by purchase, they are an excellent
source of arms. One wonders if the Soviets have ever considered leaving the propagation of Communism to the more
orthodox of our old-line Latin American hands and those
who believe that wherever there is a soldier he should be
given an American gun. If Communism must be encouraged,
perhaps it is best done by proven talent.[4]

IV

In the Model III countries, prescription comes much closer
to what we have come to consider the standard policy for
underdevelopment. The cultural base in these countries being wide, this requires no urgent action. Education is important; no one would argue against its further development.
But it does not remove the prime barrier to advance.[5] The
social structure is, as everywhere, imperfect. But the claims
of nonfunctional groups and the absence of reward for those
who have function are also not the decisive barrier to ad-

---

[4] I have long felt that more is to be attributed here to political innocence
than to reactionary economic interest. The traditional Latin American officers in the State Department identified themselves with the power structure of these countries. They had little experience with the inner political
life of the United States and the pressures here created by unions, minorities
and the poor and hence little sympathy for and less understanding of these
aspirations when encountered in other countries. To this was added the
condescending belief that Latinos were hopelessly oratorical and unserious.
A new and more sophisticated generation of public officials is now coming
into positions of influence. But it would be unduly sanguine to suppose
that the old attitudes, with their infinite capacity for mischief, have disappeared.
[5] Technical assistance in industrial, educational and agricultural fields is, at
best, of marginal importance in the model. However, it is my feeling that
in countries such as India, it has, in fact, been overemphasized. It can be
useful in specific areas where, despite the ample cultural base, specific
technical or other intellectual resources are limited.

vance. One is spared the delicate task of recommending the right kind of revolution.

In these countries the simple fact is that too many people struggle to make a living from too few resources. As a further consequence, little can be saved to enlarge the capital base — factories, power plants, transport — by which production is increased. The obvious remedy is to provide resources for immediate consumption if these are patently insufficient, to provide capital for expansion of existing agricultural and industrial plant, and, most urgently, to limit the number of people who must live from these perilously scarce resources.

Translated into specific measures, this means that all feasible steps must be taken — by encouraging individual savings, encouraging the retention and reinvestment of earnings, and by judicious use of taxation — to mobilize internal savings. The amount so made available will almost certainly be small. And these countries have the cultural resources to use considerable amounts. This is the meaning of the common statement that India, Pakistan and Egypt have large absorptive capacity for capital. So external capital assistance in generous amounts is of great importance in this model.

The social structure of these countries makes poverty comparatively democratic. For a very large proportion of the population, accordingly, consumption will have a larger claim on resources than saving for capital formation, for this consumption is coordinate with life itself. This sets limits on what can be squeezed out of these economies for investment.

It is obviously important that capital, being scarce, be used effectively. This means that there must be priorities and an administrative apparatus for carrying these priorities into effect. The administrative and technical resources from the wide cultural base make such planning feasible although there is no case for doing bureaucratically by administrative edict what can be accomplished with approximately equal effect by the market. In the Model III countries, as in the others, administrative skill is a scarce resource to be conserved like capital itself. Planning of capital use is both less essential and less feasible in the other two models.

It is of the highest importance in this model that the nexus between poverty and the birthrate be broken. A high birthrate is a common attribute of poverty, but it is in Model III countries that action is most urgent. For years, men of modest foresight have been warning that, in the future, the dense populations of these lands would press alarmingly on the means for supporting them. Now the future has come.

It would be wrong to wait on more studies or a better contraceptive. Such research has already been used to the limit as an alternative to determined action on birth control. Whichever contraceptive is now most practical, imperfections notwithstanding, must be provided in adequate quantity at the earliest moment to every village and with every possible encouragement and incentive to its use. Results must be measured not, as now, by pamphlets issued, speeches delivered and conferences attended, but by what happens to the birthrate. The moral choice is not between contraception and children but between contraception and starvation. The provision of food from abroad — and by a long supply line that might be cut with disastrous consequences — is justified if it enlarges consumption for an existing population. It is not so easy to justify if it induces a Malthusian increase in population with the result that people are as hungry as before but there are more people to be hungry.

v

It will be evident that in all of these models we face problems of the most formidable difficulty. There can be no talk of the poor countries catching up with the rich. Nor can we hope to keep the gap between those that grow easily and those that grow only with difficulty from widening. Our best hope is that the people of the poor countries, in comparing their position in the given year with that of the year before, will have a sense of improvement. This is not a negligible accomplishment; the basic comparison in economic affairs is with the position of very near neighbors and the year before. But to ensure even this improvement will require patience and great effort. The discovery that this is so undoubtedly has been disconcerting to those who hoped that the rescue of the poor countries from their poverty would be a quick and glamorous exercise, qualifying them for modest monuments in this world and major rewards in the next. It is not so, and like most other difficult tasks, economic development has had its summer patriots, quickly recruited when the job seemed easy, quickly lost when its true character became evident. But others remain and one can only hope that their number and support will grow. Though a hard course, it is one worth staying.

Contemporaries
and
Amusements

1

The Day Nikita Khrushchev
Visited the Establishment

A FEW WEEKS AGO Averell Harriman phoned to chat and
ask my recollections of the visit Nikita Khrushchev paid to
his Manhattan house on September 17, 1959 — a matter of
eleven years and a few weeks before. I happily complied; few
occasions are etched more vividly on my memory. Then
it occurred to me that others might be interested.

I did not remind Harriman how I happened to be present
— it was not an occasion at which I naturally belonged.
Khrushchev, having been first in Washington, had just arrived
in New York at the beginning of his American tour. He had
evinced a desire to meet the people who really run the
United States. This to a Marxist (which Khrushchev did not
omit to remind Americans he was) did not mean Dwight
D. Eisenhower, Richard Nixon, John Foster Dulles, Ezra
Taft Benson, J. Edgar Hoover, Carl Hayden, Lyndon Johnson or Sam Rayburn and our other nominal rulers in Washington. These were only the Executive Committee of the
bourgeois class. It meant the people who had the money
or, at a minimum, held the purse strings. Harriman obliged,
and established the sensible criterion that, to be present, a
man must own or control assets of (as a rough figure) $100

million or more. This was more than I could readily command.

However, the day before the meeting — the word confrontation had not yet entered the language — Harriman phoned me to talk about matters in general and to ask for some help on a speech. (Harriman's use of the telephone is beyond anything imagined by Lyndon Johnson. Johnson always had something in mind although you often couldn't be sure what it was. Harriman calls friends for no purpose but to exchange information. That can occupy pleasantly an hour or more.) I promised the speech and then guided the conversation to the affair the next afternoon. He did not respond; it was obvious that I did not qualify. I pressed the matter; perhaps one representative of the proletariat should be present. He still demurred; conceivably it was because Thomas K. Finletter, who was only a lawyer, had already been asked to attend in this capacity. But in the end he invited me. After some hesitation and a little persuasion, I accepted.

Two years later, talking of the forthcoming meeting between President Kennedy and Premier Khrushchev in Vienna, Prime Minister Nehru told me that Khrushchev had earlier confided in him that his purpose in getting out of Russia and around the world was to erase the unpleasant and fearsome impression that all countries had formed of the Soviet Union from Stalin. I am sure this was so, although during my years in India I discovered that another reason heads of government travel is that they love to travel. Dozens came to India for no conceivable reason of state. But the guns, bands, banquets, parades, crowds, cheers, speeches and sights are a perquisite of high position; it is for such that a man seeks or seizes office. And so often there is a warmth and enthusiasm about foreign crowds that a man does not experience at home. One thinks even of Mr. Nixon. Unfortunately, the leading members of the Executive Committee then in Washington, Mr. Dulles in particular, suspected Mr. Khrushchev of other and less innocent ambitions — they thought he was here to make Cold War propaganda at the expense of the United States, and this was a contest, in those days, that was very closely scored. There was also fear that he would somehow allay the very natural and justified suspicions of the American people as to Communist wickedness. (A reporter asked President Eisenhower at his press conference on the day Khrushchev reached New York if he didn't worry that millions of Americans would see the Soviet leader on television and conclude that he was a pretty good fellow after all. Ike discounted the danger. The *Washington Post* ran this news on the front page under an eight-column headline.) There was also concern that Khrushchev would seize on some of the insignificant flaws in American society to conclude that the country was ripe for revolution — or that the Soviets had more support from the masses than was conceded by the classes. These fears were liberally communicated to the reporters, many of whom were fiercely involved in the Cold War battle tactics, where they added appreciably to the tension of the tour.

The Administration's fears were also communicated to Henry Cabot Lodge, Jr., who was currently getting good notices for his philippics against the Soviets in the Security Council. He was told to remain by Khrushchev's side throughout the visit and to correct, promptly, any misinformation coming from, or accruing to, the Soviet leader.

This did not add so much to tension as to a kind of inspired silliness. At a luncheon at the Waldorf given by Mayor Wagner on the day of the Harriman party, Ambassador Lodge thoughtfully advised Mr. Khrushchev that in New York people of every race, religion and color lived side by side. He went on to say that "you may as well know that one American national trait which irritates many Americans and must be convenient for our critics is that we relentlessly advertise our imperfections." As an example Mr. Lodge turned to what the *New York Times* called the Negro problem. Conceding that "racial discrimination in the United States has not ended," he pledged that the day would come when "legal segregation would completely disappear." That evening at the Economic Club of New York he rose to even greater heights. He told (speaking a trifle carelessly) of our "strict laws" against monopoly and our high taxes for welfare and advised the Soviet leader not again to refer to our system as "monopoly capitalism." "Economic humanism" was much more accurate, he said. While the new designation seems not to have caught on in the Communist world it so inspired his audience of economic humanists that night that they rose and, placing arms across chests, spontaneously sang "The Star-Spangled Banner." In days following, Mr. Lodge continued his civics lectures, as they were called by the press, until in Los Angeles Mayor Poulson and others were so egregiously rude to Mr. Khrushchev that he threatened to go home. Mr. Lodge thereafter concentrated on being a good host and urged his companion to ignore the insults of, as he sensibly described Poulson and others, "the provincial politicians."

II

The Harriman party was scheduled for five-thirty in the afternoon. I arrived at 16 East 81st Street at five-fifteen. It occurred to me that I should not be too early — I would be showing my eagerness to belong, letting down my side. I walked around the block and arrived back at the house at five-twenty. It was still too early but someone was going in so I followed. Except for the Russians, I was the last to arrive.

The Harriman house was large and handsome and filled with lovely pictures — the famous Harriman collection of Impressionists and Post-Impressionists — and we were marshaled into a large, somewhat elongated circle in the library on the second floor — with others, Frederick H. Ecker of Metropolitan Life; W. Alton Jones, head of Cities Service; George Woods, head of the First Boston Corporation; Dean Rusk, head of the Rockefeller Foundation and John D. Rockefeller III. (It is possible that the Rockefellers had drawn lots.) Presently the Russians — Khrushchev, Ambassador Menshikov, the interpreter — arrived. Harriman took them around the circle for introductions and it was evident before he was more than halfway around that the Soviet leader was well in command of the situation. He warmly embraced Herbert Lehman (there as former Senator as well as for the Lehman millions) and called him "my boss." Although they had never met, Khrushchev, following World War II, had been in charge of UNRRA operations (United Nations Relief and Rehabilitation Administration) in the Ukraine. Lehman had been the head of the agency, in the work of which he had taken much pride, and it was clear that he was well pleased with the salutation. For some of the others present it might not have been completely reassuring, for Lehman was considered a rather damaging radical, his money notwithstanding. I was standing next to Henry Heald, the President of the Ford Foundation (several hundred millions and thus eminently qualified). Khrushchev, on being introduced, shook hands perfunctorily. Then his face lit up, somewhat in the manner of an indigent college president, and he shook hands again, saying, "Oh, Mr. Heald of the *Ford* Foundation." Everybody shook hands.

Mr. Khrushchev then took a seat before the fireplace and beneath a large Picasso. Harriman and the interpreter were nearby. The scene — the very shapeless man in a rather shapeless suit with a very large pink head and very short legs beneath the Picasso — still shines in my memory. Harriman made the introductions pointing out that both Republicans and Democrats were present in the audience but omitting to add that it was somewhat less than a perfect cross section of the two parties. Then there was an interruption while he offered his guest a drink. All politicians feel they must cherish home-grown commodities and the cliché evidently transcends ideology. Khrushchev asked for some Russian vodka. Harriman explained that he had none and then in a truly inspired political gesture offered Khrushchev a glass of New York State (sic) brandy. In an even more heroic gesture Khrushchev sipped it.

Over the last half century the most persistent as well as the most durable advocate in either country of closer Soviet-American relations has been Averell Harriman, but he has always moved in his own remarkable way his wonders to perform. It is the movers and shakers in both countries that he has sought to move. This he considers to require not attention-catching oratory, or flamboyance of any kind, but the extremes of tact. Capitalist and Communist ideologues alike, he feels, must be provided with a formula for getting along which they can reconcile with their deeper commitment to suspicion, dislike, intransigence, bad manners and natural belligerence. That evening, resuming after his reference to the bipartisan character of the occasion, he went on to say that all present were united in support of President Eisenhower's foreign policy. That brought approving nods from the audience — all took for granted that as a good American he was rallying to the support of Dulles and the tough line. Then came the Harriman touch. He said that this approval extended strongly to any steps President Eisenhower might take to relax tensions between the two great powers. Were the Democrats to win the Presidency in 1960, he assured his visitor, they would honor Republican agreements to this end. Everyone continued to nod more or less automatically. Mr. Khrushchev said a few unmemorable words about Democrats and Republicans and expressed his belief, possibly even his satisfaction, that those present did, if often through their agents, rule the United States. Somebody demurred but in perfunctory fashion. Then began the questions.

A week or so after the meeting Harriman wrote a brief account of it for *Life*. Rereading this I find my own memory to be reasonably accurate as to what was said but very different as to mood. Harriman's tact was in evidence, as ever, in telling of the performance of his American guests. Their questions were, in fact, incredible.

Almost all began with a disavowal of Communist sympathies and a strong affirmation of faith in the American free enterprise system. In light of the asset position of the speakers, neither disavowal nor avowal seemed absolutely essential. All of the questions were phrased to convey information, not elicit it. A Ring Lardner parent once responded to his offspring, " 'Shut up,' he explained." On that afternoon there was a slight variation. " 'I would like to tell you something,' they asked." However, the questions did not convey much information and not because they were brief. As he spoke, each interrogator covertly eyed the others present to see whether he was making a decent impression.

The first question came, as a matter of official precedence, from John J. McCloy who was present both in his asset capacity as Chairman of the Chase Manhattan Bank and also as the current chairman of the Establishment itself. Many people have speculated over the years as to the source of Mr. McCloy's extraordinary eminence. I have always held that it owed much to the rocklike self-confidence that he has always brought alike to truth, error and even nonsense. He was never better than on that afternoon. Wall Street, he assured Mr. Khrushchev in his question, was without influence in Washington; if it supported some legislation, that was the kiss of death. And it was a particular mistake to assume that anyone in Wall Street or anywhere else wanted the arms race to continue. Harriman afterward quoted him as saying that "No one among the American people is trying to preserve international tension for profits. No one in this room knows of any such person." This was in pretty healthy contrast to the kind of stuff that Khrushchev encountered in Communist propaganda.

In response to Mr. McCloy's question, Mr. Khrushchev spoke sympathetically of the helplessness of Wall Street — he referred to it as a poor relation of the United States. But he stuck discouragingly to his belief that arms were good for business, some business anyhow. Already there was indication that, while the questions might not be good, the answers would be better. They were succinct and improved by the extraordinarily apt translation provided by Oleg Troyanovsky, the good-looking, youthful, Quaker-educated son of the first Soviet Ambassador to the United States. Troyanovsky's eyes sparkled in harmony with Khrushchev's thrusts and, as Russian-speaking reporters had already discovered, he frequently toned down a riposte that he thought a bit too abrasive. After McCloy came Frank Pace, one time Director of the Budget, onetime Secretary of the Army and now Chairman of General Dynamics, a giant among the weapons producers. Pace's question involved a novel twist. He made a compelling case for the American system by recounting in detail what it had done for him — how it had facilitated his passage from an Arkansas farm (or some economic equivalent) to Washington and the Bureau of the Budget and the Pentagon and on to the leadership of one of the nation's greatest corporations. The nub of his question was that General Dynamics would gladly liquidate its military business, if circumstances only allowed, as a contribution to the peace of the world. It is possible that Pace was better on promise than he would have been on performance. As he spoke, the Convair division of General Dynamics was on the verge of reporting the largest losses in American corporate history as the result of an ill-managed venture into the civilian air transport market. The company was saved from bankruptcy by its weapons business on which henceforth it concentrated. In the course of the salvation, Frank Pace got fired. Mr. Khrushchev expressed his appreciation of what capitalism had done for Mr. Pace and said that he well understood why Mr. Pace supported the system.

The next question I subsequently estimated at twenty minutes — but this could have been an impression. It was put — perhaps one could better say composed — by the Chairman of the Radio Corporation of America, General David Sarnoff himself. Mr. Sarnoff's manner (at least to Khrushchev) could best be described as imperial. He made it clear at the outset that no disagreement would be tolerated. He began with a detailed outline of the free American system of broadcasting. He continued with a warm tribute to its freedom — and some statistics on the number of stations currently on the air. This question was punctuated by some pounding of the Sarnoff breast. No mention was made of commercials. The question was itself a commercial. The General then depicted the refined and varied blessings that would accrue were Russia to adopt a similar system employing a maximum of American programming. When he finished there was silence — a total solemn silence. On this question Khrushchev rose to the greatest heights of the meeting, perhaps indeed of the entire visit. After a general word or two he said, "Things have changed in Minsk since you were a boy."

From this point all was downhill. Mr. McCloy re-entered with a question that was almost a question. Was the Soviet Union willing to give up the idea of revolution in the non-Communist world? Khrushchev's reply was indistinct. Dean Rusk remained silent. Harriman nodded to me and I came through with a question urging Khrushchev to accept the thesis of American Keynesians, such as myself, that the capitalist crisis was now under control. I developed the question with care and at considerable length for I had concluded that the other men present could do with a lecture on modern economics. Many were still very suspicious of Keynesian fiscal policy; they, as well as Mr. Khrushchev, needed to understand the true foundations of American well-being. As my question continued I watched my audience out of the corner of my eye. I could see that they were following me closely. Presently I finished. Mr. Khrushchev replied that I was entitled to my views, that he was sure that I took them seriously and that he was glad I had confidence in the system. He added that economics is a subject that does not greatly respect one's wishes.

Outside it was still daylight, a lovely autumn evening, and a large crowd of newspapermen and cameramen were waiting. I walked out with Tom Finletter. Several reporters sensed that we might be the soft underbelly of the Establishment and tried to pump us. We remained loyal — a sense of class solidarity is quickly acquired. But it was not quite complete. As we turned down 81st Street, Tom said, "Do you have any doubt as to who was the smartest man in there tonight?"

2

Dean Acheson

IN THE LATE FIFTIES, I served for a couple of years with Dean Acheson on a highly inefficacious adjunct of the Democratic National Committee called the Democratic Advisory Council. He was captain-general for foreign affairs. I was chairman of the counterpart committee on domestic policy. When, as happened on occasion, he made guerrilla forays into my domain, it was, invariably, to express views somewhat to the right of Ezra Taft Benson, then one of the heavier ideologues of the Eisenhower Administration. On foreign policy he believed that the danger of nuclear destruction was something to be minimized, not threatened — an important distinction. Otherwise his principal quarrel with Mr. Dulles was in seeing the Cold War as a secular not a religious phenomenon and in believing the Secretary to be a pompous, vainglorious, moralistic and essentially clumsy operator who wanted a big policy at low cost. Dulles had a better view of himself.

The meetings of the Democratic Advisory Council were extensively devoted to toning down Acheson's ultimatums which were drafted, or rather processed, to his specifications by Paul Nitze. In perfecting this function over the years, Nitze had earned Acheson's very great admiration. All of these documents advised the Soviet government and the American people of the terrible trials awaiting them if the Democrats ever got back in power. The moderating efforts were pressed by Harriman, Stevenson and Lehman. Acheson thought them an outrageous concession to political acceptability. Only on one occasion in those years did we agree. At a meeting in New York the then Governor of Michigan, G. Mennen Williams, was reflecting with approval on a document before us. "It has," said Soapy, "a good solid slug of idealism which is what I like." I couldn't help noticing that the Secretary had the same favorable reaction to this expression that I did. Our area of agreement soon diminished again.

I report all this for I could hardly have come to Mr. Acheson's account of his years in the State Department[1] — as an Assistant Secretary in the war years, Undersecretary under Byrnes and Marshall and then as Secretary from 1949 through 1952 — with less inclination to be favorable or even unnecessarily fair. Yet sometimes the truth must be faced; it is impossible to describe these memoirs as less than superior. I thought them superb. There are more meetings of foreign ministers on NATO and kindred affiliations than one can bear to read about for pleasure or even information. Professorial humor tends to be bad because it is tested by the responses of students who will laugh at anything. There is occasional evidence here that a State Department staff meeting is equally dangerous. The author reaches compulsively for erudition. And, needless to say, he is a terrible snob. "My friendship is not easily given or easily withdrawn," he told a Senate committee in 1949 with a perfectly straight face, and he repeats the thought in this book. As regards the

[1] *Present at the Creation* (New York: Norton, 1969).

rich and well-born and more especially the well-positioned, it is not entirely true. He claims to have found interest and intellectual refreshment from the British Royal Family which suggests a certain susceptibility. But the statement does describe the author's view of his relationship to the common run of humanity. People are entitled to exist and he is prepared to bless them with his personality in accordance with their merits. But he is the sole judge and they must expect him to judge sternly.

These are, however, cosmetic faults and some of them, like the story of those infinitely dreary meetings, are doubtless needed by the thesis writers who will distill even greater dreariness from it all. On the other side are three great virtues, each of which, on reflection, I thought greater than the others.

There is first the luminous view of the Americans the author encountered, or who had the misfortune to encounter the author, during these years. Men of good character will like his affectionate treatment of Harry Truman and George Marshall. Others will rejoice in his disposition of Edward R. Stettinius, Bernard Baruch and Douglas MacArthur. Stettinius and Baruch were, without question, two of the great comic figures of the last fifty years. Stettinius — young, with radiant white hair, contrasting black eyebrows, beautiful and vacuous face — was extensively invented by Harry Hopkins to prove that a really big businessman (besides Harriman who was real) could love FDR. The culmination of this effortless career as a defector from his class was the post of Secretary of State. Acheson notes gracefully that before coming to Washington, Stettinius "had gone far with comparatively modest equipment." The equipment, he then explains, consisted of enthusiasm, good nature, the aforementioned white hair and a gift for public relations. Some businessmen, he observes, need staff to survive. Some need brains. Stettinius, he concludes, did well without either.

Baruch, in his own way as handsome as Stettinius, was altogether a greater artist. While Stettinius wisely recognized the limitations of his genius and relied on his public relations men, Baruch, with some help from Herbert Bayard Swope, handled himself. Had he devoted the same talent to being the real thing that he lavished on becoming the most successful humbug since Henry Ward Beecher, his horizons ' would have been limitless. Here is Acheson on Baruch:

> I protested . . . dissenting from Mr. [James] Byrnes's — and the generally held — view that this so-called "adviser to Presidents" was a wise man. My own experience led me to believe that his reputation was without foundation in fact and entirely self-propagated. Mr. Baruch was undoubtedly a money-maker through shrewd stock market speculations, as he himself has claimed. He made equally shrewd political use of his fortune, rarely squandering it on large party contributions, but dispensing it judiciously — and often nonpartisanly — in small individual contributions to senatorial and congressional primary or election campaigns. This practice multiplied his admirers in the Congress . . . My plea was useless. Mr. Byrnes, like his successor, General Marshall, had fallen victim to Mr. Baruch's spell.

Mr. Acheson neglects to add that no carelessness had caused Baruch to overlook Mr. Byrnes's own campaigns for the Senate.

Douglas MacArthur was, of course, in a class by himself. He raised self-approbation by a quantum jump. And where Stettinius induced praise and Baruch purchased it, MacArthur was not permissive. In befitting military fashion, he commanded it. Comedy is separated only by a hair from tragedy and one's enjoyment of this God-Emperor as he regarded himself, and of his courtiers and eunuchs as they were forced to regard themselves, is diluted by reflection on the catastrophe he nearly caused. For, as Acheson tells in the most graphic chapters of this book, when in the terrible last months of 1950 the Chinese in Korea punctured the MacArthur myth, there remained a frightened, distraught and desperate old man who was willing to risk almost anything for self-requital.

The second great virtue of this book is the narrative skill with which Acheson tells such tales. That of the collapse and recall of MacArthur is the best. But it is closely followed by the accounts of the inter-agency struggles in wartime Washington, the Marshall mission (of which Acheson was the Washington backstop) and the Chinese Revolution, the problems of peacemaking with Japan, the Congressional onslaught on Truman and Acheson by the legislators whom, with nice precision of phrase, he calls the primitives, and many others. As I have said, I found the accounts of the endless meetings to organize Europe after the war of less interest. But even here the author manages so faithfully to slip something of interest into each report that one is badly advised to skip.

The third virtue of this book is in reminding all who have disagreed with Acheson in recent times how much we are in his debt for the period of which he writes. On the evening of the news of the bombing of Hiroshima, he wrote, "The news of the atomic bomb is the most frightening yet. If we cannot work out some sort of organization of great powers, we shall be gone geese for fair." During these years he was a moving force behind the Food and Agricultural Organization, UNRRA and the Bretton Woods agreements, and he guided the United Nations charter through the Senate. No other man did as much on behalf of the international organization he thought necessary. Later he was to be less proud of this effort than of organizing Western Europe against Stalin. Partly no doubt this resulted from the standard affliction of middle-aged intellectuals; at a certain age, nothing conveys such a feeling of forthright masculinity as a commanding involvement in military decisions. But Acheson also saw how many liberals would rather make speeches about supporting the United Nations than do anything useful about its weaknesses or even admit to their existence. And as the Chinese Revolution and the Cold War came, Acheson (the case of German rearmament possibly apart) was strongly and bravely on the side of restraint. He was the relentless opponent of the classical Washington coward. That is the man who calls for heroic and reckless action abroad because he is terrified of criticism here at home for showing sensible restraint. Time has vindicated good sense. Here is an extract from the once greatly criticized China White Paper summarizing his views on that earth movement:

The unfortunate but inescapable fact is that the ominous result of the civil war in China was beyond the control of the government of the United States. Nothing that this country did or could have done within the reasonable limits of its capabilities could have changed that result; nothing that was left undone by this country has contributed to it. It was a product of internal Chinese forces, forces which this country tried to influence but could not. A decision was arrived at within China, if only a decision by default.

Can anyone doubt our misfortune in not having in office men as wise and as indifferent to right-wing criticism when the same thing needed to be said about events (including civil war) similarly beyond our reach in Vietnam?

Acheson fought off the pastoralists in Germany, those who wanted a punitive peace with Japan and the Pentagon which wanted no treaty at all. Only President Truman had more to do with lassoing MacArthur and though Acheson (not uncharacteristically) now thinks he might, as Secretary of State, have pressed harder sooner, he did enough to earn the gratitude of all survivors. He saw before anyone else that the best hope for peace in Western Europe was capital on a massive scale and from this foresight came the Marshall Plan. And so it was on many other matters. No man in Washington in the late forties and early fifties was his equal as a target for those who wanted no solutions or violent solutions or both. Partly this was resentment of superior ability and greatly superior manner, neither of them concealed. Partly it was because Acheson, unlike Dulles after him, defended his friends and subordinates when they were charged with sodomy, subversion, treason or some other imaginative defect. He knew that many of these shafts were meant to wound him. But mostly, one must conclude, the right-wing radicals chose well. Acheson was, indeed, their most formidable enemy. From their point of view, they were right to go after him.

Dean Acheson was fortunate in his enemies and also in many other things. So, with reason, he cherishes the world in which he had power. And like many others he has assumed that, by not changing himself, he could keep the world from changing in accordance with the designs of all kinds of immature, disorderly, incoherent, ungentlemanly, demagogic and otherwise unsatisfactory people. By this means also he kept faith with men who, twenty or so years ago, acquired a reputation in foreign policy by accepting his thoughts and leadership and who could not change. In consequence, as I myself have certainly held, Dean Acheson in these last years has been, or allowed himself to seem, out of touch. It is a minor fault considering how much he was in touch with his own time.

3

Dwight D. Eisenhower, General

HAD I BEEN told last March that I would spend my odd moments in this ardent spring reading prose, much of it militarily processed, ostensibly of Dwight D. Eisenhower, I would have been surprised and also depressed. Memory of his wavering homilies and eccentric syntax are still with us even though dimmed by the Titan II rhetoric and the Procter and Gamble sincerity which we have had from the White House since. But his wartime papers, just published, *The Papers of Dwight David Eisenhower: The War Years*,[1] tell the story of tremendous years — of years when thousands had a damaging brush with destiny, many at a dangerously vulnerable age. Though I was only marginally involved, I found the documents irresistible. And they were partly so because, with all else, they are firmly and unpretentiously literate.

One's first thanks must go to the Johns Hopkins scholars who sorted and arranged the papers and, in footnotes, tell all you need to know (and then some) to follow the action. There has been a little censorship. Eisenhower's adverse opinions of military subordinates who are still alive were deleted. So were his letters to his wife as, one senses, were a

[1] Alfred D. Chandler, Jr., ed. (Baltimore: John Hopkins Press, 1970).

few other personal papers. These personal papers are no loss. Ike seems to have answered faithfully all letters from all people he had ever known, especially if they lived in Abilene. But apart from reporting conscientiously how long the incoming letters took to arrive — the volumes are a major source on the achievements of the army mail service — he was relentlessly perfunctory. Sometimes he senses this and explains that because of military censorship he must not say anything about anything. Still, the very number of these letters tells something of the thoughtfulness of the author or sender. And so do the letters of congratulation, commendation, felicitation and praise which, in that war at least, the generals exchanged in such volume.

The period covered is from a few days after the attack on Pearl Harbor (when Eisenhower joined the War Plans Division of the War Department with special responsibility for the Pacific) through London, North Africa, Sicily, London again and France until May 7, 1945. A great many staff documents — plans for Torch, Husky and Overlord setting forth requirements, shortages and orders of battle often with hints of the probable alibi in the event of failure — are here and these I mostly skipped. Similarly the directives to the subordinate commanders. No doubt they will be needed by military historians though such needs are probably occasioned by the absence of more useful occupation. The rest of the papers report his transactions as diplomat, bureaucrat, public relations expert, conscientious citizen and the great captain of World War II. He may not have been outstanding in every one of these roles but few men have combined so successfully so many of them.

The most rewarding documents by far are his letters to General Marshall. Even if someone else helped with the drafting, they bear throughout the mark of a single personality and it is, unmistakably, that of Eisenhower. They leave no doubt, whatever the myth, that he was in charge. He had a clear view of the larger issues and a brilliant sense of the smaller matters that at any moment might smite him. His rule was to keep one eye on the Germans, one eye on his generals and both ears bent back toward Washington. At the precise moment when General Marshall would begin to worry lest everyone in the ETO (and especially in the Air Force) would come home as brigadier general or better, a letter from Eisenhower would go back condemning excessive promotions among staff officers. Often he would use the occasion to press for a particularly urgent promotion or two. (An astonishing number of these pages have to do with promotions.) Let there be some breach of security or some particularly silly press story from some subordinate headquarters — some general depicting himself unduly to the disadvantage of Alexander the Great — and Ike would have a forestalling letter in Washington expressing his own outrage. But he was no simplistic blame-shifting bureaucrat. Let there be an attack on a subordinate and you could count on word from Eisenhower explaining that the responsibility was really his. A letter might then go to the guilty party telling him he'd better do better or go home.

But to suggest that these papers are principally important for their picture of Eisenhower as a superb organization man would be quite wrong. He was that. But he also comes through as a determined leader who chose men carefully and preferred to encourage his subordinates but did not hesitate to put them aboard a boat when they failed. The presence of men like Bradley or Patton in his armies or Bedell Smith on his staff was no accident. The papers tell how he fought to get and keep them. These pages also affirm (were it needed) Eisenhower's determination to prove that he could lead British and American forces and enjoy equally the confidence of both. His formula was simple: It was to act on all matters, large or small, so as to show that he deserved that confidence. He did not anger easily although he loved to suggest the contrary. But word that an American general had criticized the British, or that American soldiers were behaving badly in London or driving badly on English highways, or even that clubs were being segregated along what he called "nationalistic" lines sent him into a rage that was probably contrived but possibly real.

And deeper still is the sense of responsibility that pervades these papers. It flows out from Marshall to Eisenhower and on from Eisenhower to his subordinates and back again to Washington. Neither general ever separated himself for a moment from the political responsibilities of his principals — in Ike's case both FDR and Churchill. Repeatedly Eisenhower makes clear his understanding that his civilian principals must answer to a different and demanding constituency. In all these papers there is scarcely a reference to the separate concerns of soldiers and politicians. And there is not a single criticism of the political leaders for acting politically — the oldest of military beefs. (Ike did make it clear that he preferred to have politicians remain in Washington or London and not come to visit him in Europe or Africa.)

It is this sense of total responsibility which gives these volumes their contemporary interest — and which causes them, in light of the contemporary scene, to read like communiqués from another world. Lyndon Johnson is now resting on the Pedernales and Richard Nixon may be well on the way to some similar resort because their generals pressed upon them in Vietnam, Laos and Cambodia military actions, on military grounds, that were politically unacceptable — that the people of the United States would not buy. (Not even a simple majority is enough. Wars must be fought on something closer to a unanimity rule.) It is hard to imagine FDR or Churchill yielding on Vietnam or Cambodia. But it is equally impossible for anyone who has read these papers to imagine George Marshall or Dwight D. Eisenhower pressing such action. (The next volumes, I am told by Malcolm Moos, make clear how vigorous was his opposition to the Indochina involvement in 1954.) Both Marshall and Eisenhower looked at the military problem in the whole context of national policy and national opinion.

And they saw this as necessary for the Services themselves. Both, and perhaps more remarkably Eisenhower as a field commander, were deeply worried about any action (such as the Patton face-slapping) which would cause criticism of the Army. And anything that might alienate the civilian community from the Army was unthinkable. In a secret paper to General Devers on the problem of redeployment in 1945, during what must have been one of the busiest weeks of the war at SHAEF, Eisenhower said:

> Failure to return all those eligible for discharge to the United States at the earliest possible date will not only result in a loss of confidence by the soldier in the Army, but will also develop an unfavorable public opinion which could well result in a loss of the good will built up by the Army in its successful campaigns.

He wouldn't like what his successors have accomplished in loss of good will. To both Marshall and Eisenhower the alienation over Vietnam would have seemed an unparalleled disaster to the Service they so loved. No military gain in those jungles could have justified it.

Arthur Larson tells of the pride, pedantic but genuine, that Eisenhower took in his writing. Reminding him that he had been MacArthur's staff officer, Eisenhower once asked Larson who he supposed had drafted the MacArthur prose poems back then. These volumes bear Larson out. Even if much was done by staff, it was done for a man who understood how things should be said. His associates have remarked that between the war and the Presidency he aged greatly and perhaps this accounts for the lesser reputation of his Presidential prose. Certainly these documents are by (or for) an exceedingly vigorous and articulate leader and administrator who shows himself throughout to have been also a very conscientious and sensible man.

4

Richard Nixon

To My New Friend in the Affluent Society . . .
Greetings

The family which takes its mauve and cerise, air-conditioned, power-steered and power-braked automobile out for a tour passes through cities that are badly paved, made hideous by litter, blighted buildings, billboards and posts for wires that should long since have been put underground. They pass on into a countryside that has been rendered largely invisible by commercial art . . . They picnic on exquisitely packaged food from a portable icebox by a polluted stream and go on to spend the night at a park which is a menace to public health and morals. Just before dozing off on an air mattress, beneath a nylon tent, amid the stench of decaying refuse, they may reflect vaguely on the curious unevenness of their blessings. Is this, indeed, the American genius?

THE ABOVE PASSAGE was in *The Affluent Society* which came out originally in 1958. It received something more than modest notice and, in consequence, I have lately been asked how I feel about the intense interest that has now developed in the problem there specified. In 1970, President Nixon devoted much of his State of the Union Message to the subject. A man in Wall Street with a long memory found that part of it was an excellent paraphrase of an address I had given there in 1965. In consequence, I find myself being asked how I feel about President Nixon as a disciple. None of this means, of course, that people necessarily want a reply. It's the beginning of wisdom to realize that most who make such inquiries don't. President Truman once made a similar point some years ago when he said of George Romney, "That fellow isn't going anywhere. He's answering questions that haven't even been asked." Still, if one is asked, one has an excuse to answer.

As to President Nixon, it was for him only the short step from protégé to apostle. In 1941, when he was fresh out of law school, he came to Washington looking for a job. He applied to the FBI and, alas, they rejected him. This could have blighted his whole interest in a public career and, worse still, he would have spent his entire life resenting J. Edgar Hoover. But the Office of Price Administration saw that he was a man with a future and rescued him — and hired Mrs. Nixon too. The primary credit goes, I believe, to Thomas I. Emerson, later Professor of Law at Yale, a valiant supporter of Henry A. Wallace and by all odds the most radical member of this very liberal agency. But Leon Henderson, who was in overall charge, gets bureaucratic credit and as the man in charge of price control, so do I. Mr. Nixon was for many years rather reticent about his association with OPA. In official biographies he said that his service was in the Office of Emergency Management, the administrative holding company for the war agencies. This was even more oblique than being in the Marines but saying that you worked for the Department of Defense. He has recently however been telling how deeply (though adversely) he was influenced by what he learned about price control under my direction. So, clearly, he has at least as much satisfaction as I have in our association. That he should have gone on from regulating the economy to being an apt student of *The Affluent Society* was entirely to be expected.

As to both his and the larger public interest in our surroundings, it is good. I would have welcomed his conversion had it come sooner; as it developed, I got a reputation for being unsound for urging things that now seem extravagantly trite. But that was to be expected. It is the mark of the sound, prudent leader that he never gets too far out in front. People think him reckless and they continue to be uneasy about him even when they catch up. The gifted statesman waits until the parade is about to pass his door. Then he grabs the baton and marches out ahead. That inspires real confidence.

That is the kind of leadership that we now have on the environment and I for one greatly admire its timing. In other respects, it is less encouraging. For one thing, it seems too well balanced — to involve an unduly shrewd blend of prayer, incantation, political oratory and public wailing. There are four further faults which I would like to list:

1. There is clearly an impression that we can combine environmental improvement with inspired public economy. In fact, for cleaning up the streets, the air, the riparian waters, the old cars that are about to cover the entire landscape, and to preserve the countryside from further architectural and commercial abuse, the great and primary need is money. Nothing else is so important. All who speak about the environment and neglect to advocate the increased taxes (state and local as well as federal) to pay for improvement should be rewarded with loud and insulting laughter.

2. There is an even stronger impression that we can retrieve the environment without in any way invading the sacred prerogatives, as they are called, of private enterprise.

This is fantastic. The tendency of the modern economy is to serve not the wishes of the public but the convenience (and other interests) of the more powerful producers. And it is convenient and in accord with producer interest to make automobiles that poison the air, and to dump industrial waste that poisons the waters, and to use chemicals that poison birds, fish and people along with the worms, and to allow the cities to engulf the countryside in an unregulated sprawl, and to give the highways over to billboards and the purveyors of gasoline, exotic inedibles and sundry places of rest and assignation. This, alas, is the nature of unregulated private enterprise. That nature can only be changed by public regulation of such enterprise and of private land use. Orators who evade this unpleasant truth should also be accorded a raucous laugh and a delicately thumbed nose.

3. We have yet to realize that to rescue the environment, we will have to restrict production and consumption of some goods. Increasing production and consumption, and the single-minded concern for increasing them still more, was what got us into this mess. To get out we must ask what things are a cause of more public sorrow than private joy. This involves a radical reversal of form. For years, as an election theme, praise of motherhood has run a poor second to praise of the American standard of living. Were the Declaration of Independence now reissued, it would speak of life, liberty and the pursuit of an ever-increasing Gross National Product.

Yet within the next five years at most, we will have to begin limiting private automobile use in the big cities. (Since I first wrote that sentence, the Swedes and John Lindsay have said they intend to do so.) And there are other straws. The population experts have begun to argue that the environment cannot sustain continuing population growth with prospective levels of consumption. From this they make the case for contraception. (Continence, sodomy or self-abuse would presumably be just as serviceable.) But it would be simpler and certainly much more logical not to consume so much.

4. Finally, one hears from those who are aroused on the left that the remedy is some radical but unspecified revision of the system. Alas, there is no system that elides the environmental problems of high level industrialization. These plague the Soviets. They will plague the Chinese, the Cubans and also the Albanians when they reach the same level of industrial production. It will be a problem in Heaven if that is a high production, high consumption society as right-thinking members of the silent majority assume it will be. Unstructured talk of revolution is one way of avoiding reality.

For the average citizen, there are some simple tests which will tell him when, in fact, we have passed from oratory and incantation to practical action on the environment. One I've already mentioned will be when something practical is done about private automobile use in the big cities. Another will be when the billboards, the worst and most nearly useless excrescence of industrial civilization, are removed from the highways. Yet another, of course, will be when one can step into the lower Detroit River without having a doctor urge immediate amputation. Yet another will be when telephone and electric wires everywhere in the cities go underground and we accept the added charge on our bills.

My own personal test, for what it may be worth, concerns the gasoline service station. This, without rival, is the most repellent piece of architecture of the past two thousand years. There are far more of them than are needed. Usually they are filthy. Their merchandise is always hideously packaged and garishly displayed. They are uncontrollably addicted to great strings of ragged little flags. Protecting them is an ominous coalition of small businessmen and large oil companies. The stations should be excluded entirely from most streets and highways. Where allowed, they should be franchised to limit the number and there should be stern requirements as to architecture, appearance, cleanliness and advertising display. When we begin on these, I will think that we are serious about the environment.

A Retrospect on Albert Speer

IN THE SPRING and summer of 1945, life was like being on
a moving staircase which suddenly began accelerating at a
manic pace. Within weeks Roosevelt, Mussolini and Hitler
all were dead and Churchill was out of office. The Third
Reich crumpled; instead of men of fearful power there remained only a few seedy thugs. The victors met at Potsdam;
the bombs exploded; Japan surrendered; the armies were on
their way home. So much history should have taken years.

I was in Germany that heady spring and summer on the
enterprise that made me acquainted with Albert Speer. During the previous year, FDR had become suspicious of the
claims of the Air Force as to its accomplishments, which
showed that he had mastered the first principle of modern
warfare. He asked Stimson to empanel a civilian board to
assess results, not from aerial reconnaissance abetted by
imagination but from looking at things on the ground. This
knowledge was also needed for the air war on Japan. I was a
director of the enterprise; so among others were George Ball,
Undersecretary of State under Kennedy and LBJ, and Paul
Nitze, Deputy Secretary of Defense under Johnson. The late
Henry Alexander of Morgan Guaranty was the de facto head

of the United States Strategic Bombing Survey (USSBS) as it was called. The Air Force cooperated enthusiastically with a view to controlling the findings. In this it did not altogether succeed.

In February of 1944 the air war against the German aircraft factories came to its climax. The object was to deny the Luftwaffe replacements, especially for its tactical and defensive fleets. All the important factories were hit, with heavy American losses. In January, 1944, German fighter aircraft production was 1340; in February, 1323; in March after the attacks it was 1830; by September it was 3538. The ball-bearing raids had also been a failure. Production of bearings was only briefly impaired; the using industries were unhampered; the loss of planes was catastrophic. Some of the mainly RAF raids on the cities, by destroying stores, shops, restaurants, banks and other places of nonessential civilian employment, might on balance have added to the German labor supply for the war industries which was decisively scarce. This was established for the great attacks on Hamburg. Synthetic oil installations and railroads were successfully attacked but these raids had come late; until the autumn of 1944, German arms output had continued to increase. At best, the bombing was a badly flawed performance. Faced with the flaws, and notably those terrible figures on aircraft output, the Air Force first challenged the accuracy of the evidence, then sought its suppression. I led the opposition with a minimum of tact, grace or even good manners. For many days in the autumn of 1945, the row continued. Only one outcome was possible for I could always release the basic figures anyway. So truth prevailed, leaving deep wounds.

One reason our information, however appalling, could not

be challenged was that it had been assembled by the most talented economists and statisticians of the United States and Britain. Early in our efforts we found that nothing could be learned of the effect of the air attacks from looking at burned and broken factories. They all looked alike. One needed records and the men who had kept them or used them. These in turn required skilled interpretation or questioning. So, as the war came to an end, we combed the Army, Washington civilian agencies and Britain for qualified German-speaking economists and statisticians. A great number were available. As one indication of their accomplishment: In order to measure the overall effect of the air attacks they gathered and sifted the data and computed the first competent series on Gross National Product that was available for Germany.

Early in our task, we became aware — as had previously the talented staff of the OSS — of a figure in the Nazi pantheon far less notorious than Goering, Goebbels, Himmler, Ribbentrop, Ley or Streicher but far more important. He had, evidently, worked wonders with German war production and his name was Albert Speer. For ascertaining the effect of the air attacks, he quickly established himself as the man we most wanted to know.

Toward the middle of May 1945, I was in southern Germany where many of the records of the Reich had been sent and where many of the high officials and officers had taken refuge. I received a signal from George Ball to come immediately to Flensburg on the Danish border. The Doenitz government was functioning there as the last vestigial remnant of the Third Reich. A lieutenant on our staff named George Sklarz, accompanied by a technical sergeant named

Harold Fassberg, had been poking through some makeshift office buildings and come upon a door on which was the name Speer. He was our man. He was standing in — serving would not be the word — as Minister of Economics for Doenitz. Interrogation was about to begin. A plane was found and I arrived a few hours later. The colonel who was with me wore glasses and was a trifle short-sighted. He saluted handsomely the two men he took to be RAF officers who came out to greet us. Both returned the salute with real ceremony; both were Luftwaffe officers, for the field was still under German management.

General Jodl and Admiral Friedeburg had surrendered a few days earlier at Rheims and then again in Berlin. Then they had returned to Flensburg where, according to local doctrine, SHAEF was considering with care how you took the surrender of a government that had already unconditionally surrendered. An allied mission including a Russian contingent kept tabs. To this we were attached. The ensuing days remain in my memory like one of those too bright landscape paintings that one sees at a sidewalk exhibition. We were quartered on a German passenger liner in the harbor — the *Patria*, if it matters. The dining room stewards had survived the war and served us our meals on the veranda deck. The sun shone; the water was sparkling blue; the town, which was undamaged, was scrubbed and clean and the grass in the parks and gardens was ostentatiously green. One did not see much of the streets for they were a mass of field-gray uniforms, moving, moving, always moving, from wall to wall. German soldiery by the hundreds of thousands had fallen back on the Flensburg enclave. There was — I do not exaggerate or not much — scarcely standing room. I can still see this mass of men moving ceaselessly through the streets. It was impossible to imagine that Germany had ended the war with so many able-bodied men in uniform.

The Doenitz government met every morning (as I recall) at eleven. In any case, the examination of Speer began each day at twelve. It took place (as Speer tells in his memoirs) at his headquarters in Schloss Glücksburg, a lovely château moated by a lake a few miles from Flensburg. We arrived in requisitioned vehicles a little before that hour to be greeted and ushered in by a small weasel-faced officer who captained the SS detachment which was serving as Speer's bodyguard. Presently Speer would arrive — tall, in light raincoat, with dark, slightly disarranged hair, dark, bright eyes, easy smile. Here, none could doubt, was a person. Sometimes he had a comment on the cabinet meeting he had attended — "Grade B Warner Brothers," "bad opera." He told us, one day, we should put an end to this poor joke. The interrogation took place in a small room furnished in red and gold brocade and just off the Great Hall of the château. It was brilliantly led by George Ball.

One day Speer did not show up for the interrogation. His staff, including the weasel-faced SS captain, was in deep distress. His secretary was crying. They told us that unknown men had taken him away early that morning; they thought it was the Gestapo. We considered the matter. He had been talking very freely. Himmler had not yet been found. Was it possible the Gestapo was still operating? It seemed too good to be true. While we were discussing the matter, Speer came in. An OSS unit had just learned of his existence and arrested him. When he told them he had an appointment with another American outfit, they released him. "We were always having worse mix-ups than that under Hitler," said Speer.

The interrogation continued for seven days and in odd moments we extended it to lesser figures. Early on, we learned that Speer had brought out from Berlin the basic documents and statistics on German arms production and deposited them in a Hamburg bank. These documents, which were of enormous value, were retrieved. We covered every aspect of German war production and administration with, of course, lengthy attention to the effects of the air war. Then on May 22 we received word that the Flensburg charade was to be closed out the next day. That night for some reason we moved the interrogation to a small villa in Flensburg. It lasted until 4:30 A.M. and ranged widely over the history of the Third Reich. Day was breaking when I completed my notes and started back to the *Patria*. A few hours later the German leaders, booted and clattering, were called aboard and arrested; it was the third surrender ceremony for Admiral Friedeburg and, excusing himself after it was over, he went to a nearby washroom and shot himself. The major Nazis were taken to a prison at Mondorf-les-Bains in Luxembourg which had the code name of Ashcan. The more technical captives, including Speer, were taken to one called Dustbin in the vicinity of Frankfurt. George Ball and I again interrogated Speer there and Speer invited Ball to defend him at the Nuremberg trials. He recalled that young American lawyers made their reputation defending notorious wrongdoers. "Where," he asked, "could you get a more famous client?"[1] George declined.

---

[1] This quotation and those following are from two articles I wrote at the time. Speer's references to Warner Brothers and the "mix-ups under Hitler" are from memory but are, I think, textually accurate.

In ensuing months the texts of the Speer interrogation, though classified, had a circulation running in the thousands. They have since been much used by scholars. I have not been able to check back to them for this article but I was astonished on reading Speer's book at how closely his account, published after a quarter of a century, coincided in almost all particulars with my memories of the period. Hugh Trevor-Roper, who read our interrogation record and then questioned Speer at length himself, has said the same thing. On two matters only does Speer's account diverge from my recollection of what was said. In telling in 1945 of the last days of the Third Reich, he made amusing but emphatic mention of the role of alcohol. As the high Nazis saw the end coming, they eased their anxiety by getting soused: "In the last six months one had always to deal with drunken men." Ribbentrop, Funk, Ley and others, when arrested, were all at the end of a monumental bat. At Ashcan, where we interrogated them, they very much looked it. Little mention is made of this in the book.

More important, certain thoughts of Speer on how the regime might have been ended seem to have gained in stature over the years. This is especially true of his plan for introducing a highly lethal poison gas into the ventilating system of the Führerbunker with terminal effects for all within. In 1945 this was a rather fanciful thought. He mentioned it along with a proposal for loading Keitel, Jodl and the other Hitler sycophants — he called them the nodding donkeys — into an airplane and flying them over to the Allies. That, obviously, would have taken some doing. But overwhelmingly, Speer tells now what he told then.

None of this means that the book, any more than the earlier interrogations, can be read uncritically. Some reviewers have sensed a rather elaborate effort by Speer to rescue and enhance his reputation. This both George Ball and I felt to be the case in 1945 and it was the theme of an article we wrote that autumn for *Life*. (I'm not altogether proud of the piece; I've become more conservative about awarding capital punishment than I then was.) We concluded that Speer had "what amounted to a well-devised strategy of self-vindication and survival. The first part of [this] strategy was to qualify himself as a brilliant technician and administrator. He could guess that his enemies admired brains and technical ability . . . The second part of his strategy was to appear completely unconcerned over his own fate. No one admires a coward; Speer wanted us to know that he realized his danger and did not care."

I'm persuaded that this design for personal rehabilitation, or some variant of it, is brilliantly carried forward in his book. The author was faced with a nearly insuperable problem in guilt both by association and participation. He was intelligent and imaginative enough to see that he could best minimize its personal consequences by getting offsetting credit for telling the truth as he saw it or could be assumed to have seen it and by conceding his own part in the horrors. To conceal or gloss over the truth would be self-defeating — as would be any serious effort at self-justification. But his strategy did allow, perhaps unconsciously, for a certain selectivity in emphasis. The use and terrible misuse of foreign workers by his arms companies does not come in for the same attention as, for example, the self-governing system of committees and rings by which he organized the arms industry. More important, Hugh Trevor-Roper has drawn my attention to the small role played in this volume by the SS. The SS was the iron frame on which the dictatorship was built — it was the state which upheld the State. Its efforts, sometimes infantile, to organize its own economy complete with consumer goods and weapons industries bugged Speer persistently. But the SS is passed over lightly. Perhaps to dwell on it more was to associate himself the more with its bestiality. This does not keep Speer's book from being a valid historical document. It is, and one of unparalleled importance. But it is Speer's truth.

There are also a number of matters on which Speer is wrong — and on which most reviewers have been either poorly informed or too trusting. One concerns his efforts at the end of the war to frustrate Hitler's apocalyptic order to destroy everything — factories, bridges, machinery — that might otherwise fall to the advancing armies. In largely succeeding, Speer believes that he saved the German economy and people from extinction. This is nonsense.

That Speer sabotaged Hitler's orders is not in doubt. Nor is the risk he ran in doing so — although Nazi power then being in decline, it was less than it would have been earlier. What Speer exaggerates is, first of all, the ease with which earth is scorched. Armies in rapid and involuntary retreat cannot easily organize the requisite destruction. And some things like roads and rail lines cannot be destroyed. Nor, although the British and American Air Forces made a brave if involuntary try, can agriculture. But more important, industrial destruction, as the whole post World War II experience reveals, is very quickly repaired. It turns on a point that John Stuart Mill made a hundred and twenty-five years ago. Industrial capital is constantly in the process of being replaced anyway. Destruction simply speeds up this normal process. While it makes life difficult in the short run, agriculture, transportation and enough shelter — the basic essentials — survive. And in the slightly longer run, industry has new instead of semi-obsolete equipment. Perhaps destruction, dismantlement and replacement of obsolete plant do not explain the rapid recovery and development of Germany and Japan following the war. But no one can say that they prevented such recovery.

Reviewers have also accepted far too uncritically the miracle of German war production. Some, in fact, made it more of a miracle than has Speer.

Between taking office in early 1942 and the late summer of 1944, Speer achieved a very great increase in German arms production — nearly fourfold in weapons, fourfold in aircraft, threefold in munitions, almost sixfold in tanks. But three things greatly qualify this performance and the credit to be accorded to Speer.

In the first place, until 1942 Hitler's talk of "total war" was a fraud taken seriously only by his enemies. The concept of the Blitzkrieg called, rather, for a modest level of arms output to be accumulated against the day of need. Then the stock would be used up in the course of a quick (and presumptively victorious) campaign. Explicit in this idea was a minimum of interference with the civilian economy — Hitler was very uneasy about imposing sacrifices that might, he felt, alienate the civilian population from the regime. Only after the Stalingrad disaster in 1942 did Germany begin to arm seriously and in depth. The decision to do so coincided with the death of Fritz Todt, Speer's predecessor. So the ensuing increase in output was partly the result of the adoption of a new production policy — one that had already been adopted by the Soviet Union and Britain. And the ensuing increases were multiples of a very small base. British arms output in 1941 for nearly all items was above that of Germany.

Second, some credit must be given Fritz Todt. Dr. Todt, unquestionably an able organizer, was killed in an airplane accident in February 1942. (In Speer's book there is a hint that the crash was arranged by Bormann and others and that Speer was meant to be included. This thought did not, as I recall, come up in the earlier interrogations.) Some scholars, notably Alan S. Milward,[2] think that before his death Todt had largely worked out the organization — centralized responsibility for planning arms production, decentralized responsibility for execution — that served Speer so well. Speer, and those who have relied on his evidence, tend to minimize Todt's role. I have a feeling, more strongly now than in 1945, that Todt deserves more credit than Speer awards him.[3]

Finally, as Speer's own book makes totally clear, the production miracle over which he presided was a highly defective one. We think of World War II as being on a vastly greater economic scale than World War I. For the United States it was incomparably so. Not so in Germany. During the first year of the war with Russia, armaments production in Germany was only about one fourth of the 1918 level; by 1944, at the peak, it had barely reached the World War I output. Women were not mobilized despite a critical labor shortage; in July 1939, 2,620,000 women were in the German labor force. In July 1944, the number was 2,678,000. In

---

[2] *The German Economy at War* (London: Athlone Press of the University of London, 1965).

[3] Burton Klein (Germany's Economic Preparation for War. Cambridge: Harvard University Press, 1958) also minimizes Todt's role. Klein was a senior and dominant figure in the work of USSBS and his views command great respect. However, like the rest of us, he relied heavily on Speer.

Flensburg Speer said, "I was always disturbed when I saw your magazines and their pictures of factories full of women." Germany ended the war with 1,300,000 domestic servants as compared with 1,500,000 in 1939.[4] At the peak of the effort in 1944, between 80 and 90 percent of all workers were on the first shift. The factories closed up at night. Nor, some exceptional cases apart, were hours excessively long. Labor was scarce but partly because of undermobilization and partly because Speer and Fritz Sauckel, a gangster type who was in charge of labor supply, fought a notable feud which continued into captivity. In May 1945 in Flensburg, Speer let us understand that if anyone in the Third Reich was a candidate for condign punishment it was Sauckel. At about the same time, Paul Nitze was interrogating Sauckel in southern Germany. Any mention of Speer's name brought an explosion — the general import was that there was a man you should hang. (That was Sauckel's fate.) The management of German aircraft procurement was a particular disaster. In 1944, Speer won control of the industry from Goering and (as I have noted) succeeded in greatly increasing output. But continued bad management at the top (abetted by heavy combat losses) accomplished what the American bombers had failed to achieve. By now, the Germans had ready for serial production the ME 262, a twin-jet fighter, 150 miles an hour faster and an age ahead of Allied machines. It was held up for months by an insane effort to make it into a bomber. Meanwhile the Luftwaffe disintegrated into nearly nothing; "We were like telephone poles," a German air general complained after his capture, "even the little dogs didn't respect us." Many of these failures —

---

[4] During the war, some 50,000 (not half a million as Speer tells) girls were imported as domestic help from the Ukraine.

the undermobilization of women, the holdup on the ME 262 — were the result of Hitler's decisions. But when Speer did win Hitler's support, he takes credit for it. And some of Speer's own planning was very bad. Though steel was scarce in Germany, German industry ended the war with a 15 million (metric) ton hoard. Much had been squirreled away, as after 1943, firms saw the end coming. Speer's allocation system was not good enough to prevent such hoarding. German war management — the process of getting the most from the available manpower, plant and materials — was far inferior to that of Britain and probably inferior to that of the United States. I returned from Germany in 1945 to write an article for *Fortune* called "Germany Was Badly Run."

Other faults in Speer's story have been insufficiently noticed. While he has been rightly praised for his portrait of Hitler and his court, he omits to point out that the Führer was a terrible coward — that he was totally and even pathologically craven. He would not venture near the front — or even willingly into Russia. He would not face unpleasant facts; instead he closed his eyes to them or denied them, and bearers of bad news were always in trouble. (American production figures could not be cited to Hitler or even circulated to government departments. Rightly, after a time, we did not classify them.) An appreciable fraction of German cement production — something like five percent in some years, as I recall — was used to build fabulously thick shelters to protect him from bombs. He was very neurotic about bombs. And in the last months of the war, German strategy and tactics, as dictated by Hitler, were extensively motivated not by the hope of victory, not by the hope of preventing defeat, but by Hitler's effort to prolong his own life for a few months, weeks, days or — eventually — hours. Hundreds of thousands of young Germans died to buy him this time. This aspect of Hitler's character is important and deserves to be better known.

Finally, I come to one of those clichés which, at least since the New Testament, literary critics have been plagiarizing from each other. This one is that Speer was the apotheosis of the technocrat. Brilliantly in command of his craft, he addressed himself to it alone, unmindful of the political ends he served. Numerous if soggy morals have been drawn, most of them having to do with the dubious morality of the apolitical man. As far as Speer is concerned it is purest bunk.

Speer was not a technician. His technical knowledge, which was in architecture, had little bearing on his work in organizing arms production. And so far from being apolitical, he moved brilliantly through the political thickets of the Nazi hierarchy to accumulate power. This Goering, Goebbels, Bormann and numerous lesser rivals discovered to their cost and dismay. He managed, whatever the price in lack of sleep and personal boredom, to keep close to Hitler, the source of power. This also showed a clear aptitude for bureaucratic politics. And there is not the slightest evidence that he was indifferent to the political fate of the regime he served. That depended on the success of the German armies, the ability to sustain and expand war production, keeping the economy going, maintaining a tolerable position with the people. Speer saw these needs more clearly than anyone else. The book itself is a document on his concerns.

In the Western industrial countries wartime mobilization was a new task. There were lessons from World War I but they were of limited application. Success depended on a combination of planning and improvisation — on laying out the task, specifying and finding resources and devising the means for doing the job. So it was in Washington and White-hall; so it was in Berlin. In Britain the planning was the more important element; Washington was an intermediate case; in Germany, on the defensive and under the bombs, the essential feature was improvisation. With all else, Speer was a gifted improviser. He was also, let there be no doubt, a highly intelligent man. And also, it is now evident, a very literate one. No one in Britain or the United States has made the task of wartime economic mobilization come alive as has he. And he has an instinct for personal success. For, whether one wishes it or not, a quarter century after the suicide of Hitler, he now emerges from that Caligulan world with a marked aura. No other Nazi has done so. George Ball and I guessed in 1945 that he intended to end up as a Vice President of General Motors. He has done much better than that. This too is not the achievement of a bloodless technician.

6

Ed O'Connor

THE WAVE of migrants of which I was a part rolled in on Boston and its environs in the nineteen-thirties. The most recent of the many population movements into that region in the last three centuries, it was attracted, as were the others, by the prospect of economic and social advance — in the case of my migrant generation, by the demand for low-paid workers at the large educational institutions of the area and the upward mobility that, rightly or wrongly, was assumed to characterize such employment. Arriving from the farms and small towns of the Middle West (or, in my case, from rural Ontario), we found that the adjustment was not easy. The dilapidated slums in which many of us settled, to the east and north of Harvard Yard, were in dismal contrast to the clean countryside from which we came. We submitted with whatever grace we could to the disciplines of our Irish landladies, whose rents, in those depression years and by our simple agrarian standards, were merciless. We could not easily forget our position as a depressed caste, for we were in daily touch with the well-to-do, relaxed and secure young natives — the Macdonalds, Kennedys and Smiths — who inhabited Harvard College and who suffered none of our hardships.

The normal way of redressing injustice in a democracy is by recourse to political action. I am not sure that many of my generation thought of this possibility but those who did saw a searing prospect. All of the high positions in the Commonwealth and all of the lesser ones were monopolized by the earlier arrivals. In the executive, the Curleys, Hurleys and Buckleys formed an unbroken phalanx. In the legislature, there was a sprinkling of names like Saltonstall and Parkman, who differed from the dominant Irish only in being members of an even earlier migration. And one could not listen to the old Irish families without discovering that, like all aristocracies, they had a feeling of divine right. They had won their position of predominance by their own efforts and against the resistance of the yet earlier arrivals. It was now something to be defended without question, although not yet without indignation.

Obviously there was material here for a novel. Like the previous waves that as maidservants, laborers or textile hands had come similarly into the cul-de-sacs or onto the lower rungs of the social ladder, we teaching assistants and instructors were there voluntarily. But the sensitive among us could not but see that in our neglect, exploitation and exclusion from the major opportunities of the community, we were paying heavily for our chance. No one ever did write a novel about us or about the French Canadians, Poles, Italians or Jews who at one time or another also suffered the sorrows of the uprooted around Boston. The reason is that all the available writers have always been writing about the Irish. Old and superbly established though they were, theirs continued to be the only problem in movement and rehabilitation that aroused any interest. When Italians or Poles were unloaded on the beach, nothing much had been assumed to happen. But for the Irish this had been an experience of infinite complexity and lasting sadness. It would be going too far to say that novelists feel that only the Irish have a soul. Yet certainly they feel that the Irish soul is an exceptionally sensitive and friable organ that provides unlimited opportunity for study. The susceptibility of the Irish soul to more or less permanent damage has also impressed the political scientists. To this day in Massachusetts, no one would dream of discussing politics in a learned way without going into the continuing consequences of the cold shoulder the Irish immigrants were accorded by the Yankees a century ago. That one's great-grandfather came in after the famine and had a very hard time is only a little short of being admissible evidence for the defense in a trial for highway fraud. The clustering around the Church, the closing of the ranks against the outsider, the loyalty to the old sod, the difficult upward path, the occasional escape to the world outside — all of this has been material for scores of grand yarns and dozens of deeply perceptive books. On this point, it is doubtful that any subject in American letters, with the possible exception of the plight of the post-bellum South, has given sensitive writers a deeper feeling of their own worth.

In the early nineteen-sixties, the leading prophet of the acculturation of the Irish, to give the phenomenon its technical name, was Edwin O'Connor. In my view, he is an excellent novelist and a master at showing how much can be made of moth-eaten material. His *The Last Hurrah*, published in 1956, was a classic in one sense of the word: Frank Skeffington, the hero, was politically and sociologically a completely standardized phenomenon. He was a member of a racial and religious minority that had been abused and rejected. This abuse and neglect nurtured strong tribal loyalties and bred men of ability and guile. In the course of time, the minority became a majority, and it remained only for one of the men of ability and guile to mobilize the tribal loyalties and take over. Then, subject to reasonable percentage limits, the exploited became the exploiters. Things are supposed to work out this way.

O'Connor's portrait of Skeffington so impressed the late James Michael Curley, to whom, according to the author, Skeffington bore only a coincidental resemblance, that Curley was moved to write his own autobiography as a kind of companion piece. It was founded on the same sociology as the career of Skeffington and employed the same justification for off-color behavior. In this volume, it might be added, the relationship to reality was often indubitably coincidental. Thus, at one point Curley described, with considerable if not wholly justifiable pride, a religious brawl that he had tried to pick in the Capitol with the late J. Thomas (Cotton Tom) Heflin, the distinguished demagogue from Alabama, and how he had been frustrated at the last moment by an almost unprecedented intervention of his better nature. The alleged incident could have occurred only some ten years before Curley went to Congress or some ten years after Heflin had been accorded a well-merited retirement. Among Curley's many qualities was the ability to arouse a large measure of skepticism about anything he might say, and this extended to his literary endeavor. People noted that both in the book and in the movie Skeffington had been well received by the American people, and presumed that this had caused Curley to copy from O'Connor rather than from life. My own interpretation is more lenient. In considering how to present himself, it was natural that Curley should turn to the production model.

There is evidence that when he began his book, *The Edge of Sadness*,[1] O'Connor intended to leave the acculturation of the Irish for good and all, and deal with the simple but delicate problem of a priest who in his middle years turns to alcohol. The advance billing of the book made much of this theme. In fact, it forms only a small and not wholly plausible part of the story. The causes of the descent into drunkenness are not fully developed or entirely convincing. The lost weekdays are deliberately and mercifully left unchronicled. The cure, as recovery from alcoholism goes, seems to have been rather easy. In the very early pages are hints of concern about a relapse, but this disappears. There being no story here, the author turns back to the struggles and torments of the Irish. But he has to find a new twist. In recent years in New England, the challenge to the Irish by the other ethnic groups (not, I may say, including my own) has been increasingly strong. With the Italians so obviously moving in, it is not quite so easy to talk about the efforts of the Irish to establish themselves vis-à-vis the Yankees. Moreover, as the author came to the last chapters of his manuscript, he must have been struck by the distinct possibility that the grandson of one of his uprooted would soon become President of the United States. (A young Congressional candidate who enters the story in the latter pages has several of the political trademarks of John Fitzgerald Kennedy.) Election of a President from a particular ethnic group may not be final proof of full assimilation, but it surely suggests a trend. So O'Connor has had to concede what members of the much later migrant groups, including the Galbraiths, have so long taken for granted — namely, that in America the Irish are in.

[1] Boston: Little, Brown, 1961.

Because the author is not able to talk of the struggle between the Irish and their precursors, his solution is a struggle between the Irish and the Irish. He finds, or invents, a formidable tension between those who are fully acculturated and those who are not. It is a remarkably ingenious solution, for it keeps a maximum of these fragile souls in torment for some little time longer. And it makes a very good story. Those who retain their ancient traits and habits are now getting on in years, and attention centers on a wealthy eighty-one-year-old tenement-and-slum proprietor named Charlie Carmody. Charlie is described by one of his oldest friends:

> "The man is misunderstood," he would say. "There are people in this city who think that Charlie's the meanest man that ever drew on a pair of trousers. He's no such thing. In his whole life he never did anything mean just for the sake of being mean. One, there's no money in it. Two, it's not his style at all. Charlie's not the lad to jab his thumb in your eye just so's your eye will sting. But say you went into his real estate office one day to buy a little piece of land worth maybe ten dollars, and Charlie was good enough — you being an old friend — to sell it to you for a hundred. And say you went to go out of the door with your little bargain under your arm, and Charlie ran around from behind his desk to help you on with your hat — just to keep on being friendly. And say just at the moment he had your hat in the air, ready to slip it on your head, you twisted your head around of a sudden and got his thumb smack dab in your eye — well now, that's the sort of thing that makes the day for Charlie. He's not only cheated you deaf and dumb, but you almost go blind in the bargain! What sensible man could ask for more? I tell you, it's the little bonuses that count the most with Charlie. They go to prove, don't you see, that God's on the right side?"

Charlie, in turn, can be eloquent in his own defense:

"They made Little Georgie Casey's boy head of the rent control last week and before he had the chance to warm the seat with his pants he was up callin' me names in the papers! Did you read about that, Father? Did you read about Charlie Carmody the rent-gouger? Oh my, ain't that a terrible thing to be called? By the son of Little Georgie, that I knew all my life like a brother? And then the papers get on to me and say, 'Ain't it awful, Mr. Carmody, when a young feller like that calls a fine man like you names?' . . . And what do I tell them, Father? I tell them the truth. I say, 'I got no statement but forgive and forget. That's the way Charlie Carmody is and that's the way he'll always be. He holds no grudges. I got nothin' against any man, specially when he's Little Georgie Casey's boy that was brought up with practically no father at all, what with Little Georgie bein' away for so long for stealin' the penny stamps out of the post office . . .'"

To his children, Charlie is more than an anachronism. He has destroyed two of them; the other two, one of whom is a priest, he has managed to scar for life. Much of the book is devoted to a clinical examination of the wounds. The patient listener to all this is the priest, Father Kennedy, who tells the story in the book. After his conquest of alcohol, he has returned to a rundown parish called Old St. Paul's, in the city of his birth and now, for reasons that are not quite clear to him, is being cultivated by Charlie. This throws him back in touch with the children whom Charlie has damaged. The new generation are no longer strongly committed either to the Church or to each other. The Polish curate of the parish, Father Danowski, an impressive achievement in character design and proof that O'Connor could, if necessary, work with Presbyterians, is still the shepherd of his flock. But the Irish priests, though devout, are tired, aloof and disenchanted. Charlie's politician grandson asks one of them if he can come to Mass, pass the collection basket and do a little politicking at the church door. He is refused. Skeffington and Curley wouldn't have bothered to ask and would have tried to preach the sermon. The talk of Charlie and his generation is ebullient, combative, whimsical, exhibitionist, long-winded and unrelated to conscious thought. His children tell of the damage he has done them in measured, grave and deeply introspective tones. One peculiarity does remain: There is no conversation, only speeches, and no speech is less than a paragraph long. All of the new generation are equipped with total recall and practice it on any available occasion.

This sounds dreary but it is anything but dreary. Someone has (or, more likely, many have) said of Jane Austen's novels that although the reader knows that nothing will happen, he can't wait to find out. The probing of the souls to find the damage done by Charlie produces nothing of interest but O'Connor makes it interesting. He even makes Charlie's intention in cultivating the narrating priest after so many years a matter of mild suspense, although in the end Charlie is concerned only with being told on his deathbed that he isn't universally detested. He receives this dubious intelligence, and then recovers.

O'Connor is unquestionably one of the most skillful writers of the day. He has a gift for quick description and a singular purity of style. Moreover, in his own venue he has John O'Hara's ear for speech, and a gift for just the amount of exaggeration that provides contrast without loss of plausibility. I cannot imagine that any priest in Boston speaks quite as does the parvenu Father Danowski. But his stilted and pretentious syntax is in marvelous contrast with the relaxed accents of the secure and aristocratic Irish, and it admirably and plausibly makes the point. It will be evident by now that I do not think O'Connor's theme is excessively important. But out of his slender material I do think he has written a very good novel.

William F. Buckley, Jr.:
The Unmaking of a Conservative

AT A GATHERING of like-minded citizens not long before he announced his candidacy (as it was called) for Mayor of New York in 1965, William F. Buckley, Jr., was believed by some reporters covering the proceedings to have urged New Yorkers to solve the problem of garbage disposal by throwing it out the window. In context, there was a certain plausibility about the plan. It involved the minimum of government regulation of individual behavior. It placed the solution of the garbage problem on the shoulders of the individual immediately concerned. It required no bureaucracy. Some will suggest that the social cost would outweigh the private convenience. But Mr. Buckley is a conservative and men who share his beliefs have long thought, perhaps with justification, that the plea of offsetting social cost is a wide roof under which socialists and American liberals automatically shelter any and all interference with the life of the citizen. The program would also appeal to a great many New Yorkers, as a casual inspection of the city will readily establish.

However, it turned out that Mr. Buckley had been misquoted and he disavowed the whole approach. The incident is not highly important in itself, but it neatly embodies

the twin themes of the present history.[1] The book is concerned, first, with the inability of the New York papers, the
News possibly excepted, to capture the subtleties which
characterized Mr. Buckley's campaign arguments and especially the distinctions which he sought to make. And it documents the terrible retreat from principle which was compelled by his pursuit of votes.

The second tendency is especially distressing. Mr. Buckley, to repeat, was running on the Conservative Party ticket.
And he was running, specifically, because the Republican
Party in general and John Lindsay in particular were deeply
unfaithful to conservative principles — because, in the author's stern view, they were willing to approve any government subsidy, hand-out, tax raid, public extravagance or
interference with sound market principles that paid off in
the votes of some minority or special interest group. And,
alas, Mr. Buckley the vote-getter ended up doing just that
himself. One could weep.

One weeps especially for his stand on the five-cent fare.
In New York for half a century, in one form or another, this
has been the supreme litmus for dividing the politicians from
the politically principled. In its modern form, it applies to
the Staten Island ferry which requires a subsidy that is a
levy against every taxpayer in the City of New York. It lifts
from Staten Islanders the price they should pay for the
splendor and isolation, but admitted inconvenience, of living on an island. It encourages life there and thus raises
the value of taxable property in the Borough of Richmond at
the expense of other taxpayers. But in order to capture votes
on Staten Island, Mr. Buckley came out for the five-cent
fare. He justified it by a simplistic and unprincipled calcu-

[1] *The Unmaking of a Mayor* (New York: Viking Press, 1966).

lation. The total cost for a Staten Islander of going by bus to the ferry and then taking the subway uptown should not exceed that of a ride on the mainland. The natural cost of awkward location was washed out; the claim of anyone in the remote reaches of Brooklyn for subsidized travel to a subway railhead would be just as good. Nor was this all.

In New York and elsewhere, as everyone knows, automobile and truck owners are numerous, strong and politically powerful. Mr. Buckley yielded without evident thought to their power; he accepted their unspoken contention that they should have streets, including brand-new highways, built for their travel without charge. The bicyclists are far less numerous, far less articulate and, their superior health notwithstanding, far less powerful. Mr. Buckley to his credit agreed to build them streets too. But in shocking contrast to his automatic surrender to the motorists' lobby, he proposed to charge them fifteen cents each time they went on their thoroughfare. One could go on. The pristine Buckley proposed that people go into the market, retain their own policemen and deduct the cost from the tax bill. By election time the vote-conscious Buckley was plumping for a fully socialized police force of even greater size.

All good conservatives, in moments of doubt about doctrine, appeal to Professor Milton Friedman of the University of Chicago. He is, as Mr. Buckley notes in this volume, their highest priest. He is also an uncompromising man and I shudder to think of his reaction to the foregoing, especially to that five-cent fare. Only one brief election campaign and Mr. Buckley becomes to conservatism what Leon Trotsky was to deviationism and Nikita Khrushchev to crass revisionism. If he should ever run again . . . But it is too much to think about.

The most interesting part of this chronicle, from the purely anthropological point of view, is Mr. Buckley's retreat from principle. But more of the book tells of his troubles with the press. Early in the volume he gives the reason: it is that damn market again. Nothing was ever so good in theory, so intolerable in politics as the free market. *"For reasons perfectly understandable in commercial terms* (my italics), the press cares about the scandal, much less about subsequent developments tending to dissipate the scandal — less, in a word, about exact history, exactly understood." It follows that newspapers, in the Buckley view, should be published by the state — or, at a minimum, by the Rockefeller Foundation.

For throughout the campaign, Mr. Buckley was engaged in precise and sensitive delineations which the press, in its commercial crudity, simply could not grasp and would not later correct. On the aforementioned matter of the garbage, he never advocated throwing it out the window. He merely said this was justified as a form of protest against Lindsay. In a much-reported speech to the New York socialized police under the auspices of the Holy Name Society, he did not approve police behavior in Selma, Alabama. He was merely critical of those who, on encountering rough behavior, complained. What did they expect? He did not attack any minority. He merely denounced the claim by minorities to special political consideration. He never opposed integration of schools. But he did insist (as would I, in fact) that it be subordinate to sound education.

As stated, these distinctions are quite clear. But in the heat of a New York political battle, as warmed further by Mr. Buckley, the reporters of the free-enterprise, market press missed them to a man. Now with this book they have, at least as individuals, a chance to get straightened out, and I hope they take it. Perhaps the only thing that is missing is some guide to when, as seems occasionally the case, Mr. Buckley intended to imply a trifle more than his words conveyed. He is not bad at that.

Still, one can only applaud Mr. Buckley's effort to hold the press to the highest standards of fairness and precision. And one reflects, with real satisfaction, that his own *National Review* will henceforth conform to the Justinian standards now prescribed by its editor. I wonder if it wasn't just as well that Joseph R. McCarthy did not live to see the day. Joe was not a subtle man; I don't think he could have ever risen to Mr. Buckley's new standard, to his insistence on "exact history, exactly understood." In consequence, the late Senator would have taken terrible punishment, poor man, at the hands of his old friend.

When Mr. Buckley announced his candidacy, a New York friend of mine, who is a pillar of such reform as is currently available in New York, commented that the new entry ensured, at least, that the campaign would not be without amusement. One winter day in Switzerland, Mr. Buckley, a would-be skier as am I, called to ask me to accompany him down a mountain of modest difficulty. He was then working on the book and, like football coaches who build character on the side, I found myself exploiting my position. I urged him in this book to forswear all temptation to statesmanship and give full rein to his natural talent for invective, malevolence and humor. He did not entirely reject this sage counsel. There is quite a bit of all three in *The Unmaking of a Mayor* and they are excellent. But serious purpose does intrude and, given the purpose, that is too bad.

8

John Steinbeck

UNTIL ALONG in the fifties I largely made my living out of the farm problem. This had been my concern as a student, and I taught agricultural economics at Harvard. For anyone with these interests, a giant figure just offstage was John Steinbeck. All official compassion in farm matters until the late thirties had been for the family farmer — an oaken citizen who leased or more often owned his own acres, sat proudly under his own rooftree but who was bedeviled by debt, rising costs, the two great droughts of the thirties and prices that, because of endemic surpluses, never reached that magic level called parity. The Southern sharecropper got a certain amount of ritualistic sympathy but the independent farmer was the farm problem.

A few liberals who knew about agriculture had for years been telling each other, and anyone else who would listen, that the truly forgotten man in farming was, in fact, the hired farm worker. He added all the misfortunes of his employer to a specialized collection of his own. Nor was his situation improved when his employer was not a family farmer but a big producer of fruit, vegetables, sugar beets, tobacco or cotton. Unfortunately, no one much did listen. Then *The Grapes of Wrath*, almost overnight, made the life led by these wretched people a national scandal. Thereafter, though they still might be ignored, they could not entirely be forgotten. It was a special stroke of genius to make the farm workers in this novel not the Mexicans, Filipinos, Negroes or Japanese who, as Steinbeck knew better than anyone, had long followed, and stooped, and harvested the crops, but white Anglo-Saxon Protestants (WASPs as they were not yet called) who had once enjoyed the unbelievably better fortune of the debt-ridden family farm. These were basic Americans made untouchable — Okies, for goodness sake — by economic weakness and resulting disaster. It could happen to anyone except Norman Vincent Peale.

I did not meet John Steinbeck until just after Christmas in 1953. With my wife I had been in Puerto Rico at the University and we went on to St. John in the Virgin Islands for a holiday. Caneel Bay, where we arrived late one night, was then a minor backwater of the Rockefeller benefactions; it was currently being operated as a kind of colony of Colonial Williamsburg. (Like everything else in the Western world, it has since been drastically developed.) There was a slight depression at the time — the Republicans had recently increased interest rates dramatically for no good reason and business was off. In consequence, an unprecedented number of Americans were remaining at home. My wife returned from her regulation dawn patrol to report that there was only one other couple in the hotel and adjacent cottages. Their name was Steinbeck. You don't suppose . . . ?

It was, and the beginning of a friendship. I can add little on Steinbeck as a writer for he didn't like talking about his work, at least to me. But I can tell quite a bit more about a shrewd and perceptive man, much interested in politics and contemporary political anthropology and not only droll but very, very funny. He was a large man, still clean-shaven in those days, exceedingly homely and older in appearance than I had imagined him to be or he in fact was. He spoke in a carefully subdued mumble. Elaine, his wife, was intelligent, tolerant, devoted and lovely.

At Caneel Bay, the Steinbecks too were on holiday and John regularly took a mask and snorkel and, looking from shore like some terrible accident of marine miscegenation, went out along the reef to explore the underwater life. It was an interest that had developed many years before on the California coast near Monterey and which is reflected in many of his stories. One day, however, my wife and I set out to tour the island on foot and John abandoned the sea to accompany us in a jeep that he had requisitioned for the purpose, along with its owner. (The latter was an acquaintance who had secluded himself on the island to write a novel. In face of the failure rate, it is astonishing how many people can be persuaded that solitude is a substitute for art. This was an instance, but John deferred to the unhappy man as to Proust.) We explored the ruins of the old sugar plantations and heard of the great revolt of 1733. Then the slaves seized the island and penned their erstwhile masters up in a small enclave around Caneel Bay. Eventually a commando of soldiers righteously representing the several civilized powers with interests in the area was sent in to restore law and order. It was a fine example of international cooperation. The slaves, however, had the last word. They went to a high promontory at one end of the island and dashed like lemmings into the sea. They could not be replaced and the island went back to wilderness. John thought, on any rational calculation of their personal future, that their decision was sound. He predicted that, within a measurable time, a similar calculation would be made by the inhabitants of Manhattan, and certainly of Miami Beach, with similar results.

Steinbeck differed from other novelists of his (or a slightly earlier) generation in being a controlled drinker. But he was also an appreciative one. Adlai Stevenson, in one of his great speeches in 1952, written I believe by James Wechsler, referred to the brief period every four years just before presidential elections when politics reconciles even the most obsolete men to the machine age. It was, he said, "a kind of pause in the Republican occupation that might be called 'The Liberal Hour.'" Thereafter, those of us who were working on his campaign spoke of the time when we assembled for a drink as the Liberal Hour.[1] I told John of this nomenclature. After some reflection, he told me he preferred to continue with his own term. He called it Milking Time.

Milking Time was an occasion for wonderful nonsense. I remember especially one evening when the conversation got on to a girl he had once known well. She was a frustrated circus performer. She loved lions and tigers and dressed like a zebra; she would often dream that she was riding around a ring on the rump of a horse and attempt in a limited way while asleep to do so; she could not see a curtain pole without taking hold of it as a trapeze; and she did a certain amount of damage to people's houses while swinging from their chandeliers. She hurt herself one day when she stepped out of a second-story window onto a poorly attached clothesline. Life with her was interesting. I believe his story about her had no appreciable relation to fact and that it was just as well that Aaron Hotchner was not around.

[1] I also used it as a title for a book.

We also talked a good deal about politics. John liked Stevenson and believed Joe McCarthy, then in peak form, strictly a flash in the pan. To exercise power through fear, he thought, required commanding intelligence and great diligence. Joe had neither. John also, as I recall, thought him insufficiently sober.

Then, as later, John developed a favorite theme which is that the world owes more than it realizes to shared greed. Since there is an infinity of visions of the future, and also of how any one vision can be made real, ideology divides men. But they are brought back together again by pursuit of their common interest in income, power, position or the prospect of an invitation to eat at the White House. It is a shrewd point. New York and California liberals quarrel hideously because, being happy where they are and not wanting to go to Washington, they are influenced more or less exclusively by ideas. Elsewhere shared greed makes men more tractable.

After 1954, we saw the Steinbecks at intervals and I heard from him often. As there must be many who will testify, he was (in small but legible script) one of the last good letter-writers. For John F. Kennedy's Inauguration, someone had the idea of beating out a covey of artists, writers and certified intellectuals to attend the rites, a project with a heavy portent of disaster for President Lyndon Johnson and Professor Eric Goldman. The Steinbecks were in the flock and joined us for the whole day.

We were also joined by a television crew. Its principals had come up with the idea of covering the event by immortalizing the responses of a highly unrepresentative set of spectators — as I recall, besides the Galbraiths, Scottie Lanahan (now Scottie Smith), Janet Leigh and Senator and Mrs.

Hubert Humphrey. Having Steinbeck show up was, from the point of view of the producer, roughly equivalent to discovering Toynbee in the audience at the Johnny Carson show.

To have a television camera on you all that day (and in the front seat of the car as we were stalled in the traffic jams) suggested major political status. We attracted more attention than Douglas Dillon, Dean Rusk or the Secretary of Commerce and were not a bad second to President and Mrs. Kennedy. We both made the most of it but John more than I. He told some people who got up the courage to ask the reason for the attention that he had just been named Chairman of the Joint Chiefs of Staff and had not yet got his uniform fitted. To others, he said he was the new Secretary of Public Morals and Consumer Education.

When asked by the television man for his reaction to the Inaugural Address, he said, "Syntax, my lad. It has been restored to the highest places in the Republic." Inspired by the prayers of Cardinal Cushing and other prelates, he also offered an allegory on that evening's situation meeting in heaven. The briefing angel would say, "Well, it was a pretty quiet day down there until noon, my Lord. Then we got one hell of a blast!" I was sad that John did not live to reflect on the way the doors and windows of heaven were shaken by the Reverend Billy Graham on Nixon's Inaugural Day.

A few weeks later, I received a long letter from John which impressed me as much as any communication I ever received. It was serious and said that I had no business becoming an ambassador. It wasn't necessarily that I would louse up the job or dislike it. Rather, I would like it too much. The bonds and constraints of bureaucracy would become too comfortable. Presently I would relax in them and cherish them. Thus the end. The letter covered many other matters including some fascinating observations on government, Kennedy and the first monkey in space and I think I should reproduce it in full:[2]

31 Jan. 61

Dear Ken:

Please excuse the method or rather the equipment. I've composed on yellow pads with a pencil for so long that any other way is like a translation. First, we want to thank you for the tickets and the transportation together with a few gay words in a grizzly world. I could wish that spinning time permitted us more access to talk for without talk there is no thought and without thought, the world remains what we find it. Q.E.D. And there are some basic wrongnesses to be put straight. In nearly every phase of our travail we are wrong. We think the primitive is simple. He isn't. His world is far more complicated than it seems to a civilized inquiring mind. Secondly we think of the world today as much more troubled than it ever was before. A look into the customs, practices, politics, economics, religion and mores of the middle ages, should convince us that it is not. I think that most of our difficulties arise from our failure to inspect. The unknown is always more fearful than the known and the rejected is the fiercest of all. We don't inspect our bomb, our world. Right here in America we reject thinking of the USSR or the Chinese complex and by this means render them frightful. And they, of course do the same. There's nothing like a closed border to keep people and minds afraid. Any dictator worth his salt knows that. What is happening in world economics, if it happened in a village market in Mexico, and it does, would not be found insoluble. We throw shadows and box with them and get knocked out by our own shadows. I read Kennedy's state of the nation speech and I think he oversimplified. I

---

[2] At the time this essay first appeared in the *Atlantic*, this letter was in transit to the Kennedy Library from which I have now been able to retrieve it.

think he simply faced things which were essentially simple to begin with. If it were widely known what generals do with their time and their minds, we would not need generals. No politician is going to demolish his mysteries by inspecting them. If Kennedy should do that, he would succeed until someone shot him for breaking the pattern. It seems to me that nothing is so dear to a human nor so well guarded as an error. Oh! I know the danger of the bomb, but I don't think it is really a danger. It is more likely that when we have finally decided to shoot our world to pieces that we will find we can't hit it. When by law we took skyrockets away from children and gave them to generals, we were naive.

The newspapers don't seem to accept your refusal of India. Or have you weakened? I could find it in my heart to hope you have not. You're pretty good but not that good. If I engage to write a piece for the *Ladies' Home Journal* or *Reader's Digest*, I am sure that it will warp toward the one or the other. You have the enormous, if unsuspected power of the free and inspective mind. Two years of the subtle disciplines and unfelt strictures of the State Department and even you would find your thinking limited and perhaps not even know it was so. And the strangest thing is that people very quickly learn to love their chains and in a little while begin to think of them as wings. I think I know why. It is a lonely thing, liberty, freedom, whatever you want to call the state which allows and orders you to make your own rules. It's kind of anti-human and keeps you in trouble.

That's all I wanted to say.

2 Feb. 61

On second thought, that isn't all I want to say at all. Perhaps it is all I *have* to say but wanting is another thing. Let my way go back to the free and critical mind and the gall-dipped pen. The nation needs that more than it needs another ambassador. Eighteenth-century writers knew this. Your power is much greater if you do not fly into the flame.

I did not invent my 4th law but I have reduced it at least to formulation — "Wanted loses value on becoming had." (Steinbeck's 4th Law.) And that's as true in government as it is in the movies. Once some years ago Zanuck wanted me to work for him and when I said I didn't want to, he said, "Don't try to kid me. Everyone has his price." To which I replied, "Quite right, I have no doubt I have my price but you don't know what it is. Come to think of it — neither do I."

One of the reasons I dislike government is that it cannot permit itself the luxury of humor. It must comport itself with the deadly seriousness of little boys in a schoolyard. From which grows my 5th law — "Who strives to save face demonstrates that he has no face to save." (Steinbeck's 5th law.)

Beware the germ of white houseitis. It is incurable once contracted. I've seen so many of my friends come down with it and remain forever afterward crippled. That's why I told you my loyalty to this administration had a life span of 24 hours. I'm against all governments. The best of them is brother to the worst, because both emerge from the same egg. I know the Embassy I want and I think I can get it. You have heard of ambassadeurs sans portfolio? I want to be Ambassadeur San Cullotes. I'd feel at home in that job.

Well, now we have shot an ape into the air. I wonder what Troglodytes Anthropapithecus thinks of H. Sapiens now. There must be laughter in Africa. Pentagonic perambulation is more than a dimension. The five-sided mind has one quality like the figure — no side squarely faces any other.

I am wondering what kind of nonsense those nice young men managed to record. If their record was any way complete, our political careers are finished because politics operates as does business by a process of fumbling pragmatic magic, hereinafter called Pragmag.

Do you observe closely, Ken? Did you see, or rather feel what happened in that second news conference? I haven't mentioned it even to Elaine because it was so subtle that it was gone almost before it started. It got started well and then suddenly a moment of doubt crept in, the tiniest faltering, almost like a breath of weariness. I thought I might have imagined it until this morning when the papers announced that the live shows would be discontinued for the time being. And I think that this remarkably integrated and directed young man felt a small cold wind that suggested, "What are you doing here?"

Did you see that. There's another thing also. The eyes are slightly puffed and, on the film at least, the flesh of the cheeks have that doughy lack of resiliency that is the surface diagnostic of dog weariness. I hope this isn't so because the pressures are not going to grow less but greater. I can't conceive why anyone would want to do it.

And how are you?

Yours

John

The warning remained with me. The temptation to surrender to organization is indeed very great. While a military organization compels it, the State Department has more persuasive means. Accept the approved belief and you are, as James Stevenson has said, effective. Being effective means you are called in for conferences, consulted with deference, even respect, on actions to be taken. If, however, you insist on the uncomplicated truth, you are not effective but a problem to be handled. You do not participate; you are told afterward. I would guess that the men that Kennedy brought in split about fifty-fifty between those who decided to make sense and those who opted for being effective. In any case, in the ensuing years, every time I was tempted by the thought that Taiwan was China, that Indochina was the fulcrum of the free world, or even that one should bow to protocol and proceed to Palam Airport near New Delhi to welcome any visitor of the rank of technical sergeant or above, I thought of John. In time, I acquired a reputation for being a trifle prickly. The fault, obviously, was his.

Meanwhile I began to get letters forgiving me for my decision and offering me advice. An undated one from "Babylon sur Rhone" which evidently was Avignon must have coincided with the shelter-building flap of 1961/62. He began with a reference to this. (As with the earlier letter, I have Elaine Steinbeck's permission to quote him.) On the shelters he said:

> I have my own shelter worked out in New York. At the first suggestion of a bomb, I'll pry open a manhole cover and there are a thousand miles of shelter. And the rats there aren't likely to draw a gun on me . . . Furthermore, after a couple of days, the sewers are going to smell sweeter than the upper air.

Later, proposing that all writers unite to modernize the clichés about peace — he urged that henceforth we beat swords into portable typewriters and ballpoint pens — he asked me to arrange him a diplomatic appointment. He had decided that he wanted to be Ambassador to Oz:

> Now Oz has another secret weapon we could well use on all levels of government and diplomacy. The Wizard of Oz is a fraud who admits he is a fraud. Can you think what this would do if it got into chancelleries and general staffs. There would be a major breakthrough. I can think of a dozen other advantages and rewards of my Embassy to Oz but I think these two would justify it. The simple expedient of dyeing different countries different colors so we would know whether

we were for or against them would be worth any outlay by our government. It is even possible that a discreet traffic in emeralds could make my Embassy self-supporting if not profitable.

Then came what, with some effort, I considered a compliment:

> I trust you, Ken, to handle this matter for me with your usual discretion and subtlety.

In the next letter, not having been notified by President Kennedy of his appointment, he thought probably Senator Dirksen had got it. "Maybe he can do the job better than I can . . . It's just one more small heartbreak."

A year or two later, he reported on his triumphant journey to the Soviet Union and returned to a favorite theme:

> We got home from our culture-mongering completely exhausted and with a very vague idea of what had happened . . . I developed the only diplomacy that has ever worked outside of total conquest — that of finding areas of mutual greed.
>
> I found I enjoyed the Soviet hustlers pretty much. There was a kind of youthful honesty about their illicit intention that was not without charm. And their lives are difficult under their four party system. It takes a fairly deft or very lucky man to make his way upward in the worker's paradise.

In the last year or two his letters were shorter. The X-rays which led to spinal surgery in the autumn of 1967 he reported as looking "like a snake fence after a tornado." With some misgivings I sent him a pamphlet I had written on *How to Get Out of Vietnam*. To my delight he approved, on the whole, although he thought my solution — basically that we recognize error, pull back and negotiate withdrawal, assuring ourselves only of the safety of those remaining behind — a bit reminiscent of a recommendation that came out of a big meeting in Washington in World War II. It was to consider what could be done to arrest the rapid increase in venereal disease. Everybody was stumped. Then Gene Tunney came up with an idea that "was a beauty and would work." He proposed continence.

My last letter from John was in the winter of 1968. The political prospect was then for Mr. Johnson against Mr. Nixon. He was reminded of a little Indian girl in Salinas watching a wrestling match. In great excitement she said, "Jeses Chris', they're both jus' as good." Then, though recognizing that the need had long since passed, he got back to advising me on diplomacy. He had just heard about the perfect diplomat. Two men were discussing Green Bay, Wisconsin:

First Man: It's a real nice place.
Second Man: What's nice about it? Only things ever come out of Green Bay is the Packers and ugly whores.
First Man: Now, wait just one minute, you son of a bitch. My wife is from Green Bay.
Second Man: She is? What position she play?

Points
of a
Compass

1

The Nicest Village in the Country

A HUNDRED AND TWENTY-FIVE YEARS or more ago, the village of Newfane in southern Vermont stood on the top of a high ridge, perhaps two miles from and twelve hundred feet above the site of the present town. If you are energetic, you can still walk up to where the old village stood and you will have a marvelous view over to the Green Mountains. There is some dispute as to why the village was removed to lower land. Some think the soil was better down there; hedonists think it was warmer. My own feeling is that people simply wanted a change. In any case, the present village is now in the pleasant green valley. All that was left behind was the cemetery.

Newfane is the shire town of Windham County. Vermont counties do not amount to much; they are important only for judicial purposes and for punishment of minor crime. To the first of these ends, a courthouse stands in the middle of the village common. There is a legend, which I have never checked, that it was built to designs initially published by Sir Christopher Wren. This may be so. Although it is in wood, it has the fine line and perfect proportions of a Wren church, and a resemblance otherwise that will do for an amateur in such matters. The courthouse is, indeed, one of the most beautiful buildings anywhere. On one side of the common, facing the courthouse, is the Newfane Inn, a beautiful eighteenth-century building beautifully restored and maintained. And back of the courthouse is The Four Columns, another inn which has the best restaurant in New England. As might be expected, it is run by a Frenchman. His name is René Chardain and he would not be without modest fame had he remained in France.

Across the common from the courthouse and across the highway, mercifully still not overtraveled, and across another common lies the other public appurtenance of the county seat. That is the jail. Until a few years ago, a long two-story building combined an excellent small inn with a place of confinement for prisoners awaiting trial or serving a perfunctory sentence. The food in the inn was known to be good; the food in the jail was exactly the same. All residents were happy. During World War II, when there was a shortage of labor in the community, the prisoners were allowed out each day to help clear the roads or otherwise earn a part of their keep. It is said that one prisoner was notably irregular in his habits. Eventually he was told by the landlady that if he didn't get in on time, he would be locked out. According to yet further local legend, he never thereafter offended.

Midway between the jail and the courthouse is the war memorial. This is a Civil War soldier in marching order and around the base is the story of Newfane. The dead in the Civil War cover two full sides of the monument. The dead in World War I are many fewer, and the number dead in World War II on an adjacent plaque fewer still. This is not because our wars are becoming less lethal. It is because a hundred years ago, the forests having been cleared away, this was a prosperous farming town. But no more. The population of Newfane has been steadily declining. This is another reason for recommending it as a vacation spot. If one is to rest properly, one cannot do better than to surround oneself with an aura of gentle decay.

There are a few other things in Newfane. Not far out of town there is an automobile graveyard of hideous aspect. On the edge of the village is the right-of-way of a railway line that ran up the West River Valley and is long since defunct. It is a very nice place to walk. There is another pleasant graveyard on the hill across from town, and there is Earl Morse's store. This is not the kind of country store of which Robert Frost would have approved. Earl took it over from his family after World War II and sensibly keeps it from being used as a gathering place for the local citizens by the simple device of keeping it full of good merchandise. Other than an excellent Vermont cheese, he doesn't care much for goods that reflect the local idiom. There is another store which does go in for that sort of thing. My impression is that it makes rather less money than Earl's. Such is the fate of all who sacrifice commerce to art.

A stream runs along the other side of the town, and to the best of my knowledge it is unpolluted. Newfane is in the West River Valley and a half mile or so away is the West River. One can swim, but the swimming, like the skiing, is on the whole inconvenient. The advantage of Newfane lies in the absence of things to do.

Opinions differ on the best time to go there. Many favor the winter when it is quiet and white, and one can look without envy on those driving north to spend a vigorous day on Stratton Mountain. And if one is determined to ski, the slopes on Stratton and adjacent peaks are as good as any in Switzerland. Avoid weekends. I am not enchanted by the spring when the country has a sodden and rather muddy aspect, although there are some who disagree. The summer is lovely and, except on weekends, comparatively uncrowded. The undiscriminating and garrulous have all gone to the ocean. Newfane, like the surrounding countryside, is covered by maples, and they have their special moment of glory in the fall. Then the light is taken up by the trees and given back to the eyes. I usually struggle to be different, but I am forced to confess that for me this is the best time of the year.

2

Why Do You Go to Gstaad?

PROCEEDING along the road that runs across the Bernese Oberland from Montreux on Lake Geneva to Interlaken in the region of the Jungfrau, a friend of mine of great geographical sensitivity but simple mind rolls down the window of his car at a certain point near a village called Saanemoser, carefully scrapes his throat, and then spits. The reason, he informs his passengers, is that at this point the fluid so released is equally likely to flow down various streams to the Rhone and the Mediterranean or to augument the Rhine and eventually the North Sea. In the general breadth of his intellectual conception and depth of interest[1] he would be considered by many people well suited to a small community a few kilometers back where I have lived, off and on, for the last fifteen years. That is Gstaad, Switzerland. Apart from inquiries as to my height, no question comes to me so often as why I go to Gstaad. By almost everyone it is imagined to be a kind of intellectual desert made even more barren by the moral depredations of the rich. All this is far from the truth.

[1] David Niven, who read this after I had published it in *Holiday*, contests even my friend's geographical knowledge. The place in question, he advises, is actually the dividing line between two major watersheds of the Rhine.

For one thing Gstaad has one of the most appealing locations in what our recent Secretary of State referred to feelingly as the Free World. It lies a couple of miles off the highway I just mentioned on the line of the Montreux-Oberland-Bernois (the MOB) railway where three shallow valleys, each carrying a fast mountain stream, come together to make a sheltered basin in the mountains. The basin, highly irregular in shape, is perhaps half a mile across at the bottom and three miles long but the shoulders between the streams shove their way in at various points. The bottom of the valley is at 3300 feet; the low, rather rounded mountains nearby go up to 6500 feet. But the two widest valleys extend south toward the Rhone and end with the Oldenhorn and the Wildhorn which, though some fifteen miles away, have an aspect of remote and rugged grandeur. The morning sun makes them a pale pink on one side, the sunset a rosy pink on the other.

Gstaad has the inestimable advantage in an impersonal world of a negligible population — about 2000 permanent residents and space in various hotels and chalets for 3900 more. Until sixty years ago it was a peasant village where small lumber mills (which still survive) sawed the huge straight logs which are brought down from surrounding mountain forests with only slightly less than loving care. Then the Swiss, English, Belgian and other tourists started coming and in the next few years most of the hotels, of which there are fourteen, were built.

One hotel, completed just before World War I, is the Palace. It stands on the highest of the shoulders that intrude upon the basin and in inspiration is mostly Norman although with a perceptible debt to Chambord and the American farm silo. According to legend the builder watched the carnage and destruction of the first war for several months, then concluded that no one would ever again be rich enough to afford a hotel such as his. So he shot himself too. It was a terrible miscalculation and a warning to Conrad Hilton if he is brooding deeply over Vietnam. So many people are now able to afford the rather austere apartments of the Palace that the competition to inhabit them is extreme. The really bad skiing accidents over Christmas and in February happen to people who already have rooms there; someone trips them. Many of the denizens ski rather vicariously and stories are always in circulation about some enthusiast who has hired a ski instructor to accompany her up and down on the *téléférique.* Food, concerts, dancing and backgammon also occupy the rich at the Palace but the impression of my friends who have studied them anthropologically is that their principal enjoyments are essentially tribal. One belongs to a band in which there are sachems and braves and favorite squaws in unstable equilibrium but with a strong sense of tribal solidarity. (If they don't defend the social superiority of the rich, who will?) Questions of intratribal relationship and prestige and the war paint, wampum, wigwams, favorite hunting grounds and fleshly mortification of the members of the tribe provide inexhaustibly fascinating subjects for conversation. Indeed, one of the best local experts avers that so great is this preoccupation that not much time or energy is left for either drinking or sex.

All who do ski are partial to the Gstaad slopes. No one has ever suggested that they are violent; one rarely need wait for a lift. Some years ago when I was there I received a telephone call on some business or other from Robert McNamara. On its conclusion he asked me what I was doing. I said I was working and skiing. He replied, "Well, you

certainly can't ski in Gstaad." This, however, is a very narrow view. There are in the world steep, winding and narrow
ski slopes and also broad, flat ones. Some people are inclined
to the first; some prefer the second. It is not a matter of
ability, purely one of taste. If anything, those of us who
prefer a wide gentle slope have better taste.

The village of Gstaad, a few hundred feet below the Palace, is the part with which I have affiliation. Except in size
all of the houses are the same, as also are those which cluster
on the surrounding shoulders or spread up or down the valleys. They are of heavy squared timbers, carefully mortised
at the corners under a broad, low-pitched roof which holds
the snow. All are angled so that the wide gable end with its
windows is warmed throughout the day by the sun. Across
this gable end is a generous array of balconies for further
access to air and sunshine. Since these houses are handsome,
easy to heat, capacious and comfortable, the local authorities
have rightly decided that no further improvement is desirable or even possible. So all new construction must be of the
same kind — a provision that applies also to hotels and thus
excludes the high rise structures that offend the eye in other
Swiss resorts. When we bought part of such a chalet a while
back, we had to obtain permission to put a window in my
workroom. The authorities considered the matter for some
months because the architect had previously offended them
(so I was told) by making a small aperture under the gable
vaguely rectangular when it should have been square.

I first came to live in this pleasant village in 1955 — well
in advance of the people of fashion and conceivably as the
magnet that brought them there. I was working on a book —
The Affluent Society — and since it had gone badly in Cambridge and Vermont, I had moved to Geneva. There it went

even less well. One weekend my wife and I went up to the
mountains to walk and stayed overnight in the Hotel Rössli,
a charming and modestly elegant chalet-type hotel on the
main street of Gstaad. It was all so lovely and its restaurant
was so good that later, with the book still stalled, I came
back. Contrary to all literary experience, the new location
made a difference; chapters began to take shape, the book
all but wrote itself. By the autumn of 1956 when I returned
to the United States to join Adlai Stevenson for the campaign, I had a complete draft. Ever since, whenever time
and money have allowed, I have gone back to Gstaad. All of
what I call my serious books have been written there; no
place in the world is so efficient. One works until one is
tired and then, either in euphoria or frustration, goes skiing
or walking. Neither of these recreations occupies the mind;
I have never heard of anyone who was mentally so retarded
that he could not be taught to ski and I've encountered quite
a few who could not conceivably be taught anything else.
So to fill the vacuum one continues to ponder and by next
day you often have something more to say. The rich, dividing about equally between those who are functional illiterates and those who have heard I'm a Bolshevist, leave me
entirely alone. In Cambridge when lectures, mail, telephone
calls, tourists, social life and politics take over from writing,
all mental activity comes to an end.

Other equally discriminating people have made the same
discovery about Gstaad. Natacha Stewart writes her in-
triguing and richly amusing stories for *The New Yorker* in
a house across from the Palace Hotel. Efrem Kurtz, the con-
ductor, and Elaine Shaffer Kurtz, the world's best and best-
looking flutist, live over on another shoulder in a house they
rent from Rebekah Harkness which is called naturally The

Pavilion. Yehudi Menuhin lives over on yet another shoulder, although his visits are more sparse, and Randall Thompson, the composer, is just outside my window. We share a house with Ricardo and Betty Sicre. This remarkable pair, Spanish hosts of Hemingway in his latter years (Hemingway was also partial to Gstaad), have combined service as a Spanish Loyalist officer (he) with service in the OSS (both) with great business success in Spain (he) with flying (she) with writing on the French Resistance (he) with fiction and a book on the promotion of hybrid corn (she) with yachting (he) with social work in the Bronx (she). This sort of thing does takes them away from Gstaad from time to time. David Niven, by all odds the most entertaining man in the entertainment business in the last fifty years, lives in a nearby village and not far away, in a stately twelfth-century château, is William F. Buckley, Jr. The rooms in the cellar of the Buckley château for flogging serfs and impertinent servants are now only slightly used and even the knout has been largely given up. Next to the room where he writes his political column, Bill has an even larger room where he paints. His friends and well-wishers are strongly encouraging him to give his entire time to painting. Along with lumbering, skiing and tourists, Gstaad has long been famous for its schools — among others it is the winter headquarters of Le Rosey, the most famous of Swiss private schools. So parents also find their way there. They can turn their children over to the superior moral influence of the schoolmasters without losing them entirely from sight.

As connoisseurs of the commonplace have been observing since Caesar, Western Europe has an appalling winter climate. It's a marvel that European civilization has survived it and shows that people are better when they are punished.

The sole exception is near the top of the Alps, where the mountains pierce the blanket of wet, cold, heavily contaminated and only vaguely translucent air that lies over the rest of the continent. This accounts for the popularity of Gstaad in February, for conditions everywhere else are intolerable and have been so for some months. But in years of good snow a nicer time is at Christmas when everything is white and mysterious and the lights twinkle over the deep banks and the evergreens have a spun sugar effect. It is like a postcard but with less understatement.

My favorite season, however, is the spring. Then the skiers have gone and Ruedy Müllner, who in the winter runs a grocery, a good restaurant and teaches skiing every afternoon, confines himself to his store and Oskar Rieber and his wife, who teach skiing all day and farm all night, now only farm. While the wide meadows are still wet from the snow and patches remain on the northern flanks, the blue and yellow crocuses take over as a robe. And these are soon followed by large patches of white narcissus. Both, one imagines, reflect poor pasture management but they give the countryside a great magic as do the mountain flowers that follow. And the Swiss are not entirely uneconomic. For at this season they spread out over the grass and over the flowers, too, great thick globs of the vintage cow manure which has been accumulating all winter. It does not smell; no semantic disguise can conceal the fact that it really stinks. To me this is almost the best of all. As a boy on a farm in Canada, I had to help move great tonnages of this nutrient every spring. Nothing is so nostalgic as that odor — in combination with the knowledge that someone else is doing the shoveling.

3

Berkeley in the Thirties

ONE DAY in the autumn of 1930, I was gazing at the notice board in the post office of the main men's residence at the Ontario Agricultural College at Guelph, Canada, where, at the time, I was a senior. It was usually an unrewarding vision but on this day it advertised a number of research assistantships at the Giannini Foundation of Agricultural Economics at the University of California. The annual stipend was $720 for unmarried scholars. I copied down the details and applied. Some time later I received a letter from George Peterson, Associate Professor of Agricultural Economics, saying that I had been selected. I was surprised and so were my professors who detested me and thought the people at Berkeley were crazy. I quickly accepted; in that second year of the Great Depression the monthly salary of $60, if not princely, was by far the best offer of any kind I had. In fact, it was the only offer of any kind I had. From that day on, the University of California has engaged my affection as no other institution — educational, public or pecuniary — with which I have ever been associated. One Sunday afternoon in the summer of 1968, with my wife and oldest son (who followed me to Berkeley to be an assistant at the University of California Law School), I strolled across the California campus — over Strawberry Creek, by the Campanile, down by the Library, out Sather Gate. I was taught, as were most of my generation, that no one should allow himself the weak luxury of sentiment or even emotion. To this day when I write "Love" at the end of a letter, I always remind myself that it is only modern affectation, in all respects a matter of form. I was suddenly overwhelmed by the thought that I loved this place — the paths, trees, flowers, buildings, even the new ones. I was deeply embarrassed.

In the thirties, for some reason related either to the eccentricities of the California crop year or climate, the University of California opened in August. Accordingly, in July of 1931 I borrowed $500 from an aunt, one of the few members of our rural family still to command such capital, and, almost literally, set sail for California. I boarded the steamer which plied between Port Stanley on the north shore of Lake Erie and Cleveland where, by pre-arrangement with our local jeweler and oculist, I met his nephew who had a graduate fellowship at California in astronomy. At five o'clock the following morning, we set out in the 1926 Oakland automobile my companion had acquired for this trip. The car was in terrible condition and almost immediately got worse. To save money he had bought a five-gallon gasoline tin and a one-gallon container for oil so that we could stock up on these products whenever, as happened in those days, our path led us through a region being ravaged by a price war. Such at least was the theory. About thirty miles out of Cleveland, my friend stopped to check the gas (the gauge was broken) and look at the oil. The car absorbed the whole five gallons of gasoline and the whole gallon of oil. For the rest of the trip, we averaged around a quarter gallon of gas and a half pint of oil to the mile. To this day I shudder at the cost.

The journey took ten days not counting twenty-four hours at Casey, Iowa, where we were laid up with a broken connecting rod. That too had a lasting effect. It was raining hard, and as we waited for the repairs, we listened to the local farmers, who used the garage as a club, discussing Hoover. I became a lifelong Democrat. It was about six o'clock on a bright summer evening when we got to Berkeley and drove up Bancroft Way to the International House. The hills behind were very bleached and sere but the low sun glistened on the live oaks and the green lawns and the masses of pink geraniums which elsewhere are only geraniums but in Berkeley are the glory of the whole city. The sun also lit up the vast yellow-buff façade of the International House with the large Spanish arches of the portico below. We passed into the great hall, then gleaming new, and combining the best mission style with the finest in Moorish revival. I thought it a place of unimaginable splendor.

Eventually the International House was to prove a bit too expensive even for one who earned $60 a month and was, as a result, one of the more affluent members of the community. My capital had been depleted by that terrible car. But for the first few months at Berkeley, this nice Rockefeller benefaction — it had counterparts in New York, Chicago, Paris and Tokyo — housing several hundred students of both sexes from the United States and many foreign lands, was to be my window on the Berkeley world. Never before had I been so happy.

The world on which I looked down could not be recognized in important respects by Mario Savio or his successors. I must stress that I had just emerged from the Ontario Agricultural College and this could have distorted my vision. Once not long ago, I was asked by *Time* magazine about this academy; I replied, thoughtlessly, that in my day it was certainly the cheapest and possibly the worst in the English-speaking world. This was tactless and possibly wrong and caused dissatisfaction even after all these years. (No one questioned my statement that the college was inexpensive.) At OAC students were expected to keep and also to know and cherish their place. Leadership in the student body was solidly in the hands of those who combined an outgoing anti-intellectualism with a sound interest in livestock. This the faculty thought right. Anyone who questioned the established agricultural truths, many of which were wildly wrong, was sharply rebuked and if he offended too often he was marked down as a troublemaker. A fair number of faculty members had effectively substituted the affable and well-clipped manner and mustache of the professional countryman for the admitted tedium of science. But unquestionably the place did build health.

At Berkeley I suddenly encountered professors who knew their subject and, paradoxically, invited debate on what they knew. They also had time to talk at length with graduate students and even come up to International House to continue the conversation. I first discovered at Berkeley from Henry Erdman, who had until recently been the head of the Agricultural Economics Department, and Howard Tolley, who had just succeeded him as the Director of the Giannini Foundation, that a professor might like to be informed on some subject by a graduate student — might not just be polite but pleased. So profound was that impression that I never stopped informing people thereafter. The pleasure I have thus given has been very great. (Howard Tolley, after a year or two, went on to Washington to become head of the Agricultural Adjustment Administration under FDR. I shall mention him again in a moment. In 1968, after the elapse of a third of a century, I was back in Berkeley one Sunday to urge the case and more important, since everyone was persuaded, to raise money for Eugene McCarthy. I was not at all surprised to see Henry Erdman in the front row. He believed strongly in keeping informed.)

Although we had a stipend, we agricultural economists were second-class citizens. Our concern was with the prices of cling peaches, which were then appalling, and the financial condition of the Merced irrigation district, which was equally bad, and the prune industry which was chronically indigent, and other such useful subjects. I earned my research stipend by tramping (sic) the streets of Los Angeles and also Oakland and San Jose to ascertain the differing preferences as to package and flavor — sage, orange blossom, clover — of Mexican, Jewish, Negro and (as we then thought of them) ordinary white Americans, for honey. No differences emerged. This kind of work was not well regarded by the nonagricultural or pure economists. Thorstein Veblen was still being read with attention in Berkeley in the thirties. He distinguishes between esoteric and exoteric knowledge, the first having the commanding advantage of being without "economic or industrial effect." It is this advantage, he argues, which distinguishes the higher learning from the lower. Ours, obviously, was the lower.

We suffered from another handicap. Agriculturalists, in an indistinct way, were considered to be subject to the influence of the California Farm Bureau Federation and much worse, of the opulent and perpetually choleric baronage which comprised the Associated Farmers of California. Actually our subordination was not all that indistinct. Both organizations told the Dean of the College of Agriculture and the Director of Extension what they needed in the way of research and also conclusions. They were heard with attention, even respect. No one was ever told to shape his scholarly work accordingly; men were available who did it as a matter of course.

The nonagricultural economists, whatever their differences in other matters of doctrine, were united in regarding the farmers, even more than the bankers or oil men, as an all-purpose class enemy. In time I acquired a certain reputation in economic theory and other branches of impractical knowledge and also as a rather circumspect critic of the agricultural establishment. So I was accorded an honorary status as a scholar, my agricultural handicaps notwithstanding. I was then even more happy.

The Department of Economics at Berkeley has never been considered quite as eminent as that at Harvard. The reason is that the best Californians have always eventually come to Harvard. As this is written in the autumn of 1968, of the twenty-three full professors of economics at Harvard no fewer than seven, nearly one-third, were recruited at one stage or another in their careers from the University of California at Berkeley. And economics at Berkeley has long had a marked personality. In the early thirties, years before the Keynesian revolution, Leo Rogin was discussing Keynes with a sense of urgency that made his seminars seem to graduate students the most important things then happening in the world. I learned Alfred Marshall from Ewald Grether who taught with a drillmaster's precision for which I have ever since been grateful. Marshall is the quintessence of classical economics and much of what he says is wrong. But no one can know what is wrong if he does not understand it first. My memory also goes back to M. M. Knight's seminar in economic history, a gifted exercise in irrelevancy. Once Robert Gordon Sproul, then the President of the University, said in one of his booming speeches that, after all, a university was run for the students. Knight, a brother of the even more noted Frank H. Knight of the University of Chicago, attacked this doctrine for two full sessions. A university, he argued with indignation, was run for the faculty and to affirm the point, he announced his intention of introducing a resolution at some early faculty meeting to exclude the students from the library. They got in the way.

We graduate students were also fond of Paul Taylor who spoke out unfailingly for the small farmer in California, Charles Gulick who spoke out for the farm workers, who then as now aroused righteous anger for wanting a union and a living wage, and Robert Brady who was the friend of the consumer and other lost causes. Brady taught courses in the business cycle and set great store by exhaustive bibliographic research. One of my friends met this requirement by going to the card catalogue in the library and copying into the appendix of his thesis everything that appeared there under the headings, "Cycle, Business" and "Cycle, Trade." Brady sent over for some of the latter items which were new to him and they turned out to be works on bicycles, tricycles and motorcycles published by the Cycle Trades of America. We always heard there was quite a scene.

A few years after I left Berkeley, I became deputy head of the Office of Price Administration in charge of World War II price controls. This was a post with unlimited patronage

— eventually, as I recall, I had some seventeen thousand assistants. A number of my former professors, including Howard Tolley, Harry Wellman (later the Acting President of the University) and Robert Brady, turned up on our staff. Brady had scarcely arrived before he was assaulted hip and thigh by the Dies Committee — later better known as HUAC and now as HISC — for saying in a book on German fascism that American capitalism was only technically better. To complicate matters further, Dies had got hold of the edition published by the Left Book Club in England. It had something on the cover about not being for public sale. I handled the defense on the Hill with the handicap of knowing that everything I said in favor of Bob would immediately be used against me. Brady later attributed his troubles to the oil companies and said I was their tool. He had proposed that people conserve oil by not changing the crankcase for the duration or ten thousand miles, whichever was less. I did not endorse the idea. This was mostly because with everything else it never got to my attention. But if it had, I might have remembered that Oakland car and the way it changed itself and wondered if it would have made much difference.

The graduate students with whom I associated in the thirties were uniformly radical and the most distinguished were Communists. I listened to them eagerly and would liked to have joined both the conversation and the Party but here my agricultural background was a real handicap. It meant that, as a matter of formal Marxian doctrine, I was politically immature. Among the merits of capitalism to Marx was the fact that it rescued men from the idiocy of rural life. I had only very recently been retrieved. I sensed this bar and I knew also that my pride would be deeply hurt by rejection.

So I kept outside. There was possibly one other factor. Although I recognized that the system could not and should not survive, I was enjoying it so much that, secretly, I was a little sorry.

In the ensuing twenty years, many of those I most envied were accorded an auto-da-fé by HUAC, James Eastland or the late Joseph R. McCarthy. Their lives were ruined. Phrases about the unpredictable graces of God kept constantly crossing my mind.

One man who did not get called by Joe McCarthy was Robert Merriman, a vital and popular graduate student and teaching assistant who came down to Berkeley from Nevada in the early thirities. As an undergraduate he had been entirely wholesome and a power in the ROTC. But Berkeley had its effect and so (as he told friends) did the great waterfront strike of 1934 where he saw soldiers deployed against the strikers. Hugh Thomas's brilliant book, *The Spanish Civil War*, tells the rest of his story. Interrupting a traveling fellowship in Europe in 1936, Merriman went to Spain where, as an uncalculated consequence of ROTC, he commanded the Abraham Lincoln Battalion on the Jarama and then went on through many battles to be chief of staff of the XV International Brigade. Hemingway met and admired him and made him, at least in part, the model for Robert Jordan (the professor from Montana in *For Whom the Bell Tolls*). A major and by now long a veteran, he was killed in the retreat from Belchite in Aragon in 1938. He must have been the bravest of our contemporaries. The California campus has plaques for lesser heroes who died nearer home for more fashionable beliefs. There are some naïve haunting lines written by John Depper, a British volunteer, of the Battle of Jarama that might serve:

Death stalked in the olive trees
Picking his men
His leaden finger beckoned
Again and again.

A year or so ago in Chicago, I was on a television discussion program with Robert Merriam, a White House aide to President Eisenhower and once Republican candidate for mayor of Chicago against Richard Daley. He said that for many years he had been investigated assiduously by the FBI because of his name. Merriman was not completely forgotten.

I would not wish it thought that our life in the thirties was limited to politics and great matters of the mind. We roamed through San Francisco, climbed Mount Diablo, went up to the Sierras where someone was always imagining that the depression might make panning gold profitable again and consumed (I most diffidently) alcohol stolen from the chemistry laboratories and mixed with grapefruit juice and, after repeal, a blended whiskey of negligible cost called, to the best of my memory, Crab Orchard. I have difficulty in believing that the latter day intoxicants and suffocants do worse. In any case, we were all greatly impressed one night when a girl who had been overstimulated by these products ceremoniously removed her clothes in the patio of the International House and spent the late hours of the evening doing orgiastic obeisance to the heavens above and, more than incidentally, to the windows of the men's rooms around.

In those days people came to Berkeley from all over the world and, naturally enough, no one ever left. The reasons were social and economic as well as cultural. As a student, teaching fellow or even a nonstudent, one could be a respected member of the community and it counted against a person not at all to have no income. But the moment one left Berkeley he became a member of the great army of the unemployed. As such, he was an object of sympathy and lost his own self-respect. In general, graduate students avoided taking their final degrees lest they be under temptation, however slight, to depart. When, in 1933 and 1934, jobs suddenly and unexpectedly became available in Washington — NRA, PWA, AAA — almost everyone got busy and finished up his thesis. Even my Communist friends reacted favorably to the exorbitant salaries which economists commanded in the New Deal.

Among the people who appeared in Berkeley, my mind returns to a slim, boyish-looking girl who, improbably in light of her build, claimed to have been in Texas Guinan's chorus before turning to higher learning. More recently she had been in Tahiti and then in Bora Bora where she had gone native and had as proof a comprehensive suntan. Now she was doing graduate work in anthropology on the basis of credentials, partly forged and partly imaginary, from a nonexistent undergraduate institution in the City of New York. I fell deeply in love with her; on our second or third date, as we were walking up Strawberry Canyon back of the stadium, she asked me if I thought it right, as an economist, to be wasting both her time and mine. Nothing in my Canadian or Calvinist background had prepared me for such a personal concept of efficiency. A little later, after an allnight party in San Francisco, she insisted on being taken to the Santa Fe station. She had just remembered that, on the day following, she was scheduled to marry a banker in New Mexico. Much later I met her in New York. She was just back from Haiti (not Tahiti) and preparing to marry a Pan

Am pilot. She told me she was working on her memoirs and was being encouraged to the task by Westbrook Pegler. I was by then a promising young member of the Harvard faculty. I first worried that she would publish her recollections and then, after a time, that she would not.

Though we graduate students expected the revolution very soon and planned to encourage it, we did not expect any help from the Berkeley undergraduates. Not that they would oppose — they would simply, as usual, be unaware that anything was happening. A singular accomplishment of American higher education, as one reflects on it, was the creation of a vast network of universities, public and private, which for a century until the sixties caused no one any political embarrassment of any kind. In other countries they created trouble from time to time but not here. A control system which subtly suggested that whatever the students most wanted to do — i.e., devote themselves to football, basketball, fraternities, college tradition, rallies, hell-raising, a sentimental concern for the old alma mater and imaginative inebriation — was what they should do was basic to this peace. The alumni rightly applauded this control system and so, to an alarming extent, did the faculty. An occasional nonpolitical riot was condoned and even admired; some deeper adult instinct suggested that it was a surrogate for something worse. At Berkeley in the thirties, this system was still working perfectly. Coming up Bancroft Way to the International House of an evening, one saw the fraternity men policing up the lawns of their houses or sitting contentedly in front. Walking along Piedmont at night one heard the shouts of laughter from within, or occasional bits of song, or what Evelyn Waugh correctly described as the most evocative and nostalgic of all the sounds of an aristocracy at play, the crash of a breaking glass. Here were men with a secure position in society who knew it and who were content. On a Friday night they would do their duty at the pep rally shaming the apathetic; on Saturday they would be at the stadium and on Saturday night, win or lose, they joined with the kindred souls of earlier generations, men they did not hesitate to call brother, to whoop it up as a college man was meant to do. The *Daily Californian* was the approving chronicle of this world — of the Big Game, the Axe, the cards turned in unison in the cheering section to depict an Indian or a bear, the campaign to send the band to Oregon to support the team. In 1932, Norman Thomas came to the campus and spoke to a small assembly in a classroom. Neither Hoover nor Roosevelt dreamed of favoring us. Hoover did speak to a vast audience of indigent citizens from the local Hooverville down on the Oakland flats and was cheered uproariously when he told them that, at long last, the depression was over. They had not heard. Only once was there a suggestion of student involvement. The financial condition of the State of California in those days was appalling. State workers were being paid with tax-anticipation certificates. Even the Governor, James (Sunny Jim) Rolph, sensed that something was wrong. In 1932 and 1933, there were threats to cut the University budget. When it seemed that these were serious, the students were encouraged to assemble and ask their relatives and friends to petition their legislators to relent. Perhaps that was the camel's nose, the seed of the Frankenstein. As to persuading the legislature, however, it was considered less important than a promise by the University to retrench voluntarily and to begin with the much valued Agricultural Extension (Farm Adviser) Service. No one said so but we agriculturalists certainly felt that our pragmatic approach to scholarship had paid off for everybody.

In the nineteen-sixties, Dean Rusk, Lyndon Johnson, Lewis Hershey and Ronald Reagan accomplished what not even the most talented of our teachers had ever hoped to achieve — they (as I judge) brought Berkeley undergraduates into the political discussion. When the time comes to award honors to those who made our universities the center of our political life, it will be a great injustice if the men of affirmative as distinct from negative influence are featured. Now, I would suppose, Berkeley is the most intense intellectual and political community in the world; perhaps, indeed, it is the nearest thing to a total university community in modern times. As such, it would be silly to suppose that it could be altogether tranquil. Often in the years prior to Harvard's upheavals and following some exceptionally imaginative outbreak on Telegraph Avenue, I heard a colleague say, "You know, that sort of thing could never happen here." I was always too polite to say why I agreed. And the statement has now been proved wrong. As other university communities have succumbed to the concerns so long a commonplace at Berkeley, they too have ceased to be tranquil.

Not everyone is as restrained as I am about Berkeley. A few weeks ago, I shared a seat on an airplane with a young colleague newly recruited, like so many before him, from the University of California. I asked him if he missed it. He replied, "Christ, yes! At Berkeley you worked all morning in the library and then at noon you went out into the sun and there was always a demonstration going on or something. Man, that was living!"

The days passed. During my second year at Berkeley my stipend was raised to $70 a month, allowing me to save a little money and also to have a larger social life. Then in my third year I was sent to Davis which, for the benefit of non-Californians, is in the Sacramento Valley not far from Sacramento. It is now a full-fledged university but in those days it was the center of agricultural research and instruction too closely associated with orchards, insects and the soil to be carried on at Berkeley. It cultivated, in other words, the lowest of the lower learning. At Davis I was the head of the Departments of Economics, of Agricultural Economics, of Accounting and of Farm Management. I also gave instruction in all of these subjects and, with the exception of one elderly dean who gave lectures to nondegree students, I was also the total teaching staff in these disciplines. During the year I also had time to write my Ph.D. thesis and I do not recall that I was especially rushed. Certainly such was my love for Berkeley that I went there every weekend. At Davis my pay was $1800 and I was able (by way of repayment of my own college debts to my family) to send my younger sister to college.

The Davis students were also highly stable. My course in beginning economics was required for some majors. The scholars so compelled tramped in at the beginning of the period, squeezed their yellow corduroy-clad bottoms into the classroom chairs, listened with indifference for an hour and then, by now conveying an impression of manfully suppressed indignation, tramped out. Only once in the entire year did I arouse their interest. I gave some support to the textbook case for lower tariffs. Coming as they did from the sugar beet fields, olive orchards, cattle ranches and other

monuments to the protective tariff, they knew that was wrong
and told me so. My best remembered student that year was
a boy who had an old Ford runabout and spent his weekends
putting up signs on the highways which warned motorists to
repent and prepare at a fairly early date to meet their God.
In response on an examination to a question about the nature
of money, he stuck resolutely to the proposition that it (not
the love of money but money itself) was the root of all evil.
I tried to reason with him but in vain. So I flunked him for
his contention seemed to me palpably untrue. That was my
only personal encounter in those years with any form of
student dissent.

One day in the spring of 1933, I was in Berkeley putting
the finishing touches on my thesis. A Western Union boy
came into the room with a telegram offering me an instruc-
torship at Harvard for the following year at $2400. I had not
the slightest idea of accepting for I was totally happy at
California. But my rapid advance in economic well-being,
plus no doubt the defense of my faith against that student,
had made me avaricious and I had heard that one won
advances in academic life by flashing offers from other universities. I let it be known over the weekend that "Harvard
was after me," and, on the following Monday, went by appointment to see the Dean of the College of Agriculture to
bargain. I carried the telegram in my hand. The Dean, a
large, handsome and highly self-confident man named Claude
B. Hutchison who later became the Mayor of Berkeley, was
excellently informed on all matters in the College and his
intelligence system had not failed him on this occasion. He
congratulated me warmly on my offer, gave me the impression that he thought Harvard was being reckless with its

money and said that of course I should go. In a moment I realized to my horror I had no choice. I couldn't now plead to stay at two-thirds the price. The great love of my life was over. I remember wondering, as I went out, if I had been right to flunk that nut.

Index

Index

Acheson, Dean, 179; his *Present at the Creation*, 268–275; evaluation of Stettinius, 270–271; evaluation of Baruch, 271; evaluation of MacArthur, 271–272

ADA World, xi

Advertising, 73n–74n, 80. *See also* Persuasion

Aesthetics, 22–25, 158–160

Affluent Society, The (Galbraith), 65n, 68n, 79n, 114, 340–341; influence upon Nixon, 282, 284

Africa, sub-Sahara, 173, 174, 180, 219, 221; technical assistance in, 191; poverty of, 211; and economic planning, 222; underdeveloped nations of 229; obstacles to development, 231–233, 242, 243; development policy recommendations for, 243–245

Aggregate demand, 46–47, 62, 63, 67–68; regulated by state, 68–69, 85

Agnew, Spiro T., 113

Agricultural Adjustment Administration (AAA), 348, 354

Agricultural economics, *see* Economics

Agricultural Extension (Farm Adviser) Service, Berkeley, 356

Agriculture, U.S. Department of, 187

AID, 187, 188; in India, 189, 191, 200

Aircraft companies, 74, 107

Air Force, U.S., 177; panel to assess accomplishments of (1944), 288–289

Alexander, Henry, 281

Alliance for Progress, 166, 249

Alsop, Joseph, xii, 35, 167

Ambassador, American, 184–200; social life, 185–187; and American missions abroad, 187–189; standards for promotion of, 193–194; advantages of political appointees over career service officers, 194–196; and Congress, 195; modern liberal as, 195–196; and State Department, 196–198, 199; speeches by, 199–200

American Economic Association, 12n, 37, 38n–39n, 122